Noelle Burton

*The Technique and Practice of
Intensive Psychotherapy*

Also by Richard D. Chessick, M.D.

Agonie: Diary of a Twentieth Century Man (1976)

Intensive Psychotherapy of the Borderline Patient (1977)

Freud Teaches Psychotherapy (1980)

How Psychotherapy Heals (1969, 1983)

Why Psychotherapists Fail (1971, 1983)

The Technique and Practice of Intensive Psychotherapy (1974, 1983)

A Brief Introduction to the Genius of Nietzsche (1983)

Psychology of the Self and the Treatment of Narcissism (1985)

Great Ideas in Psychotherapy (1977, 1987)

The Technique & Practice of Listening in Intensive Psychotherapy (1989)

THE TECHNIQUE AND PRACTICE OF

Intensive

Psychotherapy

RICHARD D. CHESSICK, M.D.

JASON ARONSON INC.
Northvale, New Jersey
London

New Printing 1991

ISBN 0-87668-657-9

Library of Congress Catalog Number 73-81207

Manufactured in the United States of America. Jason Aronson Inc. offers books and
cassettes. For information and catalog write to Jason Aronson Inc., 230 Livingston
Street, Northvale, New Jersey 07647.

To Marcy

PATIENCE BORN OF LOVING

Contents

Introduction to the Second Edition

J OHN Kenneth Galbraith (1958) wrote, "It is a far, far better thing to have a firm anchor in nonsense than to put out on the troubled seas of thought" (p. 130). In spite of Galbraith's warning, I shall attempt in this preface to trace the development of various conceptualizations about what leads to change in psychoanalytic treatment, review the current controversies around this subject, indicate directions for future investigation, and briefly present my views as they have developed over the almost twenty years from the first edition of this book to the current printing.

BACKGROUND

Cooper (1989), in a brief historical review of the subject, begins with Freud's early "protopsychoanalytical" model, which stressed the cathartic release of dammed-up affects. These affects were sequestered from the patient's mental life because they were too painful; they consist of noxious feelings and thoughts that poison the mental system, producing conversion symptoms and hysterias.

Freud's protopsychoanalytic model assumes that overwhelmingly horrifying events or traumata occurred early in childhood. It postulates that the becoming conscious of repressed memories, fantasies, and their associated affects permits the unification of mental life and so places the adult's mind more under conscious control. The becoming conscious of repressed memories of traumatic events leads to new opportunities for the adult to solve old problems. The notion of psychic conflict, of a mind divided and warring over what should or should not be conscious or unconscious, is introduced in this initial work.

FREUD'S EARLY MODEL

The basic exposition of the drive/conflict/defense model is found in Breuer and Freud's (1893) *Studies on Hysteria*. One of the most memorable quotations in the whole of psychoanalytic literature can be found in section IV of this work, written by Freud and entitled "Psychotherapy of Hysteria." For Freud in this early model the problem was to overcome the resistance of the psyche or censor to the recovery of lost memories and to the discharge of dammed-up affects. He writes:

What means have we at our disposal for overcoming this continual resistance? Few, but they include almost all those by which one man can ordinarily exert a psychical influence on another. In the first place, we must reflect that a psychical resistance . . . can only be resolved slowly and by degrees, and we must wait patiently. In the next place, we may reckon on the intellectual interest which the patient begins to feel after working for a short time. By explaining things to him, by giving him information about the marvelous world of psychical processes into which we ourselves only gained insight by such analyses, we make him himself into a collaborator. . . . One works to the best of one's power, as an elucidator . . . as a teacher, as the representative of a freer or superior view of the world, as a father confessor who gives absolution . . . by a continuance of his sympathy and respect after the confession has been made. . . . Besides the intellectual motives which we mobilize to overcome the resistance, there is an affective factor, the personal influence of the physician, which we can seldom do without (pp. 281–283).

This sets the tone for Freud's actual practice of psychoanalytic therapy; an examination of his famous published case histories indicates that throughout his life he stayed fairly close to this attitude. In a later, similar statement, Freud (1916) stresses the role of transference love in influencing the patient to accept "aftereducation" and "make the advance from the pleasure principle to the reality principle by which the mature human being is distinguished from the child" (p. 312).

Freud's Later Model

This topographic drive/conflict/defense model with its focus on resistance to uncovering gave way eventually to

Freud's structural theory, centering on the ego and the mechanisms of defense. The goal of therapy became "where the id was ego shall be." Treatment was conceptualized as the analysis of resistances and defenses through focus on the transference, for the purpose of enlarging the powers of the ego. Conscious awareness was not sufficient, and what was crucial for change was not catharsis but the analysis of the transference, a reliving and working through of infantile complexes, especially with focus on the Oedipus complex.

In Freud's (1940) final, unfinished work, psychoanalysis is still described as "after-education," arising from an affective experience with the analyst, a consequence of the transference allowing the analyst to exert an influence on the patient that leads to the dissolution of the compromise formations that constitute the symptoms of the neurosis. The result would be new intrapsychic attitudes toward old psychic contents.

Freud's Pessimism

Freud's increasing awareness of the limitations of psychoanalytic therapy was expressed in his (1937) famous paper "Analysis Terminable and Interminable." Here he conceives of therapy as the taming of instincts, in which they are "brought completely into the harmony of the ego" (p. 225), become accessible to all the influences of the other trends in the ego, and are no longer allowed to go their own independent way to satisfaction. It follows that if the strength of the ego is diminished due to illness or exhaustion, the tamed instincts renew their demands and seek their satisfaction in abnormal ways. Psychoanalysis is thought of as making the ego only relatively stronger, and certainly not providing protection against other or future conflicts.

The pessimism deepens as Freud discusses factors that are decisive for the success of psychoanalytic treatment: not only the strength of the instincts and the influence of traumatic etiology, but most important, congenital or acquired alterations of the ego. Acquired alterations have a better prognosis; they represent certain selected habitual mechanisms of defense, which become fixed in the person's character and represent infantilisms. The patient seeks out situations to keep using them in order to justify them. In Freud's final view, psychoanalytic therapy is seen as producing change through a pendulum-like movement between id analysis and ego analysis. The defense mechanisms operate as resistances against recovery in the treatment.

Inherited and cultural dispositions, the so-called constitutional factors, Freud says, are adhesiveness of the libido, too mobile a libido (rendering the results of psychoanalysis very impermanent), a depletion of plasticity and capacity for change—which Freud calls "id resistances" and considers characteristic of older people— and finally, the ultimate force toward suffering provided by guilt and the need for punishment, and the death instinct.

Patients are imprisoned in themselves. The compulsion to repeat causes patients to seek out situations over and over again to justify and employ their same old characterologic mechanisms of defense with the same old outcomes. Self psychologists (Newman, 1988) later called this the need to reach out repeatedly to archaic selfobject figures in an attempt to re-create an early self/selfobject situation. Change in psychoanalytic therapy depends on the patient's capacity to step back and observe these repetitive strivings, whether we describe them as transferential strivings or attempts to repeat an archaic self/selfobject dyad. If the patient as a partner in the treatment, as Freud (1893) described it in *Studies on Hysteria*, can be persuaded to step back from repetition of these patterns and observe them, then after-education can occur. In this manner the ego can be altered by the analytic process.

Freud concludes by focusing on the analyst. Ferenczi had already pointed out that success depends on the analyst having learned sufficiently from his own errors and mistakes and having overcome the weak points in his personality. Freud adds that analysts do not always come up to standard as models of normality and correctness and as teachers. Since "the analytic relationship is based on a love of truth" and "it precludes any kind of sham or deceit" (p. 248), the demands on the analyst for maturity and integrity are very great. Hence his famous statement that analysis is an impossible profession, along with education and government. The fertile ideas in this paper by an 81-year-old man are truly remarkable.

Corrective Emotional Experience

A number of pioneer psychoanalysts such as Ferenczi, Rank, and later, Alexander, tried to facilitate after-education by deliberately providing the patient with selected affective experiences. It was Ferenczi who first recognized (Gedo, 1986) that after-education or alteration of the ego in many cases could not be brought about simply by interpretation of the transference. Ferenczi claimed that he learned this out of his own "introspective insights; in other words, he felt that he had made creative use of his own psychology in outlining a syndrome of archaic character pathology he called that of 'the wise baby' " (Gedo, 1986, p. 37). Many psychoanalytic patients even in those early years did not have the Oedipus complex as the nucleus of their neuroses; rather they presented preoedipal disorders with substantial personality problems and archaic difficulties. These patients, Gedo writes, "had been traumatized by parental failures in helping the child with the tasks of weaning, habit training, and renouncing the status of childhood in favor of more mature adaptive modes" (p. 39). These patients cannot trust the analyst's dependability, and repeatedly test the analyst, so that much of the treatment centers around analyzing the negative transference.

Ferenczi insisted that the most sensitive issue for these patients is abandonment, which may be defended against either through narcissistic personality traits or a precocious maturity, a capacity for taking care of themselves. Sometimes a protective role toward their parents during childhood that amounts to an altruistic surrender develops, which may be interpreted as identification with the aggressor and screens unconscious destructive wishes toward the parents.

Ferenczi argued that a kind of affective bond with these patients had to be encouraged by the analyst. At one point he experimented with actual physical contact—even kissing the patient—which was held against him even after he reported that such techniques did not work and abandoned their use. What apparently was scandalous to the early psychoanalysts was Ferenczi's active attempt to develop a bonding with the patient, rather than maintaining a passive analytic stance. But Ferenczi discovered, to his frustration, that such preoedipally damaged patients do not easily form an affective bond in the transference; indeed, their central difficulty is in bonding with another adult. In my experience, some of these patients can even deeply love children or animals but are utterly incapable of developing spontaneously an intense, powerful, affect-laden transference in psychoanalytic treatment for a long time. Instead, they begin analysis by forming the transference-like dispositions that Kohut (1971, 1977) called selfobject transferences, and even these may be silent. I have reviewed self psychology and the work of Kohut elsewhere (Chessick, 1985).

Ferenczi emphasized the crucial importance of intense affective experience in the here and now of the analytic transference, in contrast to the insights from interpretations. Ferenczi, Rank, and Alexander all attempted actively to bring about the development of maximally affect-laden transferences and to manipulate these transferences in order to produce an after-education of the ego. Opponents accused them of a form of seduction therapy and complained that active gratification of the patient renders the patient hopelessly attached to the therapist and removes the motivation to transfer that new capacity for attachment to others outside the treatment. Termination of the treatment cannot take place until the patient has developed the capacity to bond to others; in these patients a premature termination could produce a catastrophic disruption and disintegration of the newly developed ego capacities.

Interpretation and/or Experience

So begins a controversy about factors that produce change in psychoanalysis that persists to the present day. Anna Freud and her followers in the ego psychology school placed the analysis of the ego squarely at the center of psychoanalytic therapy, in contrast to the early psychoanalysts who focused on id analysis. For them, therapy is to enable the ego to use more and better and "higher level" defenses, a favorable alteration of the ego. They attempt to analyze the ego defenses, permitting more flexibility, less stereotyped responses, better assessment of reality, and improved adaptation. They seek structural change: a broader and stronger ego, a less archaic superego, and easier access to the id.

Reich (1949) added the concept of ego-syntonic character armor, a subtle barrier to the development of the analytic process. This was the forerunner of our current concept of "defense transference," the characteristic personality stance that the patient initially takes toward the analyst as representative of anyone who threatens the patient, and which must be analyzed. For traditional ego-psychology analysts, insights from interpretation, especially about the transference neurosis, and the corresponding reconstruction of early experiences are the crucial factors that produce change in treatment.

Another group of analysts focuses on the affective experience the patient has with the analyst, both "here and now" in the treatment and in the experiential re-living of the transference. The relationship with the analyst enlists the patient as an ally in the analytic process and provides the motivation to undergo the pain, vulnerability, and inevitable disappointments with the therapist's minor failures in empathy that pervade the analytic process.

Freud did not have great difficulty balancing these various factors, as any study of his behavior toward his patients reported in the case histories makes quite clear. Freud did not always follow his own recommendations for psychoanalytic technique, which were aimed at producing a transference that could be interpreted to provide insights and the reconstruction of early experiences. Although in his writing he emphasized the importance of these factors for change in psychoanalysis, there was always a background of powerful affect-laden interaction with the patient that Freud never hesitated to engage in throughout his treatment procedure. In fact, there are a number of instances where Freud carried this obviously too far; for example, during analysis he (Gedo, 1986) prohibited Ferenczi's marriage to the woman Ferenczi loved, a nonanalytic intervention that led to an underlying irreducible tension between Freud and his analysand Ferenczi.

Multiple Function and Over-Determination

For Wälder (1936), humans are driven impulsively by the id and purposefully by the ego. Every one of a person's actions is an attempt by the ego to solve a problem; even an apparently impulsive act is such an attempt. The ego must deal with (1) the claims of instinct and (2) the compulsion to repeat, as well as (3) the superego commands and prohibitions and (4) the outer world. It not only has to mediate among each of these, but it has its own disposition to dominate and overcome them and to join them to its organization by active assimulation. So each of the four poses two problems for the ego. Thus Wälder arrives at his principle of multiple function: any solution of one of the eight problems represents simultaneously an attempted solution of all the others. Each psychic act to some degree attempts to solve all the problems, although it always represents a compromise. On account of this, says Wälder, all people are perpetually dissatisfied.

Overdetermination means that several trends are expressed by, and there is a multiple meaning to, every action, symptom, and psychological expression. Multiple function implies that a definitive number of solutions are always expressed. Even in character formation, says Wälder, the solution must gratify the instinct as well as defend against it. A neurosis attempts solutions of all the problems. Every solution must be for the claims of the outer world, for instinctual pressure, for superego demands, and for the pressure of the compulsion to repeat, as well as for the attempt to master and assimilate all of these. Symptom formation and the neuroses are seen as having multiple meanings, multiple functions, and an overdetermination of meanings. This enormously complicates the interpretive process and also allows us to understand why there is such resistance to alteration of the ego, a resistance that even Freud (1937) recognized when he pointed out that the ego treats recovery as a danger. If so many things are being solved by any given symptom, a great deal is lost when the compromise formation is given up, and a whole Pandora's box of unresolved intrapsychic tensions is reopened.

The Mutative Interpretation

Would insight alone allow a patient to reendure such tensions? Or did some alteration of intrapsychic structure through the interaction with the analyst have to occur to make this possible? The next major step in understanding the factors that lead to change in psychoanalytic therapy was taken by Strachey (1934). His work is based on Kleinian theory and represents a direction followed by Kleinians and neo-Kleinians such as Kernberg in their characterization of factors that produce therapeutic change. Strachey begins by pointing out that 1912 to 1917 was the era of "resistance analysis," represented by Freud's papers on technique and Chapters 27 and 28 of the *Introductory Lectures on Psychoanalysis* (Freud, 1915–1917). Resistance analysis derived from the early concepts described in *Studies on Hysteria*, which assume that if one makes the unconscious conscious by an interpretation, the symptoms will disappear. When the symptoms did not disappear, this was explained as resistance, and due to the fact that the insight was only intellectual. The problem became one of how to get rid of the resistance. The idea at the time was that this would be a function of the will to recovery in the patient, of arguing with the patient about the importance of removing the resistance, and above all, of the transference, which allowed the analyst to influence the patient.

Strachey claimed that the part of the ego Freud wished to modify was the superego, the analyst taking the place of the superego. In the Kleinian view, the neurotic superego is sadistic and savage due to cycles of introjection and projection. The introjected image of the analyst is kept separate from the savage superego and functions as an auxiliary superego. The danger of this is that the arrangement can break down at any time, in which case there is a projection of the sadistic superego on the analyst that leads to a sudden sharp negative transference, a common clinical phenomenon.

A mutative interpretation, said Strachey (1934), calls attention at this highly affectually charged point to the difference between the reality of the analyst and what the patient is projecting onto the analyst. It breaks the vicious cycle, as what is now introjected will be more realistically benign and less hostile. Repeatedly, the harsh superego and the projection of it onto the analyst leads to a cycle of rage, projection, defense, and more rage. This is broken up by mutative interpretations involving these aspects of the transference. By the analyst's interpretation of primitive id impulses, the patient comes to realize that these are at an archaic fantasy object, not at the "real" analyst. So small doses of reality modify the patient's superego through the internalization of the analyst, better perceived as a benign object, into the superego.

Strachey described two phases of a mutative interpretation. The first is the patient's bit-by-bit realization that a quantity of id energy has been directed to the analyst, and the second is that the patient must be able to distinguish between the real analyst and a fantasy object. Of course this assumes that the analyst must avoid behavior that confirms the projection. Reassurance and encouraging the patient to see the analyst as good—affect-laden active approaches such as those of Ferenczi—are of no help because according to the Kleinians, the good object is then just introjected to defend against the bad object, and so the negative impulses will never appear, never be projected, and cannot be analyzed.

An important factor producing change in psychoanalytic therapy, said Strachey, is that every mutative interpretation must be at the emotional point of urgency and made deeply in spite of anxiety. According to the Kleinians, this is the safest way to eliminate the anxiety. The interpretation must be specified, detailed, and concrete. Reassurance, inexactness, and vagueness all blunt the mutative effect. Abreaction does not bring about alterations in the ego or superego. Extra-transference interpretations are not to the point of urgency and the object is not present, so that the patient cannot compare the real and fantasy object. For Strachey, therefore, extra-transference interpretations at worst can represent wild analysis; at best they are less effective but less risky and so can be essential, but they are not mutative.

The crucial factor in the therapeutic action of psychoanalysis, according to Strachey, is the modification of the superego by innumerable small steps through mutative interpretations. This approach, which rests on Kleinian theory and conceives of the analyst being internalized as a temporary new object, is still based on the notion that cognitive insight leads to an alteration of the ego. It implies an affect-laden interaction between the patient and the therapist in which the therapist is the arbiter of reality and has the responsibility to point out "distortions of reality" to the patient.

The Holding Environment

Winnicott and Fairbairn contended that not only does there have to be a change in the superego, but a change in self and object representations must come about through interpretations and through the experience of the analyst as a benign object in a holding environment.

Winnicott only partially subscribed to Kleinian metapsychology, for he emphasized providing an ambience or holding environment that did not foster the projection of all bad self and object representations. As explained above, a benign environment or a warmly benign analyst tends to be introjected, according to the Kleinians and neo-Kleinians, and may serve as a defense against the "all bad" self and object representations, which then do not get projected. Winnicott stressed an attitude of the therapist free from anxiety, to allow the patient self-discovery. He argued that with average expectable mothering, the ordinary baby would not be enraged or terrified by innate sadism. For Winnicott the paranoid–schizoid position of Klein was that of a baby kept waiting too long by an inattentive mother (Phillips, 1988). He also stressed that if environmental factors failed the child, it would develop militant self-sufficiency, what Winnicott called excessive mental functioning and loss of the psyche-soma couple. The child lives as if it had no mother and takes responsibility for the failed environment.

Winnicott said that psychoanalysis is connecting dissociated parts of the self, not modifying repression of the instincts (Phillips, 1988). He saw the mother–infant relationship as the primary model for psychoanalytic work; the psychoanalytic setting would restore the environment and allow the patient's development to resume. For Winnicott therapy required noninterference, providing a holding environment in order to allow natural growth processes to reassert themselves. His model was the rapport between the mother and the baby, and he thought of the analytic setting as a transitional space for collaborative exchange, an intermediate area of experiencing that allowed the patient to mature and develop the capacity to tolerate the continual illusionment and then disillusionment process that takes place throughout everyone's life. Winnicott feared that the deep Kleinian interpretations represented a form of indoctrination, and produced compliance in the patient rather than maturation. Thus it is clear that his conception of the factors producing change in psychoanalytic therapy was really quite different from that of analysts who based their work on the theories of Melanie Klein.

Modell (1976) emphasized the analyst's analytic attitude in the manner of Winnicott, and suggested that the analytic process itself becomes a transitional object. Especially in patients with preoedipal or narcissistic disorders, the first phase of analysis, according to Modell, might be called a cocoon in which the analyst has to wait because interpretations are not heard; the patient enjoys the illusion of being protected by the magically powerful therapist. Modell then described a middle phase in which narcissistic rage appears as the patient realizes that his or her idealization of the analyst is incorrect. At this point, Modell suggests that the analyst be more

confronting of the patient's grandiosity and of the cocoon fantasy. Here he disagreed with Kohut (1971, 1977),
who would leave these constructions alone until they
drop away by themselves. The end phase of analysis for
Modell is like the classical case, with focus on the transference neurosis and interpretations.

Modell's contribution was to emphasize the ambience
or holding aspect of the psychoanalytic process itself as a
factor producing change in psychoanalytic therapy. In
the psychoneuroses it provides the necessary background of safety for the transference to unfold; in the
character disorders, especially narcissistic and borderline, it "facilitates necessary ego consolidation so that
mutative interpretations may be eventually effective and
a therapeutic alliance may be established. It is only then
that elements of the transference neurosis emerge in a
form that can be analyzed" (p. 305). It follows that
whether one attempts an active affectual approach to
the patient or not, there is a substantial modicum of
gratification in the psychoanalytic treatment process;
attempts to ignore this as a crucial factor inducing
change, especially for preoedipally damaged patients,
can lead to a serious misunderstanding of what is happening in the treatment process.

The "Real" Relationship

As the focus on factors that produce change in psychoanalytic therapy shifted from cognitive insights to the
interaction between the patient and the analyst, including the setting in which analysis occurs, the time was
ripe for a theoretical paper that would remain clearly in

the mainstream of psychoanalytic theorizing while at the same time recognize the importance of the new relationship that the patient has with a new object, the analyst. As a pupil of Heidegger, Loewald was also exceptionally well suited to take a more philosophical perspective toward the analytic process. Although his (1980) paper follows the traditional view that understanding is communicated to the patient by interpretation, he goes on to explain that understanding represents an act to which the patient must be open and lend him- or herself. For Loewald, understanding is an act that involves some sort of mutual engagement or meeting of minds between the patient and the psychoanalyst, so that even understanding is no longer thought of as a purely cognitive process but as having an interpersonal quality to it. Loewald stresses the interaction itself, the new experience of appropriate parenting, as permitting distorted development to be corrected and to resume.

Loewald (1980) places himself squarely in the traditional psychoanalytic camp by claiming that ego development resumes in psychoanalysis, but he argues that this resumption is contingent on the relationship with a new object, the analyst. He attempts to explain how this takes place, using terminology that is not predominantly Kleinian. The interaction between the patient and the analyst leads to a situation in which, although the analyst makes himself available as a new object, as a result of the transference the patient experiences the analyst as an old one. The analyst must interpret this correctly, making it possible for a new object relationship to develop. However, the analyst cannot be detached if this is to happen; neutrality and objectivity are not the same as detachment.

Loewald utilizes the parent–child model. The parent has a more integrated vision of the child and their relationship, and the child, according to Loewald, internalizes this through identification and introjection. This leads to a greater ego integration. The analyst functions as the representative of a higher stage of organization and mediates this to the patient—at the same time interpretation is taking the patient toward regression by uncovering compromise formations and defenses.

The patient wants unsublimated gratification, but interpretation and language mediate a higher organization to the patient. By the use of language, the analyst reveals him- or herself as more mature, and as one who understands the patient's experiences as something more than they have been for the patient. This "something more" in organization and significance is represented and mediated by the analyst. The patient strives to reach this something more, which produces an integrative experience.

For Loewald, transference has two meanings. First there is the object cathexis, a transfer of libido and aggression to the analyst as object. Second, there is the transfer of relationships with infantile objects to later objects such as the analyst. A revival and reenactment of the early relationships with the parents takes place, an interaction process that is internalized in ego development. For Loewald, not only objects but interaction processes are internalized, both in childhood and in analysis as correction of alterations in the ego takes place. The analyst also mediates better integration through his or her own maturity and his or her capacity for controlled regression, that is, a greater freedom to move between the unconscious and the preconscious, "and thus of higher, interpenetrating organization of both" (p. 252).

Cooper (1988) compares the views of Strachey and Loewald. Strachey and the Kleinians claim that innate oral aggression leads to the formation of hostile introjects and a harsh superego. This results in the further projection of aspects of these orally aggressive introjected objects back onto the external object, which will now be experienced as even more dangerous and frightening, leading in turn to a more destructive introject. Mutative transference interpretations break this cycle by changing the superego. For Strachey, writes Cooper,

> This model of therapeutic action seems straightforward, based on classical instinct theory and resistance analysis, and interlarded with a bit of Kleinian object relations theory. The role of the analyst is as a neutral benign interpreter of reality, internalized as a temporary new object, helping to make the unconscious conscious, and modifying the superego. Classical analytic neutrality is preserved (p. 19).

Loewald, on the other hand, presents a drastic reform of instinct theory because for him the id is seen as originating in the interaction with the mother. He greatly expands the interactive role on the basis of his conception that object relations are constitutive in structure formation rather than just regulative for the patient. The concept that motivation comes not from drives but arises out of an interaction of the subject and object is crucial to understanding Loewald's view of the factors that produce change in psychoanalysis. Cooper (1988) continues, "Loewald believes as strongly as Kohut ever did that the empathic milieu of the child during development and of the analyst during analysis are the vital ingredients for the development of psychic health" (p. 23). Kohut, however, viewed empathy as the primary method of psychoanalytic data gathering, but Loewald conceived of it as the provision of a new integrative experience for the patient. The ambiguity arises, as Cooper points out, from the two prevailing descriptions of analytic activity: "the metapsychological description of goals, and the interactive and phenomenological description of process" (p. 26). These two descriptions are very difficult to translate into each other or even to integrate or be presented in a complementary manner (Chessick, 1985, 1988).

Loewald (Fogel, 1989) views the analyst as a new object for the resumption of development; the analyst reflects reality and structures and channels the patient's experience. For Loewald, there is no neutral objective analyst and there is a parallel between the psychoanalytic treatment process and the mother–infant interaction, in which there is a tension between the higher organization of the analyst and the lower organization of the patient across which the patient reaches. All this takes place in the context of the transference neurosis that Loewald (1980) describes as "due to the blood of recognition, which the patient's unconscious is given to taste so that the old ghosts may reawaken to life" (pp. 248–249). The work of analysis is equated with laying to rest these revitalized ghosts so that they may be transformed into ancestors, a metaphor borrowed from Chapter 7 of Freud's (1900) *Interpretation of Dreams.* This transformation of ghosts into ancestors takes place through cycles of disorganization followed by regression and deconstruction, and then interpretation and reconstruction with reorganization at a higher level. The motivation for this comes about from a tension arc between the lower form of organization in the patient and the higher form of organization in the analyst, across which the patient reaches and which impels the patient to higher and higher phases of integration and development. This viewpoint puts the personality of the analyst and the interaction with the analyst at the center of the correction process for alterations of the ego.

The conservative opposition to this form of theorizing is provided by Eissler (1953), for whom the analyst must be confined to questions and interpretations; everything else represents "parameters" that must be interpreted. The attempt to codify analytic orthodoxy has been carried to its extreme by the work of Langs (1982). Eissler's paper forms a contrasting viewpoint to Alexander's concept of corrective emotional experience, but it could also be used for comparison with the conceptions of Loewald. It remains an excellent statement of the so-called "traditional" psychoanalytic view.

Analyst as Selfobject

An opposing direction to traditional psychoanalysis, and which resembles the work of Winnicott, was developed by the self psychologists. Empathic understanding of the patient's experience of what the patient takes to be failures in the analyst's empathy becomes central to the treatment. In Kohut's (1971) early view, transmuting internalizations as a consequence of these experienced empathic failures after selfobject transferences have formed leads to strengthening of the structure of the self; in his later view empathy itself as experienced from the analyst is the central curative factor (Chessick, 1985).

Kohut's conceptual shift from transmuting internalizations, based on dynamics and energetics in Freud's metapsychology, as curative in psychoanalytic therapy to empathy as curative, represents a shift from a focus on mechanisms to a focus on the experiential and the transactional in the treatment. Terman (1989) points out that self psychologists can be classified on the basis of this shift. The explanatory–interpretive group, in which he includes Basch, Lichtenberg, and Post, claims that the curative process in psychoanalytic therapy occurs when a self psychologist recognizes and interprets the vicissitudes of the selfobject transference. The assumption is that change will occur on the basis of this alone. The crucial function of the analyst is to articulate archaic affect states for the patient. Terman explains, "The weight of emphasis, then, is on the explanatory–interpretive aspects of the therapeutic process—not as they facilitate a different experience in a relationship nor as they permit internalization of functions but as they foster inner cognitive transformations" (p. 92).

Terman calls the other group the relationship or experiential group, in which he includes himself as well as Ornstein, Stolorow, and Bacal. This group believes that a happy archaic transference enables development to resume. It emphasizes optimal responsiveness, not optimal frustration, as crucial. The experience of a new relationship becomes central to the patient's resumption of development. So even among self psychologists, the same polarization occurs between those who emphasize cognition and articulation as crucial factors in altering the ego and those who emphasize experience, relationship, and interaction. One of the disadvantages of self psychology is that neither group presents a very convincing specific metapsychological formulation of how the self is altered either by optimal frustration with transmuting internalization or by optimal responsiveness and empathy. This refinement remains for the future.

Certain analysts who are not self psychologists also insist that crucial noninterpretative elements must be provided in the psychoanalytic process in order for change to take place. Although Stone (1981) believes that interpretation is the crucial factor for change in the psychoanalytic process, he insists that it is effective only in the proper ambience. He also emphasizes the importance of clarification, properly timed questions, and the interruption of silence—all of which he considers "preparatory or ancillary to mutative interpretation" (p. 96).

Noninterpretive elements in the situation that contribute to the process are embedded in the analyst's attitude, providing it is reasonable and decent; such aspects include the tone and rhetorical quality of the analyst's verbal interventions, his or her facial expression at the beginning and end of the sessions, and the affectual tone in which realities such as hours, fees, absences, intercurrent life crises, and so forth are dealt with.

A certain kind of elasticity in the analyst's personality is needed. Lipton (1977, 1979) produced an excellent study of the climate of Freud's analyses, which preserves a real adult object relationship, although restricted, and a natural friendly and appropriate interaction between the patient and the analyst. In another publication, I (Chessick, 1988) have discussed the details of Freud's (1909) treatment of Paul Lorenz in the light of Lipton's attention to Freud's actual practice of psychoanalytic therapy.

Empathy is an extremely important factor in the psychoanalytic process, although Stone, in contrast to Kohut, does not feel that it makes up for maternal deficits. The indestructibility of the analyst is another important factor, and Stone gives Winnicott (1969) the credit for bringing this to our attention. In his conclusion, Stone (1981) reminds us that the psychoanalytic process begins and ends between two adults. The patient has every right to ask the question, "What sort of person is this to whom I am entrusting my entire mental and emotional being?" (p. 113). The entire argument of Stone's paper is directed against "the superfluous iatrogenic regressions attendant on superfluous deprivations, whether or not the patient is aware of suffering as such" (p. 113). He wishes to produce a natural interpersonal ambience as a consequence of the analyst's natural attitude toward the patient, which he does not view as curative per se, but provides an optimum ambience for effective interpretive work.

CONTROVERSIES

Osman and Tabachnick (1988) begin their survey of "Essentials of Psychoanalytic Cure" with Freud's view that the establishment and resolution of the transference neurosis is the crucial curative factor in psychoanalytic work. But Glover argued at the 1936 Marienbad Symposium that for interpretations to be efficacious, especially in the "deeper pathological states, a prerequisite of the efficacy of interpretation is the attitude, the true unconscious attitude, of the analyst to his patient" (Glover, 1937, p. 131). At that symposium (Osman and Tabachnick, 1988) Sterba described the meliorative function of introjection in a mutative interpretation as altering the ego rather than the superego, since the patient could imitate the therapist's analytic attitude of objective observing and in consequence alter his or her ego to conform to this example. The concept of the therapeutic alliance was brought up by Zetzel (1956) and later studied by Greenson (1965) as the "working alliance." Loewald (1980), as we have seen, conceived of the new object relationship as useful in the resumption of development and the correction of reality distortion. The maturity of the analyst becomes crucial and represents a higher stage of integration for the patient, just as the mother mediates this for the child. Stone (1961) stressed the affective bond or "primordial transference" as crucial in facilitating understanding and integration for the patient. He advised analysts to permit the patient to experience their physicianly vocation as "an integrated reality—syntonic representation of parental functions" (p. 110).

At the Edinburg symposium in 1961, Gitelson and Nacht emphasized the patient's emotional attachment to the analyst as a significant facilitator of the integrating or restructuring outcome of successful analytic work. Most of the participants in the conference, however, sided with such Kleinians as Segal, who emphasized the acquisition of insight through interpretation and again argued that emphasis on the positive affective aspect of the relationship makes it impossible to analyze the patient's inherent sadism and aggression. In contrast to this, Nacht (1962) viewed the affective interaction of the analyst with the patient as the most crucial factor in effecting a cure when he claimed, "What matters is what the analyst is rather than what he says" (Osman and Tabachnick, 1988, p. 106).

This controversy resurfaced in the 1977 debate (Scharfman, 1979) between the followers of Kernberg, who utilize a contemporary object relations viewpoint based on an arbitrary selection of some of the aspects of Kleinian theory, and the self psychologists, who emphasize the primordial or archaic self/selfobject bond that forms between the patient and the analyst as the patient experiences the analyst's empathic capacity.

The Role of Countertransference

The psychoanalytic process is both conflict resolution via interpretation leading to insight and working through, and a development-enhancing experience in a new object relationship. Shane and Shane (1989) suggest an inevitable interrelationship and interdigitation between these two aspects of the psychoanalytic process:

Resolution of unconscious conflict liberates an arrested or skewed developmental process in the patient. The structure-building consequences of this development enable the patient to face with greater courage and confidence dangerous dysphoric affects inherent in even more deeply buried conflict. And so on. The effect is an increasingly authentic engagement in the analytic relationship. This, we believe, is the meliorative circular ascending spiral discoverable in any productive analytic relationship (p. 337).

If this is correct, the special characteristics of the analyst, as already emphasized by Winnicott, including consistent interest in the patient, benign neutrality, capacity to forego expected retaliations, ability to maintain integrity despite attacks or seductions from the patient, and his or her "consistent and persistent curiosity about and attempt to interpret the meanings of the patient's neurotic behaviors, both outside the treatment and in the transference" (Cooper, 1989, p. 12), lead directly to focus on the role of countertransference. Slakter (1987) reviews our evolving understanding of countertransference, which comprises a complex system of unconscious cues, both given and received, and arises out of a dynamic interaction between the patient and the therapist.

Without reference to Moliere's play in 1666 describing *The Misanthrope,* Newman (1988) explains:

The tragedy of character is that it so often works to interfere with what the subject needs most—a usable object. This is most poignant with people who have suffered significant early traumata and therefore have reorganized their psychic structures with highly protective mechanisms. Frequently, the pathological character repetitively works to achieve the conviction of the unusability of the current objects through evoking complementary responses from the companion object. . . . Whether intentionally induced or not, whenever the external object enacts the complementary role to the patient's character, once more the patient gains conviction that distance must be maintained. Thus, the new object in the patient's mind becomes identified with and contaminated by the original object, and is thereby disqualified for use as a new object" (p. 251).

For Newman, patients in this manner produce countertransference, which in turn tells us about their internal objects. The analyst typically experiences negative attitudes, painful affects, and a profound sense of being demeaned and considered useless. Out of the intense interaction, patients can learn about their archaic objects if the analyst can manage his or her countertransference.

In pathological development the child's disappointment and consequent rage and protest are not soothed. The parental object is viewed as nonresponsive and unable to contain the results of nonresponsiveness, so it is seen as doubly dangerous. The patient is fixed at the level of intense primary or archaic need states. The character structure that results from these early developmental failures wards off the internal pain of needs and the attachment to "an intrusive, critical, excessively narcissistic, unavailable object" (Newman, p. 257). The character so formed provides the illusion of connectedness to objects but controls the attachment to new objects for distancing either through compliance or control, a phenomenon known as the "defense transference," which is immediately experienced at the beginning of psychoanalytic therapy as the patient uses the same characterologic maneuvers toward the therapist. The analyst's reactions to this allow the analyst to sample the faulty objects of the patient's childhood, and if the analyst can manage the countertransference, it will facilitate "an authentic recognition of the patient's inner world and in effect supplies a missing function" (Newman, p. 274). Therefore, the proper mastery of countertransference facilitates the process of change in psychoanalytic therapy.

But Newman (1988) carries this further by insisting that in the treatment of some patients this enmeshment in the transference–countertransference experience is *necessary*, a drama that must be repeated with affective participation by both parties to the relationship in order for the patient to come to grips with the psychic reality of what happened in the past. Kligerman, in the discussion that follows Newman's paper, points out, "A decisive amount depends on the empathy, skill, and honesty of the analyst who . . . is only too prone to feel bruised and narcissistically wounded himself, and, in subtle or not-so-subtle ways, tends to blame the patient" (Newman, p. 278). But this does not only involve reacting to the aggressive attacking and demeaning patient; Terman, in discussing Newman's paper, reminds us it may also apply to the compliant patient. The greatest difficulty in such situations is in the analyst's having to dislodge both parties "from a position of comfort to one of greater tension and uncertainty" (Newman, p. 281).

The whole issue of what constitutes countertransference remains unresolved and is beyond the scope of this introduction (see Chessick, 1986); a shift toward a more inclusive conceptualization has been traced by Abend (1989). For Freud, countertransference was simply a block to listening, representing certain blind spots in the analyst. Winnicott (1949) and the Kleinians Heimann (1950) and Little (1951) insisted that *all* the analyst's responses to the patient be included under countertransference. Abend argues that the current widened definition of countertransference is a phenomenon of the general de-idealization of authority in the world, and he correctly maintains that transforming countertransference into empathy and understanding is a crucial skill of the analyst, "perhaps the ultimate test of the gifted analytic clinician" (p. 389).

Blatt and Behrends (1987) stress the "gratifying involvement" that takes place between the patient and the therapist in the analytic process, which they see as the first step in the internalization process that allows the patient to change through the replacement of pathological introjects by the analytic introject. For them, progress in treatment occurs through the same mechanisms as normal growth, and therefore both the relationship and interpretation are essential components. At the same time as the therapy is experienced as a series of gratifying involvements, the analytic process is experienced as a series of incompatibilities "that facilitate internalization, whereby the patient recovers lost or disrupted regulatory, gratifying interactions with the analyst, which are real or fantasied, by appropriating these interactions, transforming them into their own, enduring, self-generated functions and characteristics" (p. 293).

Current Traditional Positions

Boesky (1988) regards the ego as a conceptual abstraction of great explanatory power, a group of functions. In the technical theory of Freud's structural model, the analyst interprets in order ultimately to help the patient achieve an alteration in his or her "pathological compromise formations in the direction of less defensive rigidity, more realistic pleasure, less affective pain, and the best possible conditions for the adaptive and flexible functioning of the patient" (p. 307). Resistance from the modern structural point of view is "a compromise formation between defenses, drive derivatives, painful affects, the need for punishment, and considerations of reality" (p. 309). Boesky insists that it is not true that our sickest patients suffer from pathology that is outside of conflict. Our task as analysts is to interpret these conflicts, and nature will build the psychic structure. What really "propels the psychoanalytic process," writes Boesky, is "examining, describing, and interpreting alterations in a variety of resistances" (p. 314).

For Rangell (1989), the unconscious ego makes choices, which he considers to be "an ongoing core process of mental functioning" (p. 190). This exercise of unconscious choice by the ego is very important for understanding the psychoanalytic process, because active unconscious ego choices determine the selection of defenses and the nature of external behavior. This assumes secondary process functioning in the unconscious, an idea not generally accepted. Rangell argues that there is a full range of secondary process unconscious activity, "evaluating, planning and executing action" (p. 200). These functions are affected by interpretation in the analytic process, during which the ego continuously judges what repressed material may be allowed into expression. The analytic process provides a strengthening of the ego through interpretation. This allows it to decide to face further repressed material, which, when interpreted, leads to further strengthening. Using the concept of unconscious choice, the method in which the ego is altered in the psychoanalytic process can be characterized in a specific fashion.

Arlow (1985) believes that certain central infantile unconscious fantasies are so important that they determine in their derivative manifestations the patient's symptoms, character, life history, object relations, and even creative endeavors. The decisive step Freud took from his early theory that neuroses were caused by literal sexual abuse of children during the first few years of life, to his focus on the central role of sexual fantasies that had a psychic reality in the patient's unconscious is carried to its logical conclusion by Arlow's work, as I (Chessick, 1988) have discussed elsewhere. What is crucial to produce change in psychoanalysis, if Arlow is correct, is that the patient must eventually become aware of this basic, unconscious infantile fantasy life and how it utterly pervades his or her past and present.

Focus on the Curative Fantasy

Ornstein and Ornstein (1977), in a quite different emphasis from the traditional view, stress the "curative fantasy" with which the patient begins treatment, the wish to have the past undone and made up for. When this is activated in the treatment, there occurs an inter-action or engagement with the therapist, whose re-sponses to this are crucial. According to these authors, the therapist must help curative fantasies emerge and deal with the guilt over them, allowing them to transform and mature. What is curative is not primarily nonspecific "physicianly vocation" elements in the treatment, but the increased unfolding of archaic curative fantasies, the wish to use the therapist as a selfobject (Kohut) and the hope for a "new beginning" (Balint). The curative fantasy motivates the patient toward recovery based on the as-sumption that the treatment will compensate for every-thing by bringing power, skills, and success.

The interpretation of this fantasy depends on one's theoretical orientation. For example, some would relate it to infantile instinctual aims that seek satisfaction in the transference, similar to Freud's discussion of a cure by love. The Ornsteins, from the point of view of self psy-chology, focus on the patient's new hopes, which, due to the fear of disappointment, are defended against. This is experienced by the analyst as "resistance." Patients may need to set up rejecting situations, in spite of their wish to be accepted, as a defense against the possibility of disappointment. Attempting to get the patient to face his or her hostility when these fantasies are disappointed and when projection takes place implies that the patient is unlovable and that something is fundamentally wrong with him or her. Such interpretations, according to the Ornsteins and other self psychologists, just retraumatize the patient. The rage must be accepted as appropriate to the patient's experienced reality, as a response to an experienced injury due to the disappointed wish for unconditional success, acceptance, power, and skills. For self psychologists, empathic acceptance, followed by understanding, followed by interpretation, remains the crucial set of factors in analytic cure (Kohut, 1984, Chessick, 1985).

New Directions for Investigation

Some of the later work in understanding the factors that contribute to psychoanalytic cure centers around the expectations and beliefs that the patient established from early experiences. These are *not* conceived as of fantasies or derivatives of instinctual wishes. They provide safety for the patient against being retraumatized and are tested again and again in the transference. This emphasizes actual early experiences that underlie our later remembered fantasies and wishes, and relates more to self psychology and behavioral conceptions than to Arlow's and to traditional conceptions.

Weiss and Sampson (1986) believe that control is possible over one's unconscious mental life; that one regulates it with respect to beliefs and external reality on the principle of avoiding danger and maintaining safety. For them, unconscious ego thinking is experimental action, like normal thought. We learn unconsciously from our early experiences, acquire beliefs, and on the basis of these, develop long-term goals. Due to such unconscious beliefs, we may suffer guilt, shame, or remorse, and this causes certain rigid, constricted, maladaptive behavior.

For example, the authors stress as a crucial problem in psychopathology the unconscious guilt about separation from the mother: "If I grow and develop it will hurt my mother." Indeed, they view "much of" (p. 67) adult psychopathology as caused by a child's wish to maintain the ties with the parents because of the unconscious guilt over separation that the child believes will hurt the parents. There are two ways such beliefs arise. Either the child attempts to gratify its impulse or reach an important goal and discovers that this threatens the tie to the parents, at which point parental behavior and response become crucial, or a traumatic event occurs, for which the child blames itself, believing the event was caused by his or her wish to gratify an impulse or reach an important goal. The authors claim that patients who feel that they do not deserve to be loved make rapid progress when they recognize this unconscious guilt. A deficit cannot be filled by subsequent good relationships in the ordinary course of life if the individual does not feel that he or she deserves a good relationship. This is why adult patients have persistent "deficits," for otherwise they would correct these deficits much earlier through new relationships.

For these authors, the patient works with the analyst in the psychoanalytic process to disconfirm pathogenic beliefs by testing them with respect to the analyst and by understanding them via interpretations. The motive to do this is very strong because these unconscious expectations and beliefs are very constricting and produce painful guilt. The authors argue that the roots of this theory may be found in Freud and that analysts have ignored his comments about the ego's unconscious thinking, believing, testing, and planning as emphasized also by Rangell (1989) from a more traditional standpoint, discussed previously.

Another important form of testing is by turning the passive into the active. The patient behaves to the analyst as his or her parent behaved to the patient. This is in contrast to the transference, where the patient behaves to the analyst as he or she behaved to a parent. Weiss and Sampson claim that all patients do both in order to keep traumatic memories repressed. Testing by turning the passive into the active is done with the hope that the analyst will not react by getting upset but will maintain the analytic stance. If so, the patient can identify with the analyst's lesser vulnerability and question the childhood belief that the trauma was deserved. This may be observed in extra-analytic situations also, for it is not unusual that later in life the grown child may treat the parent the way the child felt treated by the parent when the child was young. The more traumatized the patient was, the more likely he or she will begin the treatment with the test involving change from passive to active, as this is safer than the ordinary transference.

The authors believe that with testing and utilizing interpretation the ego controls the transference and keeps the expression of it appropriate and relatively safe. Thus after-education or new experiences with the analyst are the key to psychoanalytic treatment. In their emphasis on testing and new experiences, these authors, although they start with the same premise about the ego's capacity for unconscious judgment as does Rangell (1989), come up with a conception of how psychoanalytic treatment works quite different from the more traditional one.

None of the authors cited above, to my knowledge, have raised the issue of bifurcation (Davies, 1980) as a new direction for investigation. Bifurcation in physics is a phenomenon whereby the number of solutions of a certain type presented by a dynamic system changes abruptly as one of the parameters defining the dynamics crosses a critical value. This concept could be applied to Brenner's (1982) firm conceptualization of all symptoms and behavior as representing a compromise formed by the ego from among the demands of the id, the superego, and reality. Change of symptoms, change of behavior, so-called structural improvement in psychoanalysis, then, would all represent a change in the compromise formations formed by the ego. It follows that a sudden and abrupt jump in the direction of improvement could take place if one of the parameters defining the dynamics that are at play on the ego when it has to form a compromise suddenly shifts or crosses a critical value; the same would be true in the opposite direction. This explains the common phenomenon of there appearing to be a plateau or lack of progress in a psychoanalysis for long periods of time, then an apparent sudden breakthrough where compromise formations sharply shift.

An abrupt negative shift may be most commonly observed if the patient develops some kind of organic disease. The bodily needs and requirements are massively increased and the ego sometimes has to deal with them at the expense of more fortunate compromises; the onset of a bodily disease can even be heralded by the appearance of such negative shifts. For example, it is well known that pancreatic cancer is often preceded by a period of depression, and other authors have reported either depressive or hypomanic behavior heralding the onset of coronary artery disease, (Chessick, 1985).

xlvi

Another such bifurcation occurs in severely damaged patients who have experienced disappointment in archaic selfobject expectations. Here the narcissistic rage is so overwhelming that a critical value is crossed; previous compromise formations such as obsessional rituals or masochism are suddenly overshadowed by massive projection and projective identification. This is an emergency and can break up the treatment if the ego's capacity to respond to interpretations is lost.

This can also occur in psychoanalysis as the patient's core fantasy activity (Arlow, 1985), described previously, is approached. In those cases where the fear of revelation of this core is overwhelming, the patient may suddenly disrupt the analysis by projection in which the analyst is perceived as an intrusive, malevolent monster. Although this perception itself is a derivative of the core fantasy activity, if there is no sufficient tension regulation and capacity for insight, the patient cannot continue the treatment. At this point the patient may insist on sitting up or even leaving therapy on the basis of overwhelming fear of the process or of the analyst. Characteristically, they go on to some other form of group or supportive therapy that does not address the core fantasy activity.

My Views

Arlow (1985) stresses that after the age of 6 or 7 everyone has a unique typical repetitive fantasy activity, and adult conscious fantasy life reflects derivatives of this. Even our perception is determined by this crucial unconscious fantasy activity, which forms "the mental

xlvii

set against which the data of perception are perceived, registered, interpreted, remembered, and responded to" (p. 526). These fantasies go through convolutions as one develops, and some later editions may even provide defensive distortions of earlier fantasies. He writes:

> In the course of treatment one can observe how the symptoms of the patient's illness, how his life history and his love relations, his character structure and his artistic creations may all represent in different ways derivative manifestations of the persistent unconscious fantasy activity of the "fantasied reality" that governs the individual's life.(p. 534).

Arlow views the analyst's behavior as a stimulus, as a day residue, but it is through the stimulation of the patient's unconscious fantasy life that the reaction we call transference occurs. Even in the transference, at least at first, we see only derivatives of the persistent unconscious fantasy activity of childhood that governs the individual's life. I agree with this out of my own clinical experience (Chessick, 1988, 1990). At the core of every patient there resides a crucial fantasy activity, interwoven with early infantile experiences to a greater or lesser degree, depending on how traumatic these experiences have been. But Arlow explains, "What constitutes trauma is not inherent in the actual, real event, but rather the individual's response to the disorganizing, disruptive combination of impulses and fears integrated into a set of unconscious fantasies" (p. 533). Certain object relations and self psychology theories tend to minimize the role of this unconscious fantasy activity and emphasize the pathogenic effect of real events and

xlviii

interactions. But the individual's experience, explains Arlow (1980), "is usually organized in terms of a few, leading, unconscious phantasies which dominate an individual's perception of the world and create the mental set by which she or he perceives and interprets her/his experience" (p. 131). Transference is not a repetition of the patient's actual early interactions with present objects, but expresses derivatives of the patient's persistent unconscious childhood fantasies, the "psychic reality" of these early interactions for the patient.

My position is that empathy with the patient that allows the selfobject transferences to arise is a vital way of beginning the treatment. Along with the physicianly vocation of the analyst, empathy sets up an ambience that is optimal for the integration of interpretations and for the development of a new object relationship. This object relationship, as it arises out of the proper ambience of the treatment, continuously provides the motivation for the patient to develop, whether one wishes to view it with Freud as love for the analyst or with Loewald as a developmental reaching out toward higher levels of integration.

The setting of the analytic treatment with the patient on the couch and doing most of the talking promotes regression. The rule of abstinence, properly applied, promotes the resurgence of yearnings for old objects, the appearance of fantasy activity, and the subsequent development of the transference. If the patient is excessively gratified, the transference does not appear, but if the patient is irrationally or sadistically ungratified in the treatment, the reaction will be one of iatrogenic narcissism and rage, which cannot properly be called transference. Everything depends on the maturation, skill, and clinical judgment of the analyst.

The interpretation of the transference and of extra-transference situations should aim at focusing on the central core of the patient through the continuous analysis of derivatives of that core. The patient's observing ego must engage with the analyst and eventually take over the search for the crucial infantile fantasies and/or traumata and identify them. However, as Arlow points out, events such as the primal scene are rarely directly remembered. What counts as the patient's psychic reality is a basic core of fantasies or traumata in some combination of intensity, woven into a unique special fantasy activity; in some patients the material will be almost purely fantasy and in others the most serious kind of abuse and exposure to real horror and death has taken place. Still, no matter how great the traumata, it is the basic unique fantasy activity woven around traumata that has the primary effect on all the patient's subsequent behavior and capacity to relate to other people.

If this vital core can be reached, identified, and worked through with the patient, it allows the past to recede into the past and no longer pervade the present. The ghosts can become ancestors (Loewald, 1980). This offers the ego new options, new choices, and new compromises in dealing with its three harsh masters—the id, superego, and reality. Thus, although change can occur in psychoanalytic therapy through a new object relationship or an empathic experience with an understanding analyst, a basic structural change that does not simply consist of identification or internalization of a more

1

benign object can only come about, in my opinion, when there has been a thorough understanding of the early infantile fantasy activity that forms the background mental set of the patient's perceptual and motor system, the core of the patient's psychic reality. Derivatives of these fantasies can be found in every aspect of the patient's choices, behavior, and relationships in later life and they persist to an amazing degree even into old age. Hence the wise saying, "If you do what you've always done, you'll get what you've always got."

It has also been my experience that some analyses are aborted as this core is approached; the treatment is covered over by a superficial and premature turn toward increased integration and maturation, giving the impression that the patient has made a recovery and suggesting termination. The uncovering of these fantasies is vigorously defended against, as they represent some kind of crucial compromise formation in an attempt to master infantile anxieties, traumata, and conflicts. To expose them renders the patient vulnerable to reexperiencing the intense dread of annihilation and overwhelming fragmentation the infant suffered at a time when it was as yet extremely incapable of dealing with such powerful affects. This, in my judgment, forms the bedrock of analytic treatment; if the patient cannot bear to have this core exposed, the treatment will abort and remain a psychotherapy even though an apparently superficial improvement in the patient may take place. This leaves the patient vulnerable to continual pervasion of his or her behavior and choices by the core infantile fantasy activity, so that the improvement is maintained only as long as the internalization of the therapist continues.

A dramatic example of that is in Freud's (1918) case of the Wolf Man, who internalized the gratification of being Freud's famous patient and imagined himself under the protection of the apparently omnipotent Freud until the time he heard Freud had developed cancer. At this point the patient broke down, and his recovery took place when he was able cleverly to establish himself not as the special patient of the omnipotent Freud, but as a sort of "mascot" of the entire psychoanalytic movement, which protected him against the sickness or death of any individual psychoanalyst. This resulted in a lasting improvement in his condition (Gardiner, 1971).

I do not wish to diminish the importance of empathic understanding of the patient and of the analysis of selfobject or archaic transferences, but this work is only preliminary to the basic analytic task of altering the ego; it must be carried through before a sufficient alliance can be formed with the patient to allow the observing ego of the patient to join in the search for the core fantasies. In Menninger's (1958) concept of the psycho-analytic process, written before Kohut's self psychology, there occurs after a suitable period of frustration of the patient's curative fantasy, a turning around, which Menninger labels *kairos* from the Greek of Hippocrates, a turning around toward maturation that takes place at a suitable or proper point in the analytic regression. The question is whether this turning around does not represent an escape from the analysis of the patient's core, and constitutes a reintegration motivated prima-rily by an attempt to avoid depth analysis. In that sense,

Menninger's process might be better labeled a psycho-therapy, as basic structural change does not occur.

I believe this accounts for the failure of many of the early psychoanalyses, in which the patient's Oedipus complex was analyzed according to the then prevailing custom, and the patient pronounced cured, after which some of these "analyzed" early analysts went on to manifest serious psychopathology, even psychosis and suicide. There is no reason why, after the influence of the analyst has passed, the early core fantasy activity should not regain its pervasive motivating power if it has not been uncovered and worked through, leaving the ego open to new options and choices.

This approach stresses conflicts more than deficits, so that situations like "alexithymia" and other alleged deficits, such as the inability to experience hunger in the eating disorders (Chessick, 1985a), that have been attributed to primary deficits in development could be at least partly understood as existing on the basis of conflict. Such disorders would then have a better prognosis in that once the conflict over the repressed infantile fantasies was resolved, the so-called "deficits," to whatever extent they are derivatives of the fantasy activity, could disappear. In the manner of Gedo (1979) we may also address and try to correct the "deficits" directly, a form of after-education therapy that, although it may be very useful for the patient, does not really constitute an investigation of the patient's unconscious by the method of psychoanalysis that Arlow (1985) says is "fundamentally . . . a psychology of conflict" (p. 525).

The disagreement between my views and self psychology is that I believe that after one has worked through the narcissistic transferences and the oedipal material begins to appear as in Kohut's (1977) case of Mr. M., the treatment is not over. Rather, the stage has now been properly set for a traditional analysis. When the walls and the roof of a house crack because they are resting on a faulty foundation, obviously one must first repair the foundation. Self psychologists maintain that in humans, in contrast to a house, there is an inherent developmental force that will take over and repair the rest once the foundation is secure. But can this occur without further psychoanalytic treatment of distortions due to the patient's pathological ego alterations in further childhood stages with their characteristic conflicts, defenses, compromises, and fantasy activities?

The foundation must be repaired first if at all possible. Here the method of empathy and the study of archaic transferences become central, and it is only after these have been worked through and understood by the patient and the building of a reasonably firm tension regulation system has been established can the patient then tolerate the development of more traditional transferences and the frustrations and tensions that the rule of abstinence entails. This was Kohut's (1971) earlier conception of self psychology, which was more consistent with traditional psychoanalysis (Chessick, 1985). In practice these days, most patients seem to need some degree of foundational repair, but in less serious cases this can go on *pari passu* with traditional interpretation. Some patients, however, need a very long period of restoration of the self first; Modell's (1976) "cocoon phase" may have to go on for years.

liv

Psychoanalytic Psychotherapy

Rothstein (1988) assembles a number of authors who concentrate on the various factors that produce change in psychoanalytic psychotherapy. The primordial meaning of the psychoanalytic situation lies in its reverberations for the preoedipal child in the patient. A strong argument can be made that this was even true for the treatments described in Freud's famous case histories (Buckley, 1989). There seems to be a general agreement (Rothstein, 1968) that the more disturbed the patient the less the treatment may be called psychoanalysis and the more it involves influencing, suggestion, correction of expectations, stabilization, superego modification, and model provision for identification or introjection, as well as holding and support, with a focus on solving specific problems. Healthier patients seem to require only a reasonable modicum of these factors and can concentrate more on reliving in the transference and reconstruction through interpretation. What is paramount in any given therapy is a function of what aspect of the patient's development is being repeated with the therapist at any given time, since, as Holinger (1989) points out, that developmental stage is what determines the meaning of a given intervention. Thus the context and not just the content of any intervention must be considered in judging the appropriateness of the intervention and whether the treatment is to be called psychoanalysis or psychotherapy. The goal of the former is reorganization of psychic structure through the formation and resolution of the transference, whereas the goal of the latter is more directly problem oriented.

Basch (Rothstein, 1988) delineates three types of therapy. The first directly addresses counterproductive behavior and is a form of behavior therapy. The second directly influences the patient's thinking, adaptation, and problem solving, and is a form of cognitive therapy. The third, or psychoanalytic therapy, influences the patient's thinking and behaving indirectly by helping the patient understand how he or she comes to function as he or she does. Bringing about change in psychoanalytic therapy depends on our empathic grasp of the particular stage of development being relived in the transference or with the therapist as an object at any given time in the process.

It is our task as therapists to be able in each case to identify the predominant transference and predominant mode of relationship that the patient is using at any given time, and to tune the emphasis in the therapy to those factors that are appropriate to that developmental phase, while at the same time minimizing or de-emphasizing those factors that are inappropriate. For example, a severely disturbed chaotic patient, as Stern (1985) points out, is manifesting preoedipal pathology in which defective coping operations and interpersonal invariants have determined the developmental course and were needed for adaptation. After language has been acquired, the so-called "defenses" that we experience from the patient are secondary reworkings of this. The original problem of such preoedipal disturbed patients is coping with reality and not, he says, due to various representations or fantasies.

Gedo (1979, 1986) emphasizes the failure of such patients to develop normal skills. This is "beyond interpretation," and the therapist must deliberately demonstrate these adaptive skills to the patient. If the therapist refuses to educate the patient, claims Gedo, then there has simply been another parental failure. These preverbal patterns are the hardest to modify because they are crucial in tension relief. There is no correlation of self and object representations with the patient–analyst exchange, claims Gedo, in direct contrast to the views of Kernberg. The transference depends on the analyst's personality, specific issues brought in by the personal qualities of the analyst, and the technical choices dictated by the analyst's psychoanalytic convictions.

Stolorow and colleagues (1987), in their "intersubjective field" viewpoint,* take Gedo's contentions to the extreme by maintaining there is no specific pathology in seriously disturbed or borderline patients. For Stolorow and colleagues the borderline patient is in an archaic need state and has a fragmentation-prone self. The therapist's failure to meet such needs is inevitable and must be analyzed, but it is clear that such patients are in a position to develop archaic transferences that require mature and spontaneous human responses for the gradual building of tension regulation, and they are not in a position to utilize interpretation until that has been accomplished.

In the management of archaic transferences, the therapist is often "forced to do something," a reluctant compliance without which the patient develops an unmanageable rage that threatens to fragment the patient and break up the treatment. The skill of the therapist

---

*The "intersubjective field" concept was first emphasized by Merleau-Ponty (1962), and based on the work of Husserl (see Chessick, in press).

is to do just enough so the patient has some sense of the therapist's recognition that words alone will not suffice, but not to afford so much gratification that the patient has no motivation to change, which would engender an artificial need for more and more gratification. Later in the treatment words alone do suffice, and it is hoped that the patient is able to tolerate interpretations and the pain of reliving early childhood experiences. Gratifying behavior on the part of the analyst at this point is inappropriate and represents seduction and countertransference acting out; if it takes place, the result is an interminable treatment. The presence of this situation can be spotted by a sufficiently trained analyst through the recognition that no depth is being achieved in the development of various transference phases; the material becomes increasingly boring and repetitive. This represents analyst failure, not patient failure.

In some cases, as Wolf (1988) points out, the fragile structure of the self has to be protected from further damage from the rough and tumble and intimacy of social intercourse by schizoid mechanisms that keep involvement shallow, or by paranoid mechanisms that surround the self with an aura of hostility and suspicion to keep noxious selfobjects at bay. It is up to the therapist to recognize and respect these protective devices and not, as Kohut (1971) explained, act like a bull in a china shop.

The Self-Analysis of the Analyst

Fichte first pointed out that "knowledge" has a hidden purpose in his famous saying, "The philosophy one holds depends upon the kind of man one is" (Solomon, 1988).

Hegel discovered the idea of alternative conceptual frameworks and pointed out that our knowledge, our self-image, and indeed all our mentation contain not a fixed essence but are substantially a product of our culture. McGuinness (1988) reminds us that science is a picture or model created by the mind, often with the utmost daring and freedom. There are different fundamental hypotheses in each scientific approach, called by Wittgenstein "networks," and these different fundamental hypotheses may equally fit the world that we experience. This is our current postmodern orientation.

Ego psychology and self psychology hope for a structural change in psychoanalytic therapy. The hermeneutic approach attempts a more coherent life narrative, an increased integration of the patient into the world and a greater sense of satisfaction with being. The object relations approach postulates changes in the internal representational world of the self and objects with better integrated internal representations and less splitting. The cognitive approach, such as that of Weiss and Sampson (1986), hopes to alter false belief systems, and another approach to psychotherapy based on the alteration of false belief systems has recently been published by Basch (1988).

Bernardi (1989) points out that theories are not just "abstract formulations but . . . concrete ways of *viewing and thinking* about what is brought about in the practice of psychoanalysis" (p. 341). These various theories, Bernardi argues, *"are neither logically compatible nor semantically congruent"* (p. 342). One of the disadvantages of analytic training, like all training processes, is that it tends to make the form of theory that is used in the training automatic. Consequently, on the one hand, our attention is quickly called to those aspects of the patient's material that fit the theory, but on the other hand, a limit or horizon is set to our understanding, to use a herme-neutic term (Chessick, 1990a). Bernardi illustrates this by comparing the Freudian, Kleinian, and Lacanian ways of thinking. He concludes, "Can we say that we choose the theory that we prefer? It seems rather that we adopt a way of thinking without quite knowing how, moved perhaps by the unconscious fantasies amassed in training analyses, supervisions and seminars with the analytic knowledge already established" (p. 354). Dif-ferent presuppositions, attitudes, values, and fantasies are brought into play in our choice of holding a theoret-ical orientation, and of focusing on various aspects of what factors bring about change in psychoanalysis.

Consistent with current psychoanalytic theory, Spira (1988) explains that our very choice of a specific psycho-analytic theory and rejection of others has a defensive function. Similarly, our choice of which factors we con-sider paramount in the psychoanalytic process also rep-resents a compromise formation made by our ego in an attempt to balance the demands of our id, our superego, and our reality. The rigidity with which one clings to a given theoretical system is a measure of how important that choice has become as a means of reducing the therapist's anxiety; the greater the therapist's personal self-knowledge and the greater the maturation of the therapist, the more open the therapist can be to the experience of data that might lead to a gradual shift in theoretical position or a bifurcation jump. Such changes in theoretical position, then, could either be mature if based on the accumulation of experience and inter-change of ideas enabling the ego to make better judgments because it has better information, or neurotic and primarily dominated by the therapist's need to avoid signal anxiety. It is up to the therapist all through life to maintain self-analysis as a way of insuring that his or her shifts in theoretical orientation or conversely, adhering to one theoretical orientation, do not have a primarily neurotic basis of some kind. Elsewhere (Chessick, 1990) I tried to illustrate how the therapist's continuing self-analysis leads to a better understanding of his or her shifts in theoretical orientation over many years of practice.

For example, one must be careful not to utilize self psychology or object relations theory beyond foundational repair in psychoanalytic therapy without considering the consequences. One must ask oneself always if one is utilizing such theories and practices and the interpretations based on them defensively in a collusion to avoid facing the patient's core fantasy activity and the reverberations of it in the analyst's core fantasy activity. Continuing self-analysis is required in each and every treatment process, which is why the analyst also learns and matures from every case.

The openness of the analyst is everything. As Meissner (1985) writes, "The analyst seeks to engage the patient in such a way that the inner melody of the patient's unconscious can begin to play itself out in a variety of derivative forms, most immediately and sensitively within the context of the analytic setting with its neutrality and diminution of external stimuli" (p. 328). This permits insight through interpretation, noninterpretive aspects

lxi

of the new object relationship or experience, regression due to the analyst's reliability, which gives the opportunity to undo developmental arrests, a symbolic holding environment, and the collaborative creation of a narrative, all of which are known to have therapeutic effects.

REFERENCES

Abend, S. (1989), Countertransference and psychoanalytic technique. *Psychoanal. Q.* 58:374–395.

Arlow, J. (1980), Object concept and object choice. *Psychoanal. Q.* 49:109–133.

_____ (1985), The concept of psychic reality and related problems. *J. Am. Psycho-anal. Assoc.* 33:521–535.

Basch, M. (1988), *Understanding Psychotherapy: The Science behind the Art.* New York: Basic Books.

Bernardi, R. (1989), The role of paradigmatic determinants in psychoanalytic understanding. *Int. J. Psychoanal.* 70: 341–357.

Blatt, S., and Behrends, R. (1987), Internalization, separation–individuation, and the nature of therapeutic action. *Int. J. Psychoanal.* 68:279–297.

Boesky, D. (1988), Comments on the structural theory of technique. *Int. J. Psychoanal.* 69:303–316.

Brenner, C. (1982), *The Mind in Conflict.* New York: International Universities Press.

Breuer, J., and Freud, S. (1893), *Studies on Hysteria.* In *Standard Edition*, Volume II. London: Hogarth Press, 1955.

Buckley, P. (1989), Fifty years after Freud: Dora, the Rat-man, and the Wolf-man. *Am. J. Psychiatr.* 146:1394–1403.

Chessick, R. (1985), *Psychology of the Self and the Treatment of Narcissism.* Northvale, NJ: Jason Aronson.

_____ (1985a), Clinical notes toward the understanding and intensive psychotherapy of adult eating disorders. *An. Psychoanal.* 13:301–322.

_____ (1986), Transference and countertransference revisited. *Dyn. Psychother.* 4:14–33.

_____ (1988), *The Technique and Practice of Listening in Intensive Psychotherapy.* Northvale, NJ: Jason Aronson.

_____ (1990), Self analysis: fool for a patient? *Psychoanal. Rev.* 77:311–340.

_____ (1990a), Hermeneutics for psychotherapists. *Am. J. Psychother.* 44:256–273.

_____ (in press), *What Constitutes the Patient in Intensive Psychotherapy.* Northvale, NJ: Jason Aronson.

Cooper, A. (1988), Our changing views of the therapeutic action of psychoanalysis: comparing Strachey and Loewald. *Psychoanal. Q.* 57:15–27.

_____ (1989), Concepts of therapeutic effectiveness in psychoanalysis: a historical review. *Psychoanal. Inq.* 9:4–25.

Davies, P. (Ed.) (1989), *The New Physics.* New York: Cambridge University Press.

Eissler, K. (1953), The effect of the structure of the ego on psychoanalytic technique. *J. Am. Psycho-anal. Assoc.* 1:104–143.

Fogel, G. (1989), The authentic function of psychoanalytic theory: an overview of the contributions of Hans Loewald. *Psychoanal. Q.* 58:419–451.

Freud, S. (1900), *The Interpretation of Dreams.* In *Standard Edition,* Volumes IV and V. London: Hogarth Press.

_____ (1909), Note upon a case of obsessional neurosis. In *Standard Edition,* Volume X:153–319. London: Hogarth Press.

_____ (1916), Some character types met with in psychoanalytic work. In *Standard Edition,* Volume XIV:309–336. London: Hogarth Press.

_____ (1915–1917), *Introductory Lectures on Psycho-Analysis.* In *Standard Edition,* Volumes XV and XVI. London: Hogarth Press.

_____ (1918), From the history of an infantile neurosis. In *Standard Edition,* Volume XVII:3–122. London: Hogarth Press.

_____ (1937), Analysis terminable and interminable. In *Standard Edition,* Volume XXIII:209–254. London: Hogarth Press, 1964.

_____ (1940), *An Outline of Psycho-Analysis.* In *Standard Edition,* Volume XXIII:141–208. London: Hogarth Press, 1964.

Galbraith, J. (1958), *The Affluent Society,* New York: Mentor Books.

Gardiner, M. (Ed.) (1971), *The Wolf-Man.* New York: Basic Books.

Gedo, J. (1979), *Beyond Interpretation: Toward a Revised Theory for Psychoanalysis.* New York: International Universities Press.

_____ (1986). *Conceptual Issues in Psychoanalysis.* Hillsdale, NJ: Analytic Press.

Glover, E. (1937), Symposium on the theory of the therapeutic results of psychoanalysis. *Int. J. Psychoanal.* 43:125–132.

Greenson, R. (1965), The working alliance and the transference neurosis. *Psychoanal. Q.* 34:155–181.

Heimann, P. (1950), On counter-transference. *Int. J. Psychoanal.* 31:81–84.

Holinger, P. (1989), A developmental perspective on psychotherapy and psychoanalysis. *Am. J. Psychiatr.* 146:1404–1412.

Kohut, H. (1971), *The Analysis of the Self.* New York: International Universities Press.

_____ (1977), *Restoration of the Self.* New York: International Universities Press.

_____ (1984), *How Does Analysis Cure?* Chicago: University of Chicago Press.

Langs, R. (1982), *Psychotherapy: A Basic Text.* New York: Jason Aronson.

Lipton, S. (1977), The advantages of Freud's technique as shown in his analysis of the Rat Man. *Int. J. Psychoanal.* 58:255–273.

_____ (1979), An addendum to "The Advantages of Freud's Technique as Shown in His Analysis of the Rat Man." *Int. J. Psychoanal.* 60:215–216.

Little, M. (1951), Counter-transference and the patient's response to it. *Int. J. Pychoanal.* 32:32–40.

Loewald, H. (1980), On the therapeutic action of psychoanalysis. In *Papers on Psychoanalysis.* New Haven: Yale University Press.

McGuiness, B. (1988), *Wittgenstein: A Life, Young Ludwig 1889–1921.* Berkeley: University of California Press.

Meissner, W. (1985), Theories of personality and psychopathology: classical psychoanalysis. In *Comprehensive Textbook of Psychiatry, IV,* 4th ed., ed. H. Kaplan and B. Sadock. Baltimore, MD: Williams and Wilkins.

Menninger, K. (1958), *The Theory of Psychoanalytic Technique.* New York: Basic Books.

Merleau-Ponty, M. (1962), *Phenomenology of Perception.* London, England: Routledge and Kegan Paul.

Modell, A. (1976), The holding environment and the therapeutic action of psychoanalysis. *J. Am. Psychoanal. Assoc.* 24:285–308.

Nacht, S. (1962), The curative factors in psychoanalysis. *Int. J. Psychoanal.* 43:206–211.

Newman, K. (1988), Countertransference: its role in facilitating the use of the object. *An. Psychoanal.* 16: 251–285.

Ornstein, P., and Ornstein, A. (1977), On the continuing evolution of psychoanalytic psychotherapy: reflections and predictions. *An. Psychoanal.* 5:329–370.

Osman, M., and Tabachnick, N. (1988), Essentials of psychoanalytic cure: a symposium. Introduction and survey of some previous views. *Psychoanal. Rev.* 75:185–215.

Phillips, A. (1988), *Winnicott.* Cambridge, MA: Harvard University Press.

Rangell, L. (1989), Action theory within the structural view. *Int. J. Psychoanal.* 70:189–203.

Reich, W. (1949). *Character Analysis.* New York: Orgone Institute Press.

Rothstein, A. (Ed.) (1988), *How Does Treatment Help? On the Modes of Therapeutic Action of Psychoanalytic Psychotherapy.* New York: International Universities Press.

Scharfman, M. (1979), Panel on conceptualizing the nature of therapeutic action of psychoanalysis. *J. Am. Psycho-anal. Assoc.* 27:627–642.

Shane, E., and Shane, M. (1989), Prologue: the developmental perspective in psychoanalysis. *Psychoanal. Inq.* 9:333–339.

Slakter, E. (1987), *Countertransference.* New York: Jason Aronson.

Solomon, R. (1988), *Continental Philosophy since 1750. The Rise and Fall of the Self.* New York: Oxford University Press.

Spira, D. (1988), The defensive function of psychoanalytic theories. *An. Psychoanal.* 16:81–92.

Stern, D. (1985), *The Interpersonal World of the Infant.* New York: Basic Books.

Stolorow, R., Brandchaft, B., and Atwood, C. (1987), *Psychoanalytic Treatment: An Intersubjective Approach.* Hillsdale, NJ: Analytic Press.

Stone, L. (1961), *The Psychoanalytic Situation: An Examination of Its Development and Essential Nature.* New York: International Universities Press.

_____ (1981), Notes on the noninterpretive elements in the psychoanalytic situation and process. *J. Am. Psycho-anal. Assoc.* 29:89–118.

Strachey, J. (1934), The nature of the therapeutic action of psychoanalysis. *Int. J. Psychoanal.* 15:117–126.

Terman, D. (1989), Therapeutic change: Perspectives of self psychology, *Psychoanal. Inq.* 9:88–100.

Wälder, R. (1936), The principle of multiple function: observations on overdetermination. *Psychoanal. Q.* 5:45–62.

Weiss, J., and Sampson, H. (1986), *The Psychoanalytic Process: Theory, Clinical Observation and Empirical Research.* New York: Guilford Press.

Winnicott, D. (1949), Hate in the counter-transference. *Int. J. Psychoanal.* 30:69–74.

_____ (1969), The use of an object. *Int. J. Psychoanal.* 50:711–716.

Wolf, E. (1988), *Treating the Self. Elements of Clinical Self Psychology.* New York: Guilford Press.

Zetzel, E. (1956), Current concepts of transference. *Int. J. Psychoanal.* 37:369–376.

CHAPTER 1 *The Evolution of Intensive Psychotherapy*

A SUBSTANTIAL body of general clinical knowledge and experience has accumulated about the technique and practice of long-term, intensive, psychoanalytically oriented psychotherapy. This book attempts to collect and present it in an organized fashion, and to focus on unresolved problems and crucial issues.

Great dangers lurk for the future of psychotherapy. Most immediate is the danger of spreading disillusionment and disappointment because poorly trained therapists attempt to do psychotherapy, encounter failure, and then adopt a nihilistic, pessimistic attitude about the whole field. There is a strange lack of logic to that sort of reaction. In other fields of medicine, if someone attempts a treatment that does not work, the usual response is to learn more about the sub-

1

ject and try again or to do research to find out why it did not work. Psychotherapists tend to get cursory or poor training, plunge into some difficult cases early in training, experience failures, and then give up the whole field in favor of something simpler, more immediately practical, and involving tangible change.

A brilliant analysis of the problem by Kubie has recently appeared (1971). He points out that the current "pain-driven flight" from patients has many roots. Work with patients *is* emotionally painful. Clinical skills are undervalued, and there is a failure to realize how long it takes to acquire clinical maturity in psychotherapy. Much propaganda—Sullivan would call it "clamor"—commands service to the community, as though this does not first require the highest degree of knowledge of individual human needs and psychodynamics.

Higher academic rewards—rank, status, and good salaries —seem destined for many other areas of psychiatry and as Kubie argues, many top-range, full-time professors set a bad example by their persistent absence from the clinical arena. He feels this will be ultimately disastrous for American medicine, as our young psychotherapists–in–training shift away from doing psychotherapy with patients toward all kinds of other less threatening aspects of the field.

Mendel (1970) warns of a tendency on the part of psychotherapists to believe the omnipotence that is attributed to them by patients. When this happens, the therapist does society a great disservice; he inflates his modest understanding of psychopathology and psychotherapy and declares himself an expert on all problems of human society, proclaiming the need to "get involved" in sociology, public health, behavior

2

genetics, criminology, education, and politics. Yet each of these disciplines are sciences with a large body of knowledge and a set of techniques in research and action; they are actually quite outside the special training, experience, and competence of the ordinary psychotherapist.

Heidegger (1962), talks about a falling away or forfeiture from one's real being and an involvement in a tranquilizing way in what he calls a life of hustle and immersion in the "they." He employs terms like *distancing, averaging, leveling down, publicness, idle talk, curiosity,* and *ambiguity* to denote activities that people generally involve themselves in to fall away from anxiety and the pain of looking directly at existential questions.

This very loose interpretation of Heidegger constitutes another way of describing danger points in the lives of psychotherapists. The first, early in training, is based on disillusionment due to poor understanding of techniques and inadequate personal maturity and is liable to drive one entirely out of the field. Later on in his middle years, when the therapist gets tired, loses his zest for his field, and longs for immediate results, he may attempt to boost his reputation and his finances by broadcasting some new short-cut method; he may even become a vociferous enemy of psychoanalytic psychotherapy.

HISTORICAL REVIEW

In the past mental illness was often viewed as a visitation from God or the gods. Therefore the approach to mental illness was founded on existing mythological systems. A conflict

3

between philosophies that tried to explain mental illness in mystical and confusing terms and the rational or skeptical attitude to mental illness that began with the Greeks and reappeared in the Renaissance has a long history. The public still confusedly views the psychiatrist as an expert on mental illness and an expert on the human predicament, since originally the high priest or official philosophers were supposed to know about both. The difference in our civilization between those who emphasize humane values and those who worship efficiency, the state, and authoritarian solutions is reflected even today in divergent views of psychotherapists.

Mental illness is described in such ancient religious scriptures as the Hindu texts or the Bible, where there is a strictly animistic approach to the subject. Mental illness is not considered to belong to the realm of medicine or disease but to that of mysticism and theology. It is characteristically presented in terms of punishment, for example, "The Lord shall smite thee, with madness and blindness and astonishment of heart." In some areas of the United States this attitude still persists. It is not unusual in teaching student nurses from a rural background to have to spend considerable time discussing whether a person who is mentally ill deserves it and is simply being punished by the Lord for sins he has committed.

The first scientific approach to mental illness belongs to the Greeks. Melampus (Graves, 1955), a famous prophet and demigod who lived three centuries before Homer, introduced the first treatments for mental illness. These were similar to some used today. For example, he employed hellibore, a cathartic medicine, giving the patient strong doses of this medicine and chasing him around until he fell exhausted. It was a cathartic experience in every sense of the word. Melampus

4

was the first mortal to be granted prophetic powers, to practice as a physician, to build temples to Dionysus in Greece, and to temper wine with water. He could understand the language of the birds and also introduced the first cure for impotence, a problem that the Egyptians had already struggled with.°

Hippocrates was the first to introduce psychiatric problems into the study of medicine, daring to challenge the concept of divine cause of mental illness. For example, he refused to accept epilepsy as a sacred disease and made numerous clinical observations of epilepsy, melancholia, postpartum psychosis, and hysteria.

The Greeks also discovered two further forms of therapy that are still in use in some parts of the world today. The first of these, sleep therapy, known today as *Dauerschlaf*, was

---

° According to legend King Phylacus had a son Iphiclus who was impotent. The king said to Melampus, "I will grant you your freedom and some first-rate cattle if you will only cure my son of impotence." Melampus agreed and began the task by sacrificing two bulls to Apollo. After he had burned the thigh bones with the fat, he left their carcasses lying by the altar. Presently two vultures arrived, and one said to the other, "It must be several years since we were last here—that time when Phylacus was gelding rams and we collected our perquisites."

"I well remember it," said the other vulture. "Iphiclus, who was then still a child, saw his father coming toward him with a blood-stained knife and took fright. He apparently feared to be gelded himself, because he screamed at the top of his voice. Phylacus drove the knife into the sacred pear tree over there for safe-keeping, while he ran to comfort Iphiclus. That fright accounts for the impotency. And Phylacus forgot to recover the knife! There it still is, sticking in the tree. But bark has grown over its blade, and only the end of its handle shows."

"In that case," remarked the first vulture, "the remedy for Iphiclus's impotence would be to draw out the knife, scrape off the rust left by the rams' blood, and administer it to him, mixed in water, every day for ten days." Needless to say, this remedy worked.

practiced in the temples of Aesculapius, the god of medicine. The mentally ill would come to the temple and sleep, in the hope of having a dream. The dreams were then told to the priestesses, who interpreted them, which frequently resulted in a cure. Certain drugs and herbs were used in the treatment of the mentally ill as well.

The Greeks also produced the first great psychological works of Western man. The *Iliad* and the *Odyssey* are worth reading for their sense of human tragedy and conflicts and their resolution. Man in these poems is portrayed in the night-bound world of insensate circumstance, all men being the source and the only principle of order and light to each other. The gods are seen only as contributing chance, fate, and doom, much like the spin of a roulette wheel.

The Greeks introduced two important concepts in approaching the problem of Western man. These expressed their rational or intellectual approach to the problems of the passions in emotional illness. The first term, *hübris*, is translated as "immoderate insubordination," and it inevitably led to a tragic fall. Moderation or temperance conceptualized as internal self-discipline that keeps the passions in check and permits a balanced development was termed *sophrosyné;* the opposite is excess or the unrestricted license of passion. The most classic example of excess, as the Greeks conceived of it, is found in the play *Medea*, by Euripides. This is the first portrayal of psychosis on the stage, and here unrestricted passion results in Medea's murder of her own children.

The Greek playwrights produced the first great psychological dramas of Western man. Aeschylus (525–456 B.C.) invented tragedy and was the first of the three great tragedians. His trilogy—*Agamemnon, The Libation Bearers*, and

6

The Furies—is as important as the better-known Oedipus trilogy. In the trilogy of Aeschylus the central theme is the murder of the mother by her son. The son, Orestes, takes revenge on the mother's lover, and on the mother for taking a lover and planning her husband's murder, by killing them both. He is spurred to this murder by his sister Electra.

Sophocles (496–406 B.C.) was the younger contemporary of Aeschylus who wrote the Oedipus trilogy. Euripides (480–406 B.C.) was a psychological realist, the first playwright to portray men as they are. He dramatized the foolishness of war and presented the conflict of reason and passion in human beings. Aristophanes (448–388 B.C.) was more comical in his writing and represented a conservative trend in Greek thought.

After the Greeks very little was contributed to the study of mental illness. With the death of Galen in 200 A.D., began the Dark Ages of medical history—a time characterized as "the age of demonology" (Zilboorg, 1941).

Throughout this age people were preoccupied with *incubi* and *succubi*. These are devils who appear at night, have sexual intercourse—an *incubus* with innocent females, a *succubus* with unsuspecting males—and disappear at dawn. Judging from the writings of the time, such creatures were amazingly frequent in their visits.

Around 1487 A.D. the German monks Sprenger and Kraemer published one of the most notorious theses in the history of psychiatry, the *Malleus Maleficarum*, or the *Witches' Hammer* (literally, *The Hammer of the Female Malefactors*). This was a textbook on how to discover, examine, and sentence witches. It resulted in the burning of thousands of women, the last of which was killed in Germany in 1775. One

7

has to read this work directly to sense the intense hatred of women that pervades every page.

Zilboorg (1941) movingly describes the *Malleus Maleficarum:*

> The thesis of the Malleus is as simple as it seems to us horrible. It is divided into three parts. The first part represents an argument which attempts to prove the existence of witchcraft and witches, or to be more correct, to prove by argumentation rather than by factual demonstration that he who does not believe in the existence of witches is either in honest error or polluted with heresy. The second part is devoted to what we would call today clinical reports. It tells of various types of witches and of the various different methods one should use to identify a witch. To use modern terminology, it describes the clinical pictures and the various ways of arriving at a diagnosis. The third part deals with the legal forms of examining and sentencing a witch. It goes into the details of legal technicalities and the technique of delivering a witch from the devil or to the secular arm of justice for execution, in most cases by burning. It is not a dispassionate, cold, legalistic treatise; it is, rather, polemical, argumentative, scornful or threatening in tone, and uncompromising. It is written with firm conviction and a fervent zeal which made the authors totally anesthetic to the smell of burning human flesh. . . . all mentally sick were considered witches or sorcerers, or bewitched. . . . Unless one keeps this attitude of profound devotion in mind, one is apt to misunderstand the fundamental reaction of many generations towards the mentally ill. It is a reaction of fear and of endless anxiety which arouses to utmost intensity the drive to self-defense, a drive which is capable of utter cruelty and revengefulness. But civilized man—and even the man of the fifteenth century was

sufficiently civilized—is not capable of giving vent to his great reservoir of bitter hatred and relentless cruelty unless he finds a good, lofty, and noble reason which will allow him to justify in his own eyes his need to hate, to destroy, and to kill. The *Malleus* is the culminating point of such rationalization; that is what made it so authoritative, so relentless, so very righteous, and so incontrovertible in the eyes of its authors, its readers, and the judges who used it as a textbook.

The revolution in psychiatry that took place in the sixteenth century was largely a reaction against the *Malleus Maleficarum,* as Zilboorg points out. Juan Vives (1492–1540), considered the father of modern associational psychology, was the first to argue for the humane treatment of the mentally ill—for gentleness, tranquility, and good individualized treatment in the hospital. Vives, a great Renaissance humanist, is poorly appreciated today.

At the same time, Paracelsus (1493–1541), an iconoclastic and cantankerous contemporary of Vives (Pachter, 1961), was the first to flatly reject the idea of demonology. He described the sexual nature of hysteria and introduced the concept of the role of unconscious fantasies in hysteria.

Johann Weyer (1515–1588), considered the father of modern psychiatry, developed methodical, systematic inquiry. He produced the first written treatise against the *Malleus Maleficarum* and flatly stated that "witches are sick." The first clinician in psychiatry and true founder of this field, he is described by Zilboorg (1941):

He was the first clinical and the first descriptive psychiatrist to leave to succeeding generations a heritage which was accepted, developed, and perfected into an observational branch of medicine in a process which culminated in the great descriptive system of psychiatry formulated at the end of the nineteenth century. Weyer more than anyone else completed, or at least brought closer to completion, the process of divorcing medical psychology from theology and empirical knowledge of the human mind from the faith in the perfection of the human soul. He reduced the clinical problems of psychopathology to simple terms of everyday life and of everyday, human, inner experiences without concealing the complexity of human functioning and the obscurity of human problems. He left no theory, no dogmatic philosophy of his own. His was the task of combating misguided dogma, and he studied the field of human relations through free observation and objective evaluation of man in nature, rather than through consideration of what man might and should be and most of the time is not.

All this Weyer accomplished without developing that cold objectivity which betrays a frigid unconcern about man and which insists that the only thing which matters is the gratification of scientific curiosity. Instead, he repeatedly stressed the fact that he was a physician and that the "sacred art of medicine" must be practiced on man and *for* man. "Love man," he admonished, "kill errors, go into combat for truth without cruelty." He studied theology and history and law because these had to do with man. To those who objected to his legal arguments, he merely replied that it was the duty of the doctor to look for the truth about man wherever he could find it. In this respect Weyer was also the forerunner of the great consciousness of our day that a psychiatrist must not limit himself to a knowledge of anatomy, physiology, internal medicine, surgery, and neurology, but that he must go further into those fields of human activity which reveal man in his totality, that he must acquire sound knowledge of history, sociology, and anthropology.

10

One of the most famous figures in psychiatric history was Philippe Pinel (1745–1826), who, shortly after the French Revolution, took the chains off the mentally ill in the Bicêtre, a dungeon where the mentally ill were kept. Pinel (Zilboorg, 1941) wrote: "The mentally sick, far from being guilty people deserving of punishment, are sick people whose miserable state deserves all the consideration that is due to suffering humanity. One should try with the most simple methods to restore their reason." Pinel first took case histories and records, and his work was carried on by his famous pupil Esquirol (1772–1840).

Similarly, in England the Tuke family established humane mental hospitals in the nineteenth century. In the United States in 1783 Benjamin Rush, one of the signers of the Declaration of Independence, became the first American psychiatrist. He was the first in this country to approach mental disease scientifically, the first to propose a system of classification, and the author, in 1812, of the first treatise on psychiatry in America. Dorothea Dix, during and after the Civil War, repeatedly toured this country and encouraged a great many improvements in the care of, and the formation of many new hospitals for, the mentally ill. In 1909 a former patient, C. Beers, founded the mental health movement in the United States (Beers, 1970).

Anton Mesmer appeared in Paris in 1778. He discovered that by performing mysterious gestures and saying proper words to certain people, he could develop an influence over them. Believing that a magnetic fluid passed from him to his "clients" he felt that the power of this fluid would be greatly increased if it passed from him through and to many people, not just to one. He therefore founded the first group practice,

11

attended by an elaborate ceremony that strongly appealed to the jaded taste of his well-born clients. Mesmer made his appearance to the accompaniment of soft, mournful music, draped in a lavender silk robe. He slowly passed among his clients, fixing his eyes on them, touching them with his hands or with a long magnetized iron wand that he always carried with him.

Mesmer received a large number of enthusiastic testimonials from his clients, but his seances were brought to an end by a royal commission appointed by Louis XVI in 1784. This scientific commission, which included Benjamin Franklin and Lavoisier, declared animal magnetism to be nonexistent and Mesmer's cures entirely due to imagination.

The enormous implication of mesmerism was ignored for a long time. Finally in 1841 in England, James Braid observed a mesmeric seance and made a detailed study of the subject. In his monograph, published in 1843, he introduced the term *hypnotism*. Even as early as this Braid demonstrated that patients under hypnosis could not be made to perform criminal or obscene acts, a fear that is still held by laymen today. Braid also reported the successful treatment by hypnotism of tic douloureux, paralyses, aphasia, deafness, rheumatism, headache, palpitation, skin diseases, and other illnesses, although he realized that these cures did not last. He pointed out the use of hypnosis in surgery and dentistry. His views, however, were not accepted in England.

In France hypnotism came to be used therapeutically in the treatment of hysteria, but the method turned into a subject of bitter argument between Ambroise-August Liebeault (1823–1904) and Hippolyte Bernheim (1837–1919) of the Nancy school, who believed that most people could be hypnotized without much difficulty, and the great French neurologist Jean Charcot (1825–1893) of the Salpêtrière, who considered hypnotism a much more metaphysical issue.

Charcot did not use hypnotism for the principal purpose of therapy. His subjects, recruited from the female patients of the Salpêtrière, were already hypnotized for him and served for his neurologic studies on movements, reflexes, and contractures. One of Charcot's visitors during the height of his fame in 1886 was a young neurologist named Sigmund Freud (1856–1939), who later translated Charcot's writings from French into German.

The Nancy school rivaled and challenged Charcot's work. The doctors were more interested in the therapeutic uses of hypnotism and hypnotized their patients themselves, operating with words alone. In this way they recorded a great number of speedy cures of hysterical disorders.

The school at Nancy demonstrated for the first time a connection between the mentally ill and the normal, though this is not completely accepted even today. For example, some followers of the French neurologist Pierre Janet (1859–1947) remain convinced that all mental illness is due to a constitutional weakness of the mind, a degeneracy. They insist environmental and persuasive therapy is the answer, that it is important to demonstrate to the mentally ill that they have to get hold of themselves, snap out of it, and get back to work.

Today, however, most psychiatrists believe there is only a gradation between mental illness and normal behavior, although many psychiatrists still cling to the idea that in the psychoses there is some mysterious, organic element of deterioration.

In the nineteenth century—the era of nosological systems, of Rudolph Virchow, and of the great development of the field of pathology—all illnesses were attributed to cellular pathology. It was only natural then that psychiatrists as well turned to the study of cellular pathology and attempted to classify mental diseases on this basis. Wilhelm Griesinger (1817–1868) in Germany developed the greatest of these systems of classification, and there were quite a number of others. Griesinger flatly stated that mental diseases are somatic diseases; in his view it was only a matter of time until the proper cellular pathology would be demonstrated, a viewpoint that is still prevalent in some areas today.

The discovery that general paresis was separate and different from other mental diseases greatly advanced the science in terms of classification and understanding. In 1904 Franz Nissl and Alois Alzheimer demonstrated the histopathology of general paresis.

This era fostered a great deal of clinical study of the progress and course of mental illness, culminating with the work of Emil Kraepelin (1855–1926), who differentiated between dementia praecox and manic–depressive psychosis. This distinction—the most important that had been introduced in the study of mental disease for a long time—was based strictly on prognosis: Kraepelin believed that people with maniac–depressive psychosis recovered until the next episode, whereas people with dementia praecox never recovered. His conclusions stimulated a tremendous amount of investigative work.

The second great psychiatric revolution took place through the discoveries of Freud (Jones, 1953). Freud's work burst onto the European psychiatric scene and caused many

14

outstanding thinkers to reassess and restudy their personal experiences and clinical material. One of the most important reassessments was carried out by Eugen Bleuler (1857–1939), a Swiss psychiatrist who applied the theories of Freud—which had been developed from the study of neurotics—to his group of psychotics in Switzerland and introduced the term *schizophrenia* in 1911.

Bleuler's (1911) monograph on *Dementia Praecox or The Group of Schizophrenias* is one of the classics of psychiatry literature and makes for timely reading even today. Bleuler's work demonstrates the first application of Freud's views to another area of mental illness, and it provides an example of how dramatically Freud's views changed the thinking of psychiatrists at the time. It might be said that Freud stimulated a revolution in the treatment and approach to the neuroses, whereas Bleuler, Adolf Meyer (1866–1950), and Harry Stack Sullivan (1892–1949), working from the theories of Freud, stimulated a revolution in the treatment of the psychoses.

From a modest beginning the practice of psychotherapy was catalyzed by Freud and has become widespread today. I have reviewed the subject of psychotherapy and its position in the Western philosophical tradition elsewhere (Chessick, 1969).

Reusch (1961) views psychotherapy, as it is practiced today, as being vitally influenced by three significant traditions—the Judaeo–Christian, the Greco–Roman, and the Anglo–Saxon. He believes that the idea of mastery of the unconscious stems from the Judaeo–Christian background; he argues, "the ten commandments are anti-instinctual." The Greco–Roman tradition contributes the emphasis on human interaction (in contrast to the Judaeo–Christian stress on the

15

individual's internal struggle). Concentration on the milieu or social order and the group springs from this tradition. The third, or Anglo-Saxon tradition overlaps the second but focuses on the practical and the extroverted approach to life.

Reusch (1961) writes:

> The Judaeo–Christian tradition is upheld by psychoanalysts, who check upon one another and upon their trainees to see that each person faithfully upholds psychoanalytic principles. Purity of belief, exclusion of dissenters, adherence to an established methodology and dogmatic defense of the established theory thus become prime concerns. . . . The psychoanalytic method has taken over many features from Judaism and Catholicism. . . . The Greco–Roman tradition assumes that man is in nature, subject to its laws, and that adaptation to the unavoidable is the best solution.
>
> Finally we have the Anglo–Saxon influence with its belief that man triumphs over nature by daring, exploitation, resourcefulness, and industrial production. It is the extrovert's solution to life. He believes that as long as he does, and does right, nothing can happen to him. He depends upon the support of his peers; and as a result of this attitude group therapy, interpersonal schools of psychiatry, and the study of communication have emerged.
>
> All three traditions are found in American psychiatry. . . . It goes with out saying that these three basic trends intermingle with one another and eventually will be amalgamated, but many of the controversies and the bitter feuds in psychiatry and psychoanalysis can be traced to these different value systems and views of nature which go deeper than the individual dares to think.

Hollingshead and Redlich (1958) studied the Yale University area (New Haven) to discover what it was like to be mentally ill there. They divided the people in the area into social classes. Class I (3.4 percent of the population) contained the high-income business executives and professional leaders. Class II (9 percent) was composed of status-conscious people, the so-called junior executives who have not yet arrived. Class III (21.4 percent) was characterized by little upward mobility; that is, there was little chance the members would ever attain great wealth or influence. These were the white-collar workers, technicians, and small businessmen with only a high school education and little chance of becoming big businessmen. Class IV (48.5 percent) was made up of skilled manual workers. Class V (17.7 percent) comprised the unskilled workers, often with no union affiliation.

Hollingshead and Redlich were able to demonstrate that the total number of patients requiring admission to a mental hospital rose definitely with Class IV and enormously with Class V, compared to admission rates for Classes I, II, and III. Diagnostic differences were also apparent. Neurotics were far more prevalent in the higher classes, psychotics in the lower classes. A simple explanation, however, is not possible, for the difference. The most obvious reason would seem to be that the lower a patient's class, the longer he waited to come in for treatment. Perhaps only after a psychosis appeared was he brought for treatment, often against his will. The idea of preventive psychiatry has not taken hold at all among the less-educated classes.

Interesting differences between the classes also appeared in presenting symptoms (seen frequently in all psychiatric clinical work). The Class I or Class II patient claimed that he was *dissatisfied with himself,* he was working too hard, or he had "a strain on the nerves." The patient in Class III usually

17

THE TECHNIQUE AND PRACTICE OF INTENSIVE PSYCHOTHERAPY

denied there was anything emotionally wrong with him and could not accept even "a strain on the nerves" or overwork as an excuse. He would usually come in afraid that he had a brain tumor, a clot on the brain or some other medical problem and would demand a complete physical and neurological examination, *fearfully defending himself* against the possibility of an emotional cause for his behavior. The Class IV patient (these made up half of the sample) *ached physically*. He came in with somatic symptoms, refused to recognize emotional difficulties of any kind, and glutted the clinics with a variety of somatic problems. Finally, the Class V patient *behaved badly* and attributed his difficulties to a bump on the head or booze. This patient characteristically was dragged in by four policemen, kicking and screaming in a psychotic episode.

The types of therapy received similarly differed from class to class and were clearly related to socioeconomic status. The first two classes of patients usually underwent psychoanalysis or psychoanalytically oriented psychotherapy. Class III patients tended to receive short-term, directive therapy, while Class IV and, especially, Class V patients were often brought involuntarily to public facilities and made up the vast bulk of the psychotic back-ward patients. Class V neurotics were treated with organic therapies for neuroses five times as often as Class I and II neurotics.

This points to an obvious and currently unsolved social problem. The variety of group and individual "short-cut" psychotherapy techniques that have been developed in the past decade to deal with *symptoms* of mental illness, and that have met with various degrees of success, do not in the least contradict or scrap the basic premises of Freud or challenge

18

the relevance of intensive psychotherapy. Three factors have obscured the situation. First, it is much easier to statistically evaluate certain techniques aimed at symptom relief. The implication that some of these techniques are therefore, scientific, whereas long-term uncovering psychotherapy is not, is completely erroneous. This problem has been discussed at length by Marmor (1971). Second, certain of the recently developed techniques have a fad appeal, especially for those practioners who wish to avoid the arduous training necessary to do long-term uncovering psychotherapy and for patients who need to maintain their defenses for various reasons. Third, the sheer frustration of the long and arduous process of intensive uncovering psychotherapy, even if it is successful, drives us to constantly seek short-cut solutions.

The process of psychotherapy that originated with Freud and that with modifications, still remains our best curative technique is not obsolete, but the spirit of good, old-fashioned, rugged individualism—the doctrine that states it's a dog-eat-dog world, every man for himself, and "the devil take the hindmost"—that has long prevailed in American medical practice is out of date. Many studies show that quality of care depends on socioeconomic status and varies tremendously. Today the greatest determining factor as to whether a patient is given individual, long-term, uncovering psychotherapy is not an assessment of the patient's ego function or capacity to respond to treatment but of his ability—in time and financial resources—to maintain such a costly and time-consuming process.

This must stop. It is one thing to argue that a patient must sacrifice some time and money for psychotherapy, but the burdens of uncovering psychotherapy are simply beyond

19

the financial capacity of the entire lower class and most of the middle class of our population. Doctors, clergy, lawyers, schoolteachers, nurses, and social workers—all who deal with people in a helping capacity—could be made vastly more effective if they could be freed of their personal neurotic difficulties. Often they simply cannot afford the necessary intensive treatment, and in these situations we are repeatedly forced to compromise with symptom removal, supportive therapy on a weekly basis, group therapy, and so on. The lower-class patients sent to free clinics with long waiting lists are generally treated by inexperienced residents who rotate in their clinic assignments, thus assuring before they begin that no long-term relationship can be developed. These therapeutic decisions are based not on professional assessment of need but on bare economic factors. As such they are a violation of the basic human right to receive the best possible medical care, regardless of socioeconomic status.

Who does or does not receive psychotherapy is also affected by the psychiatrist or psychotherapist. A person who has received a training course in psychiatry, social work, or psychology is erroneously believed to be, *ipso facto,* a psychotherapist. The public at present is at the mercy of inadequate and untrained psychotherapists who do not hesitate to tackle very complex problems, with harmful and sometimes lethal results.

Given the history of psychiatry, it is not surprising to find that the psychiatrists in the area studied by Hollingshead and Redlich could also be grouped into two classes, the analytic and psychologic (A and P) psychiatrists and the directive and organic (D and O) psychiatrists. The A and P group included psychoanalysts and those who wish they were psychoanalysts. These psychiatrists tend to wear street clothes in the office, come predominantly (83 percent) from Jewish backgrounds; conduct longer and more frequent sessions with patients, and are generally introspective people who believe in a psychologic etiology of mental illness.

The D and O psychiatrists, mainly (75 percent) from Protestant backgrounds, give drugs, electric-shock treatment, and advice. They wear white coats and read a completely different set of medical journals from the first group of psychiatrists. They do not use the couch and do conduct physical examinations of their patients. Their therapy sessions are shorter and less frequent, and they hold the conviction that there is an organic etiology to most mental illness. They also make more money than the A and P group.

In experimental work a similar definitive and interesting distinction can be drawn between two groups of psychotherapists on the basis of how they approach their patients. For example, Strupp (1960) writes:

> Group I therapists appear to be more tolerant, more humane, more permissive, more "democratic," and more "therapeutic." Group II therapists emerge as more directive, disciplinarian, moralistic, and harsh. This contrast suggests the hypothesis that Group I therapists are "warmer" in their communications to the patient and that "cold," rejecting comments will be less frequent.
>
> What is meant by this distinction? On the one hand, it is a basic attitude of understanding, respect, and compassion.... It is the ability to listen without preconception, prejudgment, or condemnation. It is the ability to pierce the neurotic distortions, the socially unacceptable attitudes and acts, the more unsavory aspects of the personality, and to see behind it a con-

21

fused, bewildered, and helpless individual trying to shape his destiny, hampered and hindered by his neurotic conflicts and maladaptations. On the other hand, it is an attitude of coldness, calculation, "clinical evaluation," distance, "objectivity," aloofness, moral judgment, and condemnation. It is a readiness to take the neurotic defenses and the patient's character structure at face value and to react to them with irritation, impatience, annoyance, and anger. It is also an attitude of forming a moral judgment about the patient's illness from the beginning of the interview.

The entire concept of mental illness has traditionally been bound up in man's attitude to the human predicament. The early approaches did not recognize mental illness as an entity, and even today people mired in these ancient traditions are frightened of mental illness, regarding it as mysterious in origin, to be exorcised by religious or quasi-religious rituals. Zilboorg (1941) concludes:

> The whole course of the history of medical psychology is punctuated by the medical man's struggle to rise above the prejudices of all ages in order to identify himself with the psychological realities of his patients. Every time such an identification was achieved the medical man became a psychiatrist. The history of psychiatry is essentially the history of humanism. Every time humanism has diminished . . . psychiatry has entered a new ebb. Every time the spirit of humanism has arise, a new contribution to psychiatry has been made.

As the problem of mental illness has been separated from prepsychiatric concerns with the human predicament, a large number of existential or universal human questions have remained unanswered. There is no intrinsic reason to believe that because psychiatrists have developed new approaches to mental illness, they have simultaneously become possessed of new solutions to age-old questions about the human predicament. In fact, psychiatrists are as divided on such questions as everyone else.

CHAPTER 2 *Dynamic Psychiatry*

*P*SYCHIATRY, following Noyes (1963), can be defined as the branch of medicine that deals with the genesis, dynamics, manifestations, and treatment of such disorders and undesirable functions of the personality as disturb either the subjective life of the individual or his interpersonal relations. When we speak about personality, we use this term in its almost literal meaning, "a mask" (from the *persona* worn on the stage by actors in ancient Greece and Rome). Personality is defined by Healy and others (1930) as "The habitual patterns of behavior of the individual in terms of physical and mental activities and attitudes, particularly as these have social connotations." The personality is like a mask in that it is composed of patterns of behavior through which the individual expresses his inner and sometimes conflicting motivations, often appearing in a form of compromise behavior.

Psychiatry, as it ought to be and is usually practiced in America today, takes psychoanalysis as its basic science. Efforts to make the basic science of psychiatry a combination of biochemistry, neurophysiology, and psychophysiology have contributed to our knowledge but have not succeeded in replacing the clinically useful psychodynamic conceptions of psychoanalysis. Because modern psychiatry is based on these conceptions, it is called dynamic psychiatry.

The first of these psychoanalytic or dynamic conceptions is that of *psychic determinism*. All human behavior is conceived of as the purposeful product of an interaction between internal psychic forces and the forces and limitations of external reality. There are no irrelevent, meaningless, or purposeless thoughts, dreams, or acts.

The concept of human ideation suggests that one thought leads to or is associated with another to make up *a chain of mental events*. However, conscious and superficial thoughts and items of behavior often seem scattered, irrelevant, and unconnected. If we accept psychic determinism, chains of mental events that connect and make relevant and purposeful these seemingly scattered items must be present and exist in a functioning (not anatomical) sector of the psyche other than the conscious mind. This is defined as the *unconscious* mind, the cornerstone of modern psychoanalytic theory. A detailed account of the development of this crucial concept is presented by Ellenberger (1970).

The term *unconscious* is often confusing because it is used in two ways. In one definition, it is an adjective describing particular mental phenomena of which the person is unaware, for example, an unconscious idea. In the other

25

sense, it is a noun meaning the aggregate of such unconscious material. It is as if there is a special region of the mind in which these various unconscious thoughts, ideas, and feelings are stored and from which they exert a force. This aggregate or totality of psychic processes that we call *the* unconscious differs from other mental processes because of the subject's inability to recall or recognize this material by simply trying to pay attention to it.

The evidence for the existence of the unconscious is well presented by Freud (1901) in *The Psychopathology of Everyday Life* and reviewed more briefly by Hendrick (1948). As already implied, the unconscious cannot be known directly but must be inferred from phenomena that point to some unknown and sometimes unacceptable urges motivating behavior. Furthermore, *a very large portion of our behavior* is motivated by these unconscious urges.

Some of the evidence for the existence of the unconscious can be found in everyday behavior. The student, for example, who consistently comes late for a certain class can be expressing hostility but also a compromise with not coming at all. If we dislike doing something, we must exert greater energy to make ourselves do it; a short period of doing something we do not like can tire us out and seem endless, whereas a much longer period of time of an equally arduous activity that we enjoy seems to fly.

Slips of the tongue are classic and important examples of unconscious forces at work. In slips of the tongue two conflicting feelings merge and result in a compromise formation. For example, the chairman of the board of directors knows at the beginning of a meeting that his mistress is waiting downstairs and as soon as the meeting is over they are going to be off to the motel. He stands up to open the meeting, pounds the gavel on the table, and says, "I hereby declare this meeting closed." There are many examples of this, and they are quite useful in psychotherapy.

Another extremely important demonstration of the unconscious is *misidentification*. This is a problem throughout the field of medicine because patients misidentify the doctor with another important person in their life. Many patients get better as soon as the doctor comes into the room. They tend to identify the doctor with an omnipotent parent to whom they could turn for help.

More technical evidence for the existence of the unconscious comes from the field of hypnosis. Under hypnosis or under the influence of properly administered barbiturate drugs, it is possible to recall or bring out many painfully and automatically forgotten thoughts and acts, which are sometimes acted out graphically in front of the investigator. These often dramatic phenomena of hypnosis are, however, not completely understood.

Further important technical evidence of the unconscious is provided by asking for the patient's earliest memories, a part of every psychiatric examination. It has been found from considerable experience that when people are asked to recall memories from the early years of their lives, they tend to insert things that did not happen until later and sometimes to insert fantasies, so that one does not get an accurate reproduction of an early memory but a conglomeration of early events, distortions, and sometimes untruths.

These pseudomemories or fantasy–memories can even have an active influence on the patient's adult behavior. Patients can be quite convinced that they remember certain traumatic things that happened to them when they were little and can use these memories as reasons for certain behavior.

The most striking clinical evidence for the existence of the unconscious has come from the technique of *free association*. It has been found that if a patient is placed in an appropriate therapy situation and allowed to say whatever comes to his mind for a long period of time, thoughts and feelings begin to emerge that the patient was not aware of and that he would previously have vehemently denied were there.

Dreams in dynamic psychiatry are very important because they represent the royal road to the unconscious mind. Dreams can be described as having a manifest content and a latent content. The *manifest content* is the material that a person remembers. The unconscious material that is implicit in the manifest content is called the *latent content*. Basically the dream represents, in a condensed, displaced, and symbolized form, certain unconscious material that is disturbing the sleeper. When unconscious drives or conflicts disturb the sleeper, sleep is preserved by expressing this material in the dream, albeit in a disguised form. This serves as a temporary and moderate discharge phenomenon. When the person wakes up from a dream, it means that the dream has failed in its function. A detailed and as yet unsurpassed investigation of dreams is presented by Freud (1900) in an epoch-making work *The Interpretation of Dreams*, [later summarized by Freud (1915a)].

Unnecessary confusion has been introduced by tiresome and overworked arguments about whether the unconscious can be said to "exist" or not. For our purposes many of the

concepts used by dynamic psychiatry can be thought of as heuristic or as-if conceptions (Chessick, 1961), comparable to recent developments in physics. Born (1968, especially in the chapter "Symbol and Reality") offers a lucid and convincing presentation of the way such modern conceptions are employed.

Two sets of facts about the mind and its workings are available to us (Freud, 1938). One of these is that mental life is a function of the brain and depends on the somatic organization of the body. The brain is its bodily organ and its scene of action. Thus, if we were to have a complete understanding of mental life, we would need to understand the hereditary, constitutional, and physical–chemical aspects of the brain and the entire somatic organization of the body. A great deal of work is being done in these areas, but at present it is not possible to talk about mental functioning in such terms.

So psychiatrists have to use a second set of facts about the mind and its workings. This consists of knowledge of our conscious acts, conscious sensations, or what might be called the immediate data of the consciousness. It is through investigation of this data—our behavior, feelings, thoughts, and so on—that most of the work on psychopathology has been approached today.

In the study of psychopathology our basic data arise from the relationship set up between the physician and the patient. This is a relationship in which the physician participates and also observes. He uses the data gathered by conscious attention to try to understand the relationship. There are certain corollaries to this approach.

First, although the relationship between the physician

and the patient is of paramount importance in understanding the patient, great importance is also attached to the patient's relationships with other people throughout his life, of his feelings about these relationships, and to his methods of dealing with them.

Second, we try to understand the patient as an *individual*. We do not want to lose sight of the individual regardless of our preoccupation with dynamics, structure of the personality, and so on. We want to keep in mind that we are dealing with a living person, a continuously changing biological entity.

Third, it is important to understand the conditions and the mechanisms that are healthy in the patient, as well as the mechanisms of disease. Recognizing what enabled the patient to function optimally sometimes provides very valuable clues for understanding both the therapeutic relationship and the patient's pathology.

Fourth, we try to understand what the needs of the individual patient are as well as to delineate his conflicts. We keep in mind the importance of the patient's recent and current life situation and adjustments and the failure of those adjustments as represented by the illness. It is important to know about the past of the patient, but also, if we are to follow these basic assumptions, we want to understand present relationships and present reactions.

Finally, the fact that the patient and the psychiatrist live in a community is not to be ignored. Social factors and pressures and the cultural aspects of the relationship between the physician and the patient are important.

From these corollaries one can see why during the last fifty years (and even before) two basic views of looking at the mind and its workings have come into being. These basic

30

views are sometimes, though not necessarily, antagonistic to each other. For our purposes it is important to be familiar with both views in order better to grasp both the abnormal and the normal.

One of these views is called the *interpersonal approach*. It has probably been brought to its highest peak of sophisticated theoretical development by Harry Stack Sullivan (1935) and has been fostered by writers like Eric Fromm, Karen Horney, Alfred Adler and philosophers such as John Dewey. Here the individual is viewed as a personality that has developed in attempts to deal with other people or to deal with what some call "recurrent interpersonal situations."

I call the other view the *individual approach*. It, of course, was brought to its peak by Freud, and I think a great deal of it can be found also in the writings of many of the classical philosophers; for example, one finds, even as early as Plato, discussion of the personality's development through struggle between inner forces and outer forces.

Let us turn to the first of these two approaches, the interpersonal approach, as characterized by the psychiatry of Harry Stack Sullivan [A comprehensive review of Sullivan's views may be found in the recent text by Mullahy (1970).] In defining psychiatry as the study of interpersonal relations, Sullivan tries to make it a branch of another evolving discipline, social psychology. Sullivan's language and style are unique, and his concepts are very difficult. Throughout this survey I have tried to keep his unique words and phrases whenever possible, both to preserve the originality of his concepts and to avoid too biased an interpretation of some of his ambiguous phrases. He was a great intuitive psychotherapist, well worth careful study.

Both sociology and psychology according to Sullivan seek

31

"an adequate statement of living." The scientific psychiatrist would know "wherein and wherefore his patient fails" in interpersonal relations and whether his remedial efforts would reasonably be expected to lead to an improved facility for living.

Personality is defined by Sullivan as "the relatively enduring pattern of recurrent, interpersonal situations which characterize a human life." "The relative adequacy and appropriateness of action in interpersonal situations" is seen to constitute "extraordinary success, average living, or mental disorder." Sullivan argues that the true or absolute individuality of the person is always beyond scientific grasp and is "invariably much less significant in the person's living than he has been taught to believe."

Sullivan (1947) defines psychiatry as the study of what goes on between people: "The field of psychiatry is the field of interpersonal relations under any and all circumstances in which these relations exist." A personality can never be isolated from the complex of interpersonal relations in which the person lives and has his being. "We can study the phenomena that go on between the observer and the observed in the situation created by the observer participating with the observed." This is the subject matter of psychiatry.

On the other hand, according to the individual approach the personality is seen as developing from a struggle between inner and outer forces. Sequences of conscious and unconscious mental events take place, with the outcome of the sequence or the final result of the sequences appearing in the conscious. This outcome can be seen as the resultant vector, which occurs after the interplay of a number of opposing and conflicting forces on and from within the individual. According to this point of view, in order to understand people, psychiatry should concentrate on discovering the laws that govern the sequence of these mental events and the meaning of any mental event. This meaning is defined as the position in a sequence of events that any given mental event holds. The focus here is clearly on the individual and on *intrapsychic* phenomena.

Let us turn next to what we may characterize as the anatomy of the mental personality. This is also conceived somewhat differently by the two schools of thought. Sullivan speaks of the "self-system" or "self-dynamism," or "self." This self is built up out of experiences "of approbation and disapproval, of reward and punishment."

The self becomes the custodian of awareness. The self refuses awareness for the expression of things in the personality that are disapproved by the parent and other significant persons, and these impulses, desires, and needs become "dissociated." Sullivan (1953) goes so far as to divide the self-system, or self-dynamism into the "good-me," "bad-me," and "not-me." The good-me contains all those appraisals of the various aspects of the person that are approved by the parents and significant persons. The bad-me contains "impulses, desires, and needs" that are not approved by the significant persons but are not terribly disapproved; a moderate amount of anxiety is associated with them. The not-me is the large "dissociated" system of impulses, desires, and needs that the individual cannot tolerate as part of himself. The lack of tolerance for these takes place because the individual would be terribly disapproved of by the parent and other significant persons if he were known to have these feelings. Intense anxiety is the motivating force behind the dissociation.

These definitions lead to a conception of "mentally ill."

33

In Sullivan's view the self may be said to be made up of reflected appraisals. Any limitations and peculiarities in the self may interfere with the pursuit of biologically necessary satisfactions. When this happens, the person is to that extent mentally ill.

For example, if the reflected appraisals were chiefly derogatory, as in the case of an unwanted child who was never loved, the self will be chiefly derogatory. It will facilitate hostile, disparaging appraisals of other people and entertain disparaging and hostile appraisals of itself. Sullivan (1947) writes:

> So difficult is the maintenance of the feeling of security among his fellows for anyone who has come to have a hostile, derogatory self, that this hostile, derogatory low self appreciation must be excluded from direct communication. . . . The relative silence about the low self appraisal is achieved in part by the clamor of derogating others, in part by preoccupation with implicit reverie processes that dramatize the opposite of one's defects or protest one's rights, or otherwise manifest indirectly one's feeling of unworthiness and inferiority. . . . This selective exclusion of experience which leads to one's being occupied with or noticing only the hostile, unfriendly aspects of living not only is manifested in one's attitude toward others, but is represented in the attitude towards the self.

Careful study of this quotation explains the apparent paradox of why some people can carry on in the face of seemingly overwhelming difficulties, while others are crushed to suicide by apparently insignificant difficulties. Suicide, according to Sullivan, then becomes essentially a question of when a derogatory and hostile attitude ordinarily directed toward the outer world is directed with full force toward the self. Suicide may also fail due to "the intervention of the dissociated part of the personality, the part of the personality that has been growing up under greatest handicap and counterdistinction to the experience to which the self is receptive." For that which is excluded from awareness (dissociated) by virtue of the directing influence of the self must be quite different in some essential aspects from that which is incorporated and manifested in the self.

Let me offer some summary points about Sullivan's difficult self-system:

1. The self comes into being to preserve the feeling of security, and it is built largely of personal elements learned in contact with other significant people.

2. The self is approved by significant others, and any tendencies of the personality that are not so approved, and that are, in fact, strongly disapproved, are dissociated from personal awareness.

3. These dissociated tendencies do not cease to exist merely because they are excluded from the self; they manifest themselves in action and activities of which the person himself remains quite unaware.

4. Dissociated components of the self pursue both satisfaction and security operations. (These will be discussed later on.)

5. These dissociated tendencies were tolerated by the significant persons in the environment for a time; but as the person grows, he must dissociate some power operations, such as magical performances that were tolerated early in childhood (for example, crying, temper tantrums, baby talk).

6. It may be that whatever is useful at one stage of personality development will be dissociated in the next stage un-

35

less the "culture-carrying adults" encourage its continued elaboration within the self.

7. In general, the healthy development of the personality is inversely proportional to the amount and number of tendencies that exist in dissociation. Or the larger the proportion of energy systems in the personality that act outside the person's awareness, the greater the chances that he will meet some crisis in interpersonal relations in which he cannot act in a way we call mentally healthy. The likelihood of an acute disturbance of some interpersonal relation is greatly increased when an important system is in dissociation. The larger the not-me element of the self, the more likely an acute disturbance.

Let me turn now to the individual approach to the anatomy of the mental personality, often called the psychic apparatus. The concepts were originally presented by Freud (1923) to use as tools for understanding the psyche. Review of the history of science shows that such conceptions have always played a vital role (Kuhn, 1962). For example, the Bohr model of the atom constituted a useful set of heuristic principles and led to many fruitful discoveries in physics, although it turned out to be a false picture and was replaced by the Heisinger model. It is imperative to put aside the very dull argument about whether these conceptions are "true" or not and to try instead to learn them and employ them as heuristic tools for understanding.

The *id* arises from and represents the biological furnace of the body. From the id emanates the fury and the passion of the organism. At its base we conceive of an energy system, arising from the body's biochemical processes, that requires the body to replenish itself and to maintain physiologic equilibrium. The id may be thought of as containing all that is inherited and fixed in the constitution. It may be thought of as a cauldron of seething excitement or chaos. It represents all the somatic processes of the body reflected on a psychologic level; that is, eventually all the important somatic processes of the body have a psychic representation in the id.

The characteristics of the id are as follows:

1. The id is completely unconscious and always remains so. It consists of images, chaos, a cauldron of seething excitement.

2. The id is that part of the mind that contains everything inherited, especially the instincts, or drives. The drives, or instincts, fill the id with energy and press for immediate satisfaction. The id has no organization and no will. Its only purpose is to satisfy the needs, or the drives.

The original word that Freud used for drive or drives was *Trieb* (Fenichel, 1945). This word was originally mistranslated as "instinct," and the mistake led to a great deal of unnecessary dispute. Unfortunately, *Trieb* has remained in much of the literature as the word *instinct,* although instincts have a more specific physiologic meaning and are more fixed.

3. There is no negation in the id, only desires, which demand satisfaction.

4. The id knows no values, no good, no bad, no evil, no morality.

5. Contradictory impulses may occur in the id, and they may exist independently side by side—love and hate, for example. Such contradictory impulses do not detract from one another, and they cannot cancel one another.

6. The processes of the id are not related to reality; they are subject only to what we call the *pleasure principle,* which

37

may be described as "I want what I want when I want it."

7. The processes of the id are timeless; that is, an unfulfilled need remains unchanged and unfulfilled if nothing has been done, regardless of the passage of years.

8. Finally, the id is subject to the mechanism of displacement, which we will discuss more fully later. Ideas from it often appear in a condensed form, also.

The second heuristic concept is that of the *ego*. Freud (1938) states, "Under the influence of the real external world which surrounds us, one portion of the id has undergone a special development. From what was originally a cortical layer, provided with organs for receiving stimuli and with apparatus for protection against excessive stimulation, a special organization has arisen which henceforward acts as an intermediary between the id and the external world. This region of our mental life has been given the name of ego."

There is some controversy at present about whether the ego completely develops from the id or whether the infant is also born with certain "ego-nuclei," which develop and differentiate in the process of maturation. Freud originally postulated that the ego develops for the protection of the individual's existence when external events impinge upon the id. It begins as a "stimulus barrier" to avoid the person's being overwhelmed by pressures from within or without. On the other hand, Hartmann (1958) argues that there are certain inborn ego-nuclei and that these develop in the process of maturation (which has nothing to do with environment), although he grants that the differentiation of the ego is influenced by environmental events.

The basic functions of the ego are usually described as four in number. The first of these can be termed an internal perceptive function. The ego looks within and assesses what instincts in the id are pressing the most for expression at any given time. The second function is an external perceptive function. The ego must look to the outer world to assess what the reality situation is for the person at any given time. The third function is an executive, or integrative, function. The ego must figure out which id needs can be fulfilled in the particular reality situation that the person is in. When the ego has done this, it then carries out its fourth function and sends impulses to the body musculature, ordering certain acts to take place. It attempts to obtain the fulfillment of id needs in the particular reality situation according to the executive decrees that the ego has issued.

Thus, the ego is that part of the mind of man that is interposed between his desires and perception of his bodily needs, on the one hand, and his actions, on the other, and that mediates between them to get as many needs satisfied in any given situation as possible. The ego controls voluntary movements. It represents reason, in contrast to the id, which represents the passions. It has the task of self-preservation, although it may avoid excessive stimuli through flight. It deals with moderate stimuli through adaptation, and it learns to bring about appropriate modifications in the external world to its own advantage through muscular activity.

The ego can take itself as object. It can treat itself like any other object, observe itself, and criticize itself. In such a case, one part of the ego stands over and against the other. We shall speak more about the functions of the ego and the id when we talk about functioning of the mental apparatus.

The *superego* is the third part of the anatomy of the mental personality, according to Freud. It contains two aspects, both of which exert a pressure upon the ego to force it to act in a certain way. The first of these aspects consists of the *totality* of moral rules and regulations that the individual takes in from significant adults during the process of development. When these values and morals are transgressed, the superego installs a feeling of guilt and forces the ego by this uncomfortable feeling to change or inhibit its activity.

The second aspect of the superego has to do with the individual's ideal of how he should be. This "ego-ideal" is usually modeled on significant persons in the individual's environment, and when the individual falls short of his ego-ideal, the superego instills the feeling of shame, which may produce feelings of inferiority (these may, in turn, lead to compensatory striving). At any rate, the feeling of shame is unpleasant in itself and tends to pressure the ego to do something else or to inhibit what is being done.

It is clear that the ego is subject to "three harsh masters" —the id, the superego, and reality. It is constantly under pressure from the id to gain instinctual release, it is constantly forced to put up with a harsh uncompromising reality, and it is continually hemmed in by the restrictions of the superego. As Freud (1933) wrote:

> We are warned by a proverb against serving two masters at the same time. The poor ego has things even worse: it serves three severe masters and does what it can to bring their claims and demands into harmony with one another. No wonder the ego so often fails in its task. . . . Thus the ego, driven by the id, confined by the super-ego, repulsed by reality struggles to master its economic task of bringing about harmony among the forces and influences working in and upon it; and we can understand how it is that so often we cannot suppress a cry: "Life is not easy!"

Next let us examine the functioning of the mental apparatus. Returning to the interpersonal approach, Sullivan

40

classifies all interpersonal phenomena on the basis of certain "sought-end states." He divides all the sought-end states of the self into groups: (a) satisfactions, which have to do with the bodily organization of man, such as food, drink, sleep, and finally reducing loneliness—which Sullivan rather confusedly calls a "middling example," between the first and second groups—and (b) end states involved with the pursuit of security. These latter pursuits, according to Sullivan, pertain more closely to man's cultural equipment and have to do with the need for prestige and power. Here one can see a rather sophisticated treatment of Adler's early theory (developed under the influence of Nietzsche) that man's basic needs are to compensate for feelings of insecurity and to lust for superiority. Sullivan believes that cultural conditioning gives rise to the second group of sought-end states, pursued by "power operations," but seems to think that we are also born "with something of the power motive within us."

According to Sullivan, as one proceeds into childhood, disapproval and dissatisfaction with one's performances are more and more the tools of the significant adult in educating the infant and the child, and this disapproval is felt by the child through what Sullivan calls an "empathic linkage," which is conspicuous even in infancy. That is to say, the disapproval and anxiety of the mother are felt as a particular kind of discomfort by the infant, and this particular discomfort is the basis of what we ultimately refer to as anxiety.

There are three very unpleasant experiences that an infant can have—pain, fear, and anxiety. Anxiety is very important in the functioning of the personality, according to Sullivan's thinking, because it determines what parts of the self-system are to be dissociated into the not-me part of the personality. The more anxious the person becomes about a particular impulse, need, or desire, the more tendency there is to dissociate it from the self and store it in the not-me. It follows that the more anxious and restrictive the parents are about the impulses and needs of the infant and child, the greater the sector of the not-me part of the self is going to be in the child and the greater the tendency for difficulty in interpersonal relations later on.

Freud's individual approach, on the other hand, speaks of "modes of mental functioning" and attempts to focus on the vicissitudes of certain chains of mental events. Mental events in the id follow what Freud calls the mode of primary process. This involves the displacement and condensation of the "energy cathexis" of the instincts, or drives. Psychic energy can be freely displaced from one instinctual element to another. For example, Brenner (1955) mentions the common shift from breast seeking to thumb sucking in the infant, when breast or bottle are not available. Condensation implies that different energies and drives in the id can be condensed into one discharge object or symbolic representation.

Impulses are always trying to get out of the id, and some kind of gratification is needed, but only derivatives of these impulses can be gratified. A person must be somewhat able to drain the id impulses in order to be comfortable. Both this powerful tendency to gratification and the condensation and shifting of energy cathexes among the various impulses in the id have been referred to as primary-process mental functioning.

On the other hand, the ego functions according to a secondary process, which involves the logical organization of thoughts and ideas into a coherent and goal-directed state and implies the capacity to delay gratification. It is the char-

42

acteristic way of elaborating conscious thought and is simply another term to describe the rules and regulations of socially accepted, mature thought.

Two principles of mental functioning described by Freud (1911) are closely related to these modes of mental functioning. He describes the pleasure principle by the phrase, "I want what I want when I want it." The id operates according to the pleasure principle and strives always for satisfaction with no regard for anything else. The ego, on the other hand, operates on the reality principle. It must try to adjust what the individual does to the various demands and restrictions of his reality situation.

The energies and power of the id express the biological purpose of the individual organism's life. This purpose is to satisfy the organism's innate needs appearing as instincts, or drives. Every instinct has a source, aim, and object. The source of the instinct is the biological processes of the body, which provide the energy. The aim of the instinct is discharge, a reduction of the tension of need. The object of the instinct may easily change, depending on whatever vehicle is available for the discharge of the tension.

Freud often speaks of three qualities of mental events. First, there are conscious mental events, easy to describe, in immediate awareness. Second, there are preconscious mental events that are not immediately in awareness but that can be called to awareness with relative ease. For example, what one had for dinner the day before is information that may not be immediately available to awareness but on a little thinking can enter awareness. The third quality of mental events is unconsciousness. This includes everything else that is mental. Those mental processes that have no easy access to the con-

43

sciousness but must be inferred, discovered, and translated into conscious form are called unconscious. All of the material in the id is unconscious. Part of the ego and superego are conscious or preconscious, and part of them are unconscious.

During development of the personality the young and feeble ego must drop and push back into the unconscious certain material that had previously been conscious. We term this portion of the id the repressed and this mode of functioning—forcing down material that was conscious into the unconscious—the mechanism of repression.

Repression is one example of the many defense mechanisms that the ego may use against unacceptable impulses, thoughts, feelings, and desires. In all cases the defense mechanisms are brought into operation by anxiety. According to the individual approach (Freud, 1926), anxiety is the central motivating power in the functioning of the personality. It is defined as a signal that the ego sends out in situations that threaten the ego. Anxiety is felt as an unpleasant sensation by the individual, and it must be removed by the ego's action.

Anxiety itself constitutes energy, and this energy comes from the id. The ego borrows the energy to give itself extra impetus to deal with the threatening situation. This energy, which is first felt as anxiety, is used to deal with the threatening situation by means of psychic processes called *defense mechanisms* or by actively doing something. Since the ego very often functions unconsciously, the defense mechanisms may come into play without the individual being aware of them.

A *hallucination* is a mental image that occurs in the absence of any external stimulus. For example, a dream is a hallucination. Hallucinations are among the earliest kind of defenses used by infants. An *illusion* is a misperception of an external stimulus; something is there, but it is misperceived as something else. A *delusion* is a false belief that is not amenable to reason or evidence.

A *fixation* is a cessation in maturation at a particular stage of development. There are two reasons why fixation may occur. The first is too much deprivation; the second is too much pleasure. In both instances the anxiety aroused by going to the next stage is overwhelming.

In *projection,* also an extremely primitive mechanism of defense, one ascribes to others one's own unacceptable or undesirable thoughts, traits, or feelings. This mechanism plays an important role in the genesis of war and prejudice.

Probably the most difficult mechanism of defense to accept and understand is *introjection.* Introjection is the opposite of projection. At the most primitive level projection represents spitting out the unacceptable and introjection represents swallowing what one desires. It differs from *identification,* which is a more easily understood type of defense, and occurs later in maturation. (For details see Schafer, 1968). In identification one takes on only certain aspects of the desired person, whereas in introjection there is a total incorporation, in a cannibalistic fantasy, of both the good and the bad. For example, certain psychotic individuals who have very little strength of ego clinically appear, where the introjection mechanisms are so obvious and prevalent, to be almost a mimic, hostile caricature, or mirror image of the introject.

Three mechanisms of defense often confused are repression, suppression, and denial. *Repression* is the exclusion of unacceptable material from the conscious mind. It is a totally unconscious process. *Suppression,* on the other hand, is a conscious exclusion of unacceptable material from the mind. *Denial* is the most primitive of the three. It can be thought of as negative hallucination. Something is hallucinated away, its very existence denied.

Regression is an extremely important mechanism of defense at the core of most neuroses and represents a retreat to earlier satisfactions, to earlier stages of psychic equilibrium, when no satisfaction or insufficient satisfaction can be had at the present stage.

Magical undoing is the attempt through some symbolic behavior to abolish or control past experiences or unacceptable thoughts, the consequences of which have been painful. It might be called negative magic, that is, an undoing procedure. The individual is often unaware of what he wishes to abolish. The attempt is usually an act to eradicate an unconscious hostile wish of some kind.

Isolation is a defense process by which unpleasant experiences can be deprived of their emotional accompaniment. Clinically it can appear as colorless or flat ideation. For example, the patient calmly comes in with a straight face and no apparent emotion and says, "I feel like killing my wife." Sometimes this comes out in a cool, highly rigid intellectual formation, such as in discussions of "overkill"—how many millions will be killed on that side and how many millions will be killed on this side. It is a defensive maneuver to isolate the terror and horror of something and allow it still to appear in the conscious.

Reaction formation is the development of convictions or character traits that are exactly the opposite of the unacceptable trends in the unconscious mind. The defense is developing attitudes or characteristics that are the reverse or anti-

46

thesis of the unacceptable unconscious trends. In moderation, such a defense has considerable social value.

In *displacement* one sees a shifting of emphasis or a substitution of feeling in response to unacceptable ideas, or feelings as in the saying "Many a truth is said in jest" and "Smile when you say that." In displacement either the affect can be shifted (an angry statement made with a smile or joke), or the object can be shifted (a person really wants to kill a parent, but instead talks incessantly about the killing of the President).

In *conversion* unconscious infantile wishes are expressed through physical changes in the body. It follows that conversion takes place through the voluntary muscular system. *Dissociation* is the analogous change in the state of consciousness; the person shifts from what we would call the normal state of consciousness to a twilight, or fugue, state of consciousness or even faints. In these semiconscious states activities are carried out that would not be permissible in the normal states.

Compensation is an obvious defense mechanism related to the need for prestige. A person who cannot accomplish in one area may repress his wish to accomplish in that area and accomplish in another. Similarly, *substitution* is the reduction of frustration by getting gratification in a related area. This mechanism represents a change of aims; *turning against the self* would represent a change of objects.

Rationalization is a defense mechanism very commonly used—explaining away one's behavior or one's thoughts by finding acceptable excuses.

Finally, the most important mechanism of defense from the sociologic point of view is *sublimation,* in which the energy of an unacceptable impulse is diverted and directed to

47

socially acceptable means and goals. Sublimation is extremely important as the civilization-building mechanism of defense (Freud, 1930).

Both the interpersonal and the individual approaches to the mind and its workings lead to certain conclusions about the etiology of mental illness. *Etiological thinking from both points of view is based on the fundamental idea that disturbances in early developmental history lead to disturbances later on in life.* Here only a brief outline of Sullivan and Freud on the stages of personality development is given. The reader is also referred to Mullahy (1948) and Munroe (1955) for details and comparisons of these views.

Sullivan's approach emphasizes the career line—the direction the person has taken in interpersonal relations from early in life due to environmental experiences and that may result in trouble. Sullivan (1947) divides the developmental history of the individual into stages, which he calls "epochs" or "eras," and describes these as follows.

The first stage is the epoch of infancy, the period of "maturation, of experimentation, of empathic observation, and of autistic invention in the realm of power." In the epoch of infancy the infant is in far too immature a state to live by its own functional activity and depends, of course, on the mothering one: "The mothering one is the first vivid perception of a person relatively independent of the infant's own vague entity." The relation of the infant to the mothering one is important in terms of organizing knowledge about the world. This knowledge is organized in order to maintain necessary or pleasant functional activity within the world. For ". . . whether the objects be manageable or unmanageable, remote or immediate, one has to maintain a communal existence." Here begins the security or power concept in Sullivan's description of sought-end states.

The epoch of childhood begins with the basic acquisition of language, "an enormous cultural entity." The learning of language begins with phonemes and morphemes, certain syllables, words, or vibrations around which a meaning has been established in our culture. The world of the child is autistic and has a highly individual meaning; the process of learning language consists to a great extent of learning the cultural meaning of each phoneme and morpheme that is useful in communication and power operations. Along with the learning of language, the child experiences restraints on his freedom in the epoch of childhood. From these restraints comes the further evolution of the self-system and the generation of anxiety and subsequent dissociation. Also in childhood "consensual validation," which will be discussed later, begins.

In the juvenile epoch, there appears "an urgent need for compeers with whom to have one's existence." The child proceeds into the juvenile era of personality development by virtue of a tendency to cooperate, to do things in accomodation to the personality of others. Here the interpersonal relation between teacher and pupil in the school situation may affect the growth of the personality. There may be a seeking to go back, and the child may indicate this tendency by regressively retreating into the past and engaging in reverie processes that have been given up by other people his age.

Around the age of eight and a half to twelve comes the era of preadolescence. This is a movement from what Sullivan calls "egocentricity" toward a fully social state. It is marked by the appearance of the capacity to love in its initial form. Love is defined by Sullivan as occurring when "the satisfac-

49

tions and security which are being experienced by someone else, some particular other person, begin to be as significant to a person as his own satisfactions and security." We will return to this definition repeatedly in this book. The appearance of the capacity to love ordinarily first involves a member of one's own sex; the boy finds a chum and the girl finds a chum.

What happens then is a great increase in consensual validation. Consensual validation has to do with the comparing of notes, the checking and counterchecking of information and data about life in the world. As Sullivan describes this vitally important experience, it involves a feeling of being human in a sense in which one has not previously felt human. This feeling arises because when another person's satisfactions matter as much as your own, "it is quite possible to talk to this person as you have never talked to anyone before." That is to say, "The freedom which comes from the expanding of one's world of satisfaction and security to include two people linked together by love, permits exchange of nuance of meaning, permits investigations without fear of rebuff or humiliation," which greatly augments consensual validation.

Sullivan distinguishes between cooperation, which occurs in the earlier stages when the person plays according to his own rules of the game in order to preserve his own prestige, and the new practice of collaboration, which occurs in the preadolescent and has to do with sympathy and understanding of others.

The final epoch of development, adolescence, has to do with the coming of genital sexuality and leads to the fullest development of the human organism. Difficulties in any of these areas of living will lead to a greater not-me system in dissociation and consequently increased difficulties in inter-personal relations, which Sullivan has characterized as the definition of mental illness.

Freud's individual approach puts an entirely different emphasis on the developmental events in the life history of the individual. Freud is interested in the vicissitudes of the instincts as the individual grows up and, most especially, the vicissitudes of the sexual instinct. The energy of the sexual instinct is defined as the libido. Sexual life does not begin at puberty but starts with clear manifestations soon after birth. It is necessary to distinguish sharply between the concepts of sexual and genital. The former is the wider concept and includes many activities that have nothing to do with the genitals. Sexual life comprises the obtaining of pleasure from certain zones of the body—an activity that is subsequently brought into the service of reproduction.

These zones of the body have been called erotogenic zones (Freud, 1938), or erogenous zones (Fenichel, 1945), and they represent areas of the body from which this libido arises (Freud, 1938) or that are stimulated by certain chemical or hormonal changes to bring forth certain urgent impulses (Fenichel, 1945). The first of these zones to appear, through which the libido can be discharged, is the mouth, and the first year of life is spoken of as the oral period. During the oral period of life, in addition to maintaining biological survival, the infant experiences pure pleasure around the mouth. Not only does he suck in the milk that is necessary for his life, but he also enjoys stimulation of this erotogenic zone and subsequent libido discharge.

The first half of the oral period, or the first six months of life, is essentially passive. The infant desires to be given

51

to and to passively receive through the mouth. Essentially he wishes to suck and satiate himself, to fall asleep at the mother's breast, and to be devoured and returned inside the mother.

The next six months of life, along with the development of teeth, are characterized by an active or sadistic oral stage. Here a new pleasure is found, that of biting. Thus, anger or rage experienced in the oral period is reacted to by a hallucinatory fantasy of biting, chewing, and devouring the frustrating object. This may be originally a very pleasant retaliation fantasy ("an eye for an eye, and a tooth for a tooth") but often has to be deeply repressed by the ego because the frustrating object is most often the mother, and there would be danger if the mother were devoured and destroyed, since she is also the source of life for the infant. (Remember that fantasy and act are synonymous in primary-process thinking.)

Between the ages of one and two a new erotogenic zone becomes important. This is the anus. Many of the conflicts and problems of the two-year-old revolve around toilet training and the production of the bowel movement. The anal stage of development is also divided by some into an active, or sadistic, and a passive, or retentive, period. The active period appears first, and then the appearance of the retentive period heralds the beginning of true object-love. In the active anal or anal–sadistic stage the predominant fantasy is to expel and to get rid of objects. Thus, having a bowel movement is conceived of as a hostile expulsion of a bad object, which gives a pleasant sensation. During the passive anal stage, the wish to retain is predominant. The infant may enjoy the sensations of control over the full rectum, and battles may ensue between the infant and the mother as to when he should have the bowel movement. In the act of defecation libido is discharged around the anal erotogenic zone.

Around the age of four the erotogenic zone shifts to the genitalia. This has been called the phallic, or oedipal, phase of development. The object of the libido at the age of five is the parent of the opposite sex, and the parent of the same sex is seen as a rival. The fantasy is that of possessing sexually the parent of the opposite sex and destroying or getting rid of the parent of the same sex. Here again, although the fantasy may be pleasant, it often has to be repressed because of the fear of retaliation—especially in a boy who fears castration as a retaliation for the desire to possess the mother.

In girls the oedipal conflict centers on the struggle between the wish to mature and rival mother with sexual desires on the one hand and the desire to be dependent on mother and enjoy her protection on the other. Sometimes the latter need is stronger, and the girl renounces sexuality altogether. One also sees envy of the penis in the girl and a desire to castrate men in order to get one. This unacceptable thought may also lead to renunciation of sexuality or to a dominating, aggressive, competitive personality, sometimes called a phallic woman. Normally, the basic wish to have a baby by the father develops, the reverse of the male oedipal wish.

The oedipal phase is followed by a so-called latent phase, in which no new erotogenic zones are developed, and finally by adolescence. Thus, Freud often speaks of the biphasic nature of sexual urges. The first great increase in sexual urge occurs around the age of five years. It then falls off with the passing of the Oedipus complex and reappears again in adolescence. This is a biological phenomenon, part of the process of maturation.

Etiological thinking in Freud's individual approach is much more clear, specific, and precise than in the interpersonal approach. As the individual advances through the various stages of psychosexual development, a tendency to attach certain quantities of libido to earlier erotogenic zones and associated fantasies is left behind. Fixation depends on two factors, the amount of overindulgence a person has had at a given stage of development and the amount of deprivation a person has had at this period of development. There is always some fixation in everybody at all the various stages of development.

Later, when difficulties in living arise, there is a tendency to regress to earlier points of fixation in development. An obvious example is the child of eight years who is brought in for an appendix operation and suddenly shuts his eyes, curls up into a ball, and begins sucking his thumb, something he would never dream of doing under ordinary conditions.

A price has to be paid for this regression, however. For regression to an earlier stage of life results in a revival of problems that were unsolved and unmastered in the earlier stage. These problems give rise to anxiety because they involve the pressing for expression of unsatisfied infantile impulses and needs that are unacceptable to the ego; this forces the ego to use additional defense mechanisms to aid repression. Often the defense mechanisms used in this situation are of a drastic nature and exaggerated quantity, causing the individual much difficulty and leading to the development of the clinical picture we call a neurosis. Furthermore, guilt about the regression tends to increase the difficulties of the situation and encourage more regression.

Alexander (1948) points out, "The longer a neurosis

54

continues, the more fully a vicious circle develops. Symptoms absorb a patient's energies and make him less effective in dealing realistically with life. This is called secondary conflict and necessitates further regression and symptomatic outlets, which in turn increase conflict and absorb more energy." These considerations lead us directly to consider our current conceptions of mental health and how this vicious cycle of the development of emotional disorder can be interrupted and reversed by psychotherapy.

CHAPTER 3   *Healing Through Psychotherapy*

*F*REUD summed up his notion of mental health by the famous phrase, "to be able to love and to be able to work." In this chapter I wish to present our basic concepts of mental illness and an overview of the techniques of healing through psychotherapy. In subsequent chapters I will take up various aspects of the technique and practice of psychotherapy in more detail.

Saul and Pulver (1966) fully delineate the concepts of emotional maturity or mental health used as working hypotheses in intensive psychotherapy. Saul (1971) further presents an extended discussion of emotional maturity that is worthy of reference. Certain basic premises underlie the conception of mental health and psychological healing as it is seen here. First, the development of emotional maturity is understood to proceed of its own nature, while environment supplies only the conditions for development. Evidently ideal conditions are best, but growth can continue in the face of difficulties.

An important corollary of this is that in the process of psychological healing every person has a certain innate timetable. If the psychotherapist is not aware of each individual patient's unique timetable in the proceedings towards maturity, he may find himself abandoning patients, pressing too hard, and becoming discouraged.

The fundamental conditions for human emotional maturation, assuming adequate food and physical care, are good feelings toward the child and good examples of mature behavior on the part of those responsible for the child and closest to it—the parents, siblings, and so on.

> The proper soil, climate, protection, and freedom are, for the child, loving, understanding respect for its needs and feelings. If these favorable conditions are provided the child then develops positive feelings for and identifications with those who are responsible for and are closest to him. These good feelings are essential to maturing. If they are provided, then the child gradually becomes socialized of its own accord with a minimum of training and discipline. . . .
>
> The child's pattern of feelings toward its parents and siblings, which is formed by about age six, remains constant for life in its essentials. This pattern sets channels for the child's developing feelings toward others and toward itself. And it continues as a permanent nucleus, mostly unconscious, in the personality. *The child we once were lives on in each of us; however much the rest of the personality matures* [my italics] (Saul and Pulver, 1966).

57

Ibsen (1881) suggested much of the same thing in more poetic terms:

> I am half inclined to think we are all ghosts. It is not only what we have inherited from our fathers and mothers that exists again in us, but all sorts of old dead ideas and all kinds of old dead beliefs and things of that kind. They are not actually alive in us; but there they are dormant, all the same, and we can never be rid of them. . . . They must be as countless as the grains of the sands, it seems to me. And we are so miserably afraid of the light, all of us.

This concept of the existence of a psychodynamic nucleus or childhood core of feelings is an extremely important concept for psychotherapy. If this core is basically loving and if the relations with parents and siblings remain loving, then the child matures smoothly and adequately. "The child becomes a loving spouse, parent, friend, and citizen, a responsible productive man or woman of good will. The helpless dependent child develops into the inwardly secure, responsible, giving parent. The seedling has matured into a straight full tree." (Saul and Pulver, 1966).

Conversely, the pattern of disturbed emotional relations developed during the early formative years is the key to psychopathology—to the whole range of emotional disorders, from invisible inner suffering to frank criminal behavior. The symptoms and behavior of the individual always become intelligible in terms of his reactions as a child to how he was treated.

Of course a great many influences later in life can determine the final set of feelings with which an individual is endowed. A healthy father or a change in mother, for example, can ameliorate an impaired early childhood. A fortunate identification with an aunt or uncle or a teacher as an adolescent, marriage to a healthy, loving person, or even a lucky circumstance such as an empathic or understanding employer can do much to cover over or even neutralize a pathological childhood nucleus.

Stress is placed here on the childhood nucleus, for if intensive long-term psychotherapy is to be truly curative rather than ameliorative it *must* affect this core. Otherwise in times of stress the pathology will manifest itself again. When we speak of curative processes in psychotherapy we do not address ourself to any diseases. In psychiatry there are no specific diseases, only predominant pathological reaction patterns, appearing as personality characteristics or causes of symptoms, or both. These, in turn, are manifestations of emotional immaturity, or, to put it more formally, they reflect an impaired formation or functioning of the ego.

Mental illness is based on the unhealthy development of ego functions. The capacity of the ego to endure frustration, delay, ambiguity, separation, and misery is significantly reduced, and the "plasticity" of the ego is impaired. There is a disorder among the functioning of parts of the personality, and in consequence there is a failure in the relationships between the individual and other people.

To understand man's development as being intrinsically tied to his childhood character formation is, admittedly, rather pessimistic. As Wolberg (1969) states, in this view man emerges as a being "frustrated by the sexual impasse imposed by inimical events in childhood [who] spends the rest of his life fruitlessly trying to repair this damage. Blocked in his quest by a false friend (repression) he endlessly wanders

59

through the circuitous by-paths of life seeking vicarious and infantile satisfactions." Thus, Freud stated that the reason happiness is so difficult to find is because it is really connected with the gratification of infantile satisfactions and demands long repressed. So, while constantly casting in his present interpersonal relations and behavior the shadows of his past, man defends himself with capricious maneuvers (the mechanisms of defense), relentlessly marching on to his inevitable psychological doom, a phenomenon sometimes called the repetition compulsion.

A great many of the disagreements among schools of psychotherapy can be traced to the inability of their founders to accept this essentially pessimistic view of man. The most typical example of this can be found in the so-called existential movement, with its emphasis on the mystical, limitless potential of man, and his ultimate freedom of choice. Singer (1970) has devoted an entire book to describing psychotherapy from these opposed sides, and I will turn to this argument more fully in my last chapter.

For the purpose of trying to understand intensive psychotherapy, however, it is useful to begin, at least, with a deterministic, or mechanistic view of man, rather than a vitalistic and mystical one, no matter how this may insult narcissistic feelings.

How then does one approach a person who has *not* achieved maturity and who comes in asking for psychotherapy? Schilder (1951) delineated the problem as early as 1938. He reminds us that the physician and patient are fellow human beings. There is no fundamental difference between them. "The physician merely has more knowledge in a field of experience in which the patient happens to be not so well versed. In compensation for the advice, the patient gives money to the physician as he would give it to anyone else who serves him." The modern approach to psychotherapeutic problems stresses the necessity of gaining insight into the patient's personality and conflicts. Schilder points out that in this respect the opposing schools of Janet, Freud, Jung, and Adler are all of the same opinion. "A full social relationship to other human beings is only possible on the basis of a general good will and the acknowledgment that they are fellow human beings."

Psychotherapy has the task of not only establishing the relation between the physician and the patient but of finding out methods by which better understanding can be had of the problems of the patient. Only then is a full relation between the patient and his physician possible. The underlying conviction is that suffering due to psychic reasons is dependent on conflicts that the individual is not only unable to solve but is not even aware of. The psychotherapeutic process, therefore, must reveal the personality and the conflicts not only to the physician but to the patient himself. This is called "unveiling."

The problems of unveiling therapy or intensive psychotherapy are (a) what method is there to uncover the conflict underlying the sickness, (b) how can we bring the patient to understand his conflicts, and (c) how can one bring the patient actually to use his insights and newly acquired understanding. The psychotherapist does not "deal" with the unconscious by direct interpretations. He deals with the patient's capacity to communicate. Understanding of the unconscious of the patient is useful only when it becomes conscious to the patient, through the patient. It is always necessary to

61

work on the level of the patient's understanding. One cannot talk of what the patient is unaware of, and one cannot make a patient aware of something by telling him about it in a forceful or dogmatic way.

What is key to the therapy is what can be translated into the "you and me right here," not charismatic inspiration and certainly not wild interpretations of the unconscious. Our job is to make the patient less defensive about his feelings and to *remove resistances* so the patient can then communicate his feelings. In the process of therapy we study behavior, asking "why," and "how," and "explain." We try to help the patient to become aware of hidden motivations by beginning with the here–now current issues of his life.

Treatment may be aimed at maintaining adaptive patterns, modifying adaptive patterns, or reorganizing the whole basic personality structure. At one end of the range of treatment modes, and perhaps most easily characterized because its techniques are more sharply delineated, is psychoanalysis. In psychoanalysis insight through interpretations, especially of the transference neurosis, is considered the supreme therapeutic agent.

At the other end of the spectrum are those techniques that are characterized as supportive therapy. Gill (1951) has defined supportive psychotherapy as that designed to strengthen the defenses, in polar opposition to expressive therapy, which analyzes the defenses as a step toward an eventual reintegration. Gill names three techniques for strengthening the defenses: (a) encouragement of adaptive combinations of instincts and defense; (b) avoidance of uncovering or of interpreting defense constellations that are essential to the equilibrium of the patient; and (c) the selection of interpretations, for example, making inexact interpretations that offer a partial discharge of instinct derivatives, thus making the instinct relatively weaker and the work of defense against the remainder easier. The support of neurotic defenses in order to prevent the outbreak of psychoses is a typical example of important supportive therapy.

To put it more simply, the essence of supportive psychotherapy is the reduction of anxiety by various techniques, such as the administration of drugs, paying attention to complaints, and so forth; permitting the discharge of emotions in a nonpunitive situation (abreaction); objectively reviewing the patient's acute stress situation and assisting his judgment —reasoning together with the patient; and modification of superego and ego function by permitting and even encouraging conscious or unconscious identification with the therapist. This latter technique is especially frequent in the therapy of adolescents, where the therapist may at times consciously and deliberately present himself as a model by his behavior and by describing his ways of dealing with serious matters.

Manipulation of the environment is a highly overrated supportive measure that ignores the amazing power of the repetition compulsion. Time and again therapists have attempted to manipulate the environment either directly or through social agencies, only to be frustrated by the difficulty of doing so or frustrated by the patient's capacity to either undermine the manipulation or to go from the frying pan into the fire. This is especially true in attempts to manipulate marital situations. The therapist must be very careful to avoid trying to play God, regardless of how horrible the patient's situation or marriage seems to be. If the patient is in a bad marital situation, there is a reason for his being there. The

63

need for men and women to get into a mutual torture situation sanctified by the term *marriage* and sometimes repeated in a psychotherapy seems to be extraordinarily widespread. All sorts of rationalizations can be given for staying in these situations. In general, manipulation of the environment is valued mostly in the therapy of children and adolescents and should be used for adults only when there is a very clear-cut alternative to the patient's present position that is capable of being followed and seems definitely better.

The problem of choosing which patients require supportive psychotherapy and which patients would benefit from uncovering psychotherapy is a thorny one at times. I am not going to belabor this subject here, because I have already discussed it at length in a previous book (Chessick, 1969). DeWald (1964) has presented in detail the techniques for evaluating a patient for psychotherapy, and the reader is referred to Chapter 8 of his excellent book, or to most standard textbooks of psychiatry, for details of evaluation of the patient, testing mental status, and so forth.

It is usually possible to recognize at the beginning those patients for whom an uncovering approach at first is unreasonable. The patient must not be so comfortable as to lose motivation for further exploration nor so anxious as to be unable to function. It is ideal to try to begin all psychotherapy with primarily an uncovering approach, if this seems reasonable and practical. At least a trial of therapy should be undertaken, because it is not possible to predict on the basis of our clinical and psychological evaluation whether a given patient will respond or not to uncovering techniques (if we rule out those for whom uncovering psychotherapy is obviously impractical or impossible). In fact, the most apparently regressed or deteriorated patient can shift—sometimes after suitable supportive therapy first—and begin to utilize insight, while the most promising patients can completely frustrate their own treatment. The therapist must also be able to switch back and forth during therapy between supportive and uncovering techniques, in order to keep anxiety at an optimal level.

How does one uncover a patient's hidden or unconscious emotional conflicts? The first impetus toward this technique was given by Meyer (1951), who emphasized repeatedly the search for details in a person's life history. Meyer pointed out that medical psychology consists largely in the determination of the life history, experiences, and concrete reactions of the patient. The facts that really count, he said, are as plain and tangible, concrete and controllable, as those in any part of the medical record and examination of the human being, but they may be unwieldy and form a "long story." Before we can say that we have a clean-cut and practically useful view of "the fateful bias" indicated by the history—what we call today the childhood nucleus—it must be shown by careful scrutiny of the facts that the allegations tally with what the person actually shows objectively by his behavior and by the history furnished by others. Meyer points out that the length of the records and their apparent lack of pointedness is what makes many physicians shun the task.

This is, of course, part of Meyer's famous concept of psychobiology, based on a longitudinal life history of the patient. As we gather the facts and details we get a clearer and clearer idea of the patterns of the patient's behavior and adaptations, patterns the patient may not have noticed.

It is obvious that there are many ways of characterizing

65

THE TECHNIQUE AND PRACTICE OF INTENSIVE PSYCHOTHERAPY

the taking of a psychiatric history beside that of psychobiology, but the key to Meyer's therapy is that he was a "gentleman" and was never satisfied that he understood enough. He stressed patience, tact, and trying hard to understand the patient. The emphasis is on the utmost necessity to have thorough understanding of the details of the patient's life.

Sullivan (1954) suggested that we try to proceed along the general lines of getting some notion of what stands in the way of successful living for the person. He is quite certain that if we can clear away the obstacles, everything else will take care of itself. "So true is that," writes Sullivan, "that in well over twenty-five years, aside from my forgotten mistakes in the first few of them I have never found myself called upon to cure anybody." Sullivan insists that the patient took care of that, "once I have done the necessary brushclearing and so on." He points out that it is almost uncanny how things fade out of the picture when the reason for them is revealed. "The brute fact is," said Sullivan, "that man is so extraordinarily adapted that given any chance of reasonably adequate analysis of the situation, he is quite likely to stumble into a series of experiments which will gradually approximate more successful living."

The emphasis on recurrent patterns in the patient's life cannot be stressed sufficiently, and the only way to really understand these patterns and point them out is through a detailed historical study. Saul (1958) brings out the important fact that "the analyst, if he does not succeed in discerning the main issues, the central emotional forces which need correction, preferably in the first interview or the first few interviews may find himself beginning an analysis without knowing exactly what he is trying to correct, a situation as

potentially dangerous as that of a surgeon not knowing what
he is doing." To master the technique and achieve results
rationally and scientifically, the psychotherapist must first be
able to diagnose the central psychodynamics—what is wrong
and what he seeks to correct.

Freud (1914a) wrote that his master Charcot taught him
to "look at the same things again and again until they themselves begin to speak." The whole concept of psychotherapeutic healing is based on this idea. We get more and more
information from the patient about himself, the details of his
life, the details of his thoughts and fantasies, and, gradually,
as we are presented with this material, certain thought patterns and behavior repetitions begin to present themselves to
the therapist *if he is able to listen.* It is then the task of the
therapist to get this insight back across to the patient in such
a way that the patient can actually utilize the new information.

This technique requires a faith such as Sullivan's in the
adaptational capacities of human beings. The assessment of
the adaptational capacity of any given patient is very important, because if one feels that the patient cannot adapt,
cannot develop, and cannot heal, then one is wasting one's
time in doing psychotherapy with the patient.

It is to the everlasting credit of Sigmund Freud that he
developed the basic methods of uncovering hidden or unconscious information about the patient's conflicts and for communicating this knowledge in a meaningful way to the patient. These techniques are essentially "free association" and
the interpretation of the "transference." Free association developed out of the use of hypnosis. The patients that Freud
originally treated were hypnotized and urged to abreact or

ventilate about their emotions and their childhood conflicts. Under hypnosis it was found that they could remember things they could not remember in the normal state. It was soon pointed out to Freud by one of his more intelligent patients that hypnosis was really unnecessary. If he would simply keep quiet and encourage the patients to say whatever came to their minds, a chain of associations would take place, leading to the recovery of forgotten material and insight into unconscious conflicts.

The next great step forward took place when Freud realized that an emotional relationship developed between the patient and the therapist that seemed inappropriate to the situation. He named this transference, which he defined as a reaction to or a set of feelings about the therapist that were really appropriate to a significant parent in the past. These transference reactions were often rather dramatic, and it was the interpretation of these reactions that was found empirically to have an important effect on resolving problems in the childhood core of the patient.

Interpretations that connect the actual life situation with past experiences and with the transference situation are known as total interpretations, and the more a given interpretation can approximate this principal of totality, the more it fulfills a double purpose. First, it accelerates the assimilation of new material by the ego; second, it mobilizes further unconscious material.

A great many things demand interpretation as a basic technique in psychotherapy: resistances, transference distortions, character defenses, acting out, unconscious mental content (*after* the other things have been interpreted) and certain mental operations, such as slips of the tongue, dreams, and hallucinations. As a general principle, the therapist does not argue with the patient about hallucinations, delusions, and other such material. He simply states that he doesn't see, or hear, or believe what the patient professes to see, or hear, or believe. He tries to interest the patient in an investigation of why the patient sees or hears something different and why a difference exists between the patient's evaluation of acts and perceptions and that of the psychiatrist. For example, does the patient remember at what time during the psychotherapy or previous to it the particular distortion appeared, and can he account for real experiences in the past that produced the present distortions?

The development of psychotherapeutic technique has followed a historical line. When transference had not been discovered, the psychiatrist had simply to count on the good will or ability of the patient to reveal himself and to understand what was being said in therapy. These are very shaky factors to rely on, as the followers of Meyer discovered. With Freud's recognition of the transference, the search for infantile memories gives over in psychotherapy to the interpretation of transference phenomena. Finally, the concepts of working through and emotional after-education appeared. New relationships and experiences in the shadow play of the doctor–patient interaction in the psychotherapy became increasingly recognized as an important factor in how psychotherapy heals.

Now recovered memories are conceived to be the result of, not caused by, psychotherapy. They occur after the patient has mastered unbearable emotional conflicts in the transference, resulting in a more resilient ego that can deal with the memories, and so they appear. Thus, recovered memories

69

are more of a barometer of progress rather than a cause of progress in psychotherapy.

A variety of authors has examined the quality of the relationship between the therapist and patient, which is considered to be crucial in psychotherapeutic healing. For example, Fromm-Reichmann (1950) has pointed out that an empathic quality between the patient and therapist is at the crux of success. Therapy, she feels, should be offered in the spirit of collaborative guidance, aimed at the solution of the difficulties in living and the cure of symptoms: ". . . . the success or failure of psychoanalytic psychotherapy is, in addition, greatly dependent upon the question of whether or not there is actually an empathic quality between the psychiatrist and the patient."

The key work of the treatment is that "The dissociated and repressed material which reveals itself to patients under treatment in various connections—above all, in the realm of their relationship with the psychiatrist—must be tied together and worked through repeatedly, until awareness and understanding are finally transformed into constructive and curative insight into the basic patterns of a patient's interpersonal experiences." It is assumed that man's tendency is to move toward health, and if given a chance he will do so.

Frank (1961) has attempted to delineate the factors common to all sorts of healing situations. He emphasizes the importance of the presence of genuine care on the part of the healer, a deep commitment to bringing about the change that he feels desirable. A certain amount of power and authority that the healer inevitably has over the patient is necessary, as is also the function of the healer as a mediator between the patient and society. Thus the patient can test out with the healer patterns and changes he will use later on in society.

Strupp (1972, 1973) has carried the search for nonspecific factors in healing through psychotherapy to a more sophisticated—and controversial—level. He claims,

> A person's susceptibility to psychological influence is rooted in early experiences which are crucial in determining his responsiveness to psychotherapy in later life. Defense mechanisms regulate this susceptibility . . . a very significant amount of psychotherapeutic change occurring in all forms of psychotherapy is attributable to so-called nonspecific factors which derive their potency largely from their contact with loci of influenceability inherent in the "good" patient.

Any understanding, any new piece of awareness that has been gained by interpretative clarification, has to be reconquered and tested time and again in new contexts, which may or may not have to be subsequently approached in their own right. This is the process of repeatedly working through the dynamics and the ideational content for which awareness and understanding have been newly achieved. In the course of this working through, special interpretive attention is paid to the repetitive occurrence of patterns of feelings, thoughts, actions, and behavior that are dynamically conditioned by one and the same underlying aspect of the childhood nucleus.

We have here an explanation of why intensive psychotherapy *takes a long time.* The greatest impetus to divergence in the various schools of intensive psychotherapy has arisen simply out of frustration and impatience with the long period of time therapy takes. As I have already pointed out, there is an inherent rhythm in every human being, a tendency toward

71

health and maturity. That tendency cannot be rushed. The therapist must work slowly and patiently, working through over and over again the various insights. The patient's inherent rhythm gradually picks these up, and he matures at his own pace. There is no way to speed this up, and all varieties of symptom-removing techniques represent efforts to somehow get around this situation. In fact, one of the biggest problems that psychotherapists have is the sense of drain, frustration, and depression that develops over the long tedious years of working through emotional insights with their patients. This sometimes causes therapists, when they become middle-aged or older, to either look in different directions, seek short-cut cures, or to get out of the field of psychotherapy altogether.

Another aspect of the relationship between the patient and psychotherapist that has been recently recognized is the therapeutic alliance. This means that the therapist aims at forming a real and mature alliance with the conscious adult ego of the patient and encourages him to be a scientific partner in the exploration of his difficulties. This can be extended to overlap with the whole concept of after-education, essentially thought of as correcting the blunders of the parents (Freud, 1938), and can be described in a variety of ways —deconditioning, corrective, emotional experience, and so forth. For example, Strupp (1972, 1973) describes psychotherapy as essentially "a series of lessons in basic trust, concomitant with the undermining of those interpersonal strategies the patient has acquired for controlling himself and others."

The basic goal is to develop the patient's capacity for self-realization and his ability to form a durable, intimate relationship with others and, above all, to enable him to give and accept mature love. I define mature love as a relationship in which one is as concerned with the growth, maturation, welfare, and happiness of the beloved person as one is with one's own (to paraphrase Sullivan), and I will discuss this further in Chapter 13. By self-realization I mean a person's optimal use of his best talents, skills, and powers to his own satisfaction within the realm of his own previously established and realistic set of values. It involves the patient's ability to reach out and find fulfillment of his needs as far as they can be obtained without interfering with the law or the needs of his fellow men.

Another approach is to characterize unveiling, uncovering, or intensive psychotherapy as "evocative" (Whitehorn, 1955). In this view, psychotherapy operates by the perceptive understanding of the motivational needs behind the patient's speech and action and by evoking emotional experiences to be corrected of distorted meanings, rather than by disclosing a specific past event as "the cause" of the patient's illness.

The two approaches to therapy and its goals can be summarized in this way:

1. To learn about the noxious events or events that have happened to a person that caused a morbid emotional reaction, to discover the complex pattern that has maintained this morbid state, and to undo the cause by insight.

2. To learn about the patient's bad patterns of reaction and also about his assets and potentialities and to evoke the constructive use of these in the better handling of a crucially unresolved emotional problem or problems.

Thus we try to evoke the potential of the patient in curing his illness.

Part of this potential stems from the *emotional atmos-*

73

phere generated by a series of interpersonal events, noxious or beneficial. A child who is raised in a basically healthy emotional atmosphere can sustain a number of serious traumatic incidents without serious damage. A child who is raised in a noxious emotional atmosphere can sustain very little in the way of any kind of traumatic event and often tends to pin his difficulties on these individual traumatic events.

As Whitehorn sees it, we try to learn about the patient's patterns of reaction and about the patient's assets and potentialities and to evoke the constructive use of the patient's assets in the better handling of unresolved problems; so we evoke the potential of the patient in curing his illness. Our main allies (Alexander, 1956) are the biological striving of unconscious forces for expression and a natural integrating tendency of the ego; even if we do nothing else but avoid interfering with these two dynamic forces, we can help many patients.

In subsequent chapters more space will be devoted to various aspects of the process of intensive psychotherapy. There are, unfortunately, many unresolved problems, and it is almost impossible to present a completely consistent theory or even total description of psychotherapy. If given the opportunity to watch many patients treated by many different experienced therapists using different techniques, we would be struck by the extreme discrepancies between theory and practical application and also by a certain similarity in the percentage of therapeutic results. It may be that the different methods, regardless of their theoretical background, are equally effective and that the theoretical formulations are not as important as certain unclear common factors present in all such therapy. No one so far has been able to go into any satisfactory detail as to what these unclear common factors would be. It is equally possible that different patients respond differently to different approaches, that every method hits the jackpot in some instances and not in others. If this is the case, pure research could be aimed at trying to find out why one person responds to one approach and not to another. We have some information in that direction. Every conscientious psychotherapist knows that there are certain types of patients he simply cannot work with. As he gathers experience he rejects these patients at the initial interview and honestly advises them to seek a different therapist. There are obviously factors in the therapist that make it possible for him to click with some patients and to not click with others, and the more he knows about this, the better therapist he is going to be.

Another problem lies in differentiating between intellectual insight and emotional insight and how effective either is in curing the patient. A number of patients acquire insight into their psychodynamic mechanisms without being able to change. There is much need to understand better why this is so, what it really means to have emotional insight, and what causes people to be unable to apply such insight.

Often serious obstacles to psychotherapy exist within the patient, no matter how cooperative he may apparently be. The patient's need to suffer, or to frustrate the therapist, and form a negative therapeutic reaction are all serious problems. These factors may be operative in giving the patient greater gratification from not changing than from having a successful treatment.

We hope that it may eventually be possible to select patients in advance who will respond to psychotherapy. At present we have very few criteria to determine a patient's prognosis in response to psychotherapy. In the past this problem appeared to be deceptively simple, but it is not really so. For example, a paradox seems to exist in that some seriously schizophrenic patients may respond quite well to psychotherapy, but a number of severe neurotics, such as obsessive-compulsives, respond very poorly.

The most confusing and discouraging fact in the field lies in this unpredictability of results. Patients who according to the textbook should recover stubbornly refuse to improve. Others with an initially bad prognosis unexpectedly do recover. Perhaps the most humiliating of all is that sometimes the patient who has worked for years with an experienced psychotherapist and has been given up and sent to a public institution is treated by a beginning resident who approaches the patient with enthusiasm and messianic zeal—and the patient makes a dramatic recovery.

It thus becomes evident that there are still many areas that remain to be clarified, in this nascent discipline of psychotherapy. One of the finest recent papers on this subject is by Strupp (1969), who suggests that psychotherapy is actually a learning process of considerable complexity: "The therapist's operations are typically not very well articulated to the kinds of changes of learning hoped to be effected. Rather it seems that the therapist sets in motion a complex process whose consequences are predictable only in a very broad sense. The task of the future is to achieve greater specificity concerning the effects of particular kinds of interventions." Greater knowledge of the details of what goes on in the process of psychotherapy will hopefully lead to greater efficiency in psychotherapy. Strupp hopes for efficiency to be increased, even if it consists only of a better definition of the range of patients to whom psychotherapy is applicable. This is a somewhat pessimistic attitude. All difficulties considered, the process of psychotherapy can even now be reduced to a number of vital basic aspects, which though often described in varying terminology, share important common points. Thorough understanding of the transference mechanism and its management in psychotherapy, as well as of the various ancillary factors that are working at the same time, can produce fairly substantial information concerning the practices to be employed in psychological healing.

I hope to demonstrate that a meaningful body of information about psychotherapy can be communicated and generally agreed on by experienced therapists. One of the great problems in our field has been that various individuals try to emphasize one important factor in the psychotherapeutic process and to insist that everything in the process revolves around that one factor. This can never be the case when one is dealing with as complex a subject as individual man.

CHAPTER 4 *The Psychotherapist*
and the Therapeutic
Alliance

*K*ARL Jaspers (1969), the famous psychiatrist and philosopher, writes that ". . . the doctor himself has been called
the patient's fate in the sense of being partly brought upon
himself and partly met in the kind of doctor he will find."
The nature of the psychotherapist and the results of his conduct and personality on the patient demand attention. In his
Philosophy (1969), Jaspers gives a detailed analysis of the
doctor–patient relationship that should serve as required
reading for medical students, physicians, and psychotherapists. He emphasizes the importance of the attitude and
approach of the doctor to the patient: the influence of the
doctor's attitude on how the patient hears the doctor's communications, how the patient responds to these communications, and the subsequent effect of this response from the
patient on further communications from the doctor.

78

Jaspers (1970) stressed three vital aspects of personality that are required in a psychotherapist or in any human being who wishes to lead an authentic life. He calls these "poise," "humanitas," and "passion." *Poise* can be defined as maintaining a certain perspective on life: "It makes me keep my distance and distinguish things according to their essentiality." Poise allows us to tackle concrete tasks without fanaticism but with vigor, keeping calm if there is no success. A certain restraint the Greeks called *sophrosyné* or balance in life is involved here. *Humanitas* is open-mindedness. As Jasper's defines it, it entails, "putting myself into every other man's place, listening to reason, entering into the rationality of the case, and boundlessly expanding myself in ideas. It is resistance to sophisms, to the pressures of willful self interest, and to accidental sensitivities. It is candor, understanding, accessibility and possibility. . . . a disinclination to humiliate anyone, a courtesy in personal contact." *Passion*, the third aspect, consists of an untamed force that must be present as a driving energy to keep a person interested and emotionally invested in the world.

In *The Nature of Psychotherapy* (1964) Jaspers points out that the contemporary psychotherapist has to be a philosopher whether he wishes to or not, methodically or haphazardly. Jaspers writes, "It is not theory but his example which teaches us what manner of man he may be. The art of therapy, of relationship, gesture and attitude cannot be reduced to few simple rules. We can never anticipate how reason and compassion, presence of mind and frankness will show themselves in the given moment, nor what will be their effect." He speaks of the necessity of fundamental warmth and a natural kindness in the good psychotherapist.

A human being who is engaged in psychotherapeutic

79

activity day in and day out with a full patient load runs the risk of what could be called occupational hazards. Some of this has been hinted at by Rogow (1970), in a methodologically questionable book. Rogow sent out a series of questionnaires to practicing psychiatrists and psychoanalysts, and unfortunately only a relatively small percentage responded to these. There are, however, some interesting hints in the responses concerning the occupational hazards of doing intensive psychotherapy on a full-time basis. Some of the hazards suggested are the problem of sitting with somebody hour after hour, the passivity involved in listening and in having to postpone one's own needs until each hour is up, the problem of living by the clock and of getting patients scheduled for times in which they can realistically make their appointments, and the difficulty in pulling away from patients for vacations.

One experienced therapist points out, "Don't do full time psychoanalysis because when you get to be forty-five years old and are sitting there day in and day out listening to the patients you are going to be bored to death." I would quarrel with this, but there is no question that doing full-time, intensive psychotherapy does take its toll and has a tendency to drain the therapist in the long run. Thus, Rogow emphasizes the importance of developing hobbies, and his suggestions are echoed by many. Saul (1958), for example, stresses that exercise and large-muscle activity, as well as after-work "sociability" are essential to the mental and physical hygiene of the therapist.

A certain boredom and fatigue develops in the therapist that he carries over into family life. Rogow quotes one therapist as saying: "I have a lot of insights, but I am often too tired to apply them at home. Some days when I get home I don't want problems. I don't want to hear about low grades, menstrual cramps, lost dogs or whatever. I think insight makes me a better husband and father, but there are certain days. . . ." Here the quotation breaks off, implying that the work with the patients has a tendency to drain and exhaust the therapist, so that he cannot really apply his psychological understanding to his personal life.

There are a number of popularized and not very well substantiated reports of high suicide and divorce rates among psychiatrists and psychotherapists. It is not really possible at this time to argue whether or not the tensions, insecurities, and frustrations of psychiatric or psychotherapeutic work are responsible for this, or whether these statistics are even meaningful. It is important to realize, however, that the therapist must have continuing sources of satisfaction for himself. This is far more difficult to arrange than appears on the surface. Perhaps the primary reason for this lies in problem of human greed, which I have discussed in fuller detail elsewhere (Chessick, 1969).

The financial complications and hazards of private practice are emphasized by Saul (1958) as well. He calls private practice "the dance of the hours." Since the therapist is paid by the hour, the more hours he works, the more money he makes. Usually in middle life with wife and children, possibly in debt procured in the long training period, the therapist often feels financially insecure. He is not sure whether, when a patient finishes treatment, that available open hour will promptly be filled by another patient. He tends to try to work all the hours he can and risks slipping into equating hours and income. This equation is, of course, true, but, if not properly balanced and separated, the result can be entrapment and slavery. The therapist may feel, for example, that he can't take time for lunch, because, although the lunch may be cheap, the lost fee has to be added to its cost. Similarly, he can't take a day off, since the higher his fees the more he would be missing.

The point is, as Saul explains it, "Time off is no longer a legitimate, wholesome respite from work, the satisfaction of his proper receptive needs; it has become a frustration of his receptive needs because he is not receiving in the form of money, when he is not working." This is a dangerous twist. The therapist is driven like everyone else by the pressures of a money-based civilization in which money is thought of as a means to security, pleasure, prestige, romance—everything.

This leads us to the central issue of the maturity of the psychotherapist. One of the best tests of maturity is the therapist's capacity to be inwardly directed, that is, to resist the lure of practicing the maximum number of hours so as to make the maximum amount of money. Both the therapist and his wife have to recognize that they will never make the income of the financially successful physician in other specialities. On the other hand, as Saul (1958) points out, the therapist can devote himself to his patients, to his academic work, and to important matters in his community, and he will find that "without giving money much direct thought, he can soon have an adequate livelihood" if he is at all well trained. A little calculation reveals what the therapist can earn by working a reasonable number of hours per day "allowing for breaks for meetings, illnesses and vacations." Saul makes the significant statement: "He then can set his income and have a good life if he and his wife are not greedy." Even young men who work conscientiously with their patients report to Saul that

82

they cannot see more than six or seven patients a day without becoming fatigued.

It is much more difficult to resist these temptations than one might believe at first, especially as the pressures of middle age begin to impinge on a person. The mind is a reflection of the biological condition of the body, and the body is subjected to more strain in a day of psychotherapeutic work than the beginner may realize. Sitting all day is a strain that can injure not in days or in months but in years, unless it is balanced with adequate exercise. Saul writes: "After a million years of living by the hunt, the battle, and the soil, the human machine cannot readily substitute the analytic chair without affecting the heart, the blood vessels, the muscles, the spine, the digestion, and other organ systems."

This is no incidental matter, because if the therapist is not both mentally and physically healthy, his achievement will be problematic: *Mens sana in corpore sano.* The essence of therapy is that it represents a sample human relationship between a doctor and a patient. It is a human relationship for the doctor, too. If he has bad interpersonal relationships in life with family, friends, colleagues, and others it is doubtful whether he can be very satisfactory in the office with patients. Most of the time poor human relations in life extend to poor underlying relationships in the office. This certainly may disturb both the therapist's understanding and the therapy itself. It may influence and badly alter transference and pose countertransference problems. Conversely, Saul writes:

> If the analyst is, although no paragon, reasonably healthy and mature and has solved his major life problems reasonably well and has generally good personal relations, then he has the emotional base upon which to build his professional knowledge, skills and experience. And he has a confidence and

83

security that are genuine and give him the inner strength for an easy, natural, genuinely kind, sympathetic, personality— a respecting, human, mature attitude toward those who come to him for help with their confusions, inferiorities, insecurities and tensions.

This is a telling description of the basic problem of what the psychotherapist has to conquer in himself before he is really ready to deal with his patients.

Kubie (1971) presents more formally the requirements for maturity in the psychotherapist:

Maturity as a psychiatrist is a result of the meeting of three rivers. The individual has first to work his way out of many of the conflicts which he buried in early life and which tie him to his own childhood. In one way or another (and again I am not prescribing any one-and-only way) an evolving series of therapeutic experiences must occur if a man is to escape bondage to his own past in order to win his freedom to grow toward maturity as a human being. Secondly, maturity requires that he must have accepted such adult responsibilities as marriage and parenthood. It is in coping with these that he will encounter and master the problems which confront every adult as he emerges from youth. Emotional maturity of this kind is a necessary prerequisite for dealing with the problems of others from a mature basis.

Only after this can he begin to reach out for clinical maturity as a psychiatrist. Not reading, not diligent study, not psychological aptitude can supplant the experience of sustained relationships with patients as they fall ill and fall well again. Nothing can take the place of being a participant— observer of these fluctuating changes over weeks, months, and even years.

Fromm-Reichmann (1950) has also taken up the issue of the psychiatrist's part in the doctor–patient relationship. The

84

psychotherapist must be able to listen. This is a much more startling statement than it sounds like at first. "To be able to listen and to gather information from another person in this other person's own right, without reacting along the lines of one's own problems and experiences, of which one may be reminded, perhaps in a disturbing way, is an art of inter-personal exchange," writes Fromm-Reichmann," which few people are able to practice without special training."

If the therapist is to avoid reacting to the patient's data in terms of his own life experiences, this means that he must have enough sources of satisfaction and security in his non-professional life to forego the temptation of using his patients for the pursuit of his personal satisfaction or security. If he has not been successful in securing personal fulfillments in life, he must realize this: and his attitude toward the sources of dissatisfaction and unhappiness in his life must then be clarified and integrated to the extent that they don't inter-fere with his emotional stability and with his ability to con-centrate on listening to the patient.

A great deal could be said about this rarely discussed problem. The healthier patients are able to withstand the impact of a psychotherapist who may be using them to some extent for gratification in his own personal life. However, the usual result of therapy in these circumstances is stalemate. Not much happens, and after a certain period of time the pa-tient leaves treatment. But when one begins to work with borderline patients, character disorders of a severe nature, and certainly with schizophrenics, the problem becomes more serious and more dangerous. If a psychotherapist begins to use such patients—whether by overtly acting out with the patient or by covert methods such as indulging in autistic fantasies while the patient is talking—the latter will be placed in a

85

double-bind situation reminiscent of the early family situation. The parent, like the therapist, said one thing but his overt or covert behavior and the psychic atmosphere were sending out different messages.

Patients in the hands of such therapists will then use characteristic methods to deal with the situation: an increase of schizophrenic symptomatology, uncontrollable affect such as rages or sexual passions—which can be then either acted out with the therapist or acted out with some third party outside the therapy—addictions and alcoholism, binges and orgies, and even suicide. The fundamental responsibility of anyone who works in intensive psychotherapy with patients must be to deal first with his own needs and achieve a certain level of self-understanding. This cannot be brought about without an intensive psychotherapy of the psychotherapist. It is absolutely impossible to argue that anyone can practice long-term, intensive psychotherapy without first having undergone a long-term, intensive psychotherapy of his own. *An individual who for various reasons of his own refuses to undergo a personal, long-term, intensive psychotherapy should not attempt to practice this discipline. He is endangering himself and his patients.*

It should be noted that I have not insisted that the therapist undertake formal psychoanalysis or a training analysis. Naturally, it is ideal for the future psychotherapist to have as thorough and detailed a treatment of his own as possible. However, economic and social considerations make it impossible to demand a thorough and formal training analysis from every future psychotherapist. This leaves, on the other hand, a grave question as to what sort of psychotherapy is minimally acceptable. There is little agreement on this subject and eventually it will be necessary to set up conditions that describe what exactly constitutes satisfactory, intensive psychotherapy for a psychotherapist. Certainly, it must be required that some major transference manifestations have appeared in the future therapist's own therapy and that these have been worked through. Otherwise, the therapy will have been nothing more than a simple, superficial ventilation or adaptational therapy, in which the person has only been taught to be smoother, cleverer, and more capable of coping with his current situation than he initially was. Above all some demonstrable modification of the infantile core of the future therapist must take place for, as Saul (1958) writes, "The child lives on in the analyst as in everyone else; only one expects the child to be a little less fractious, unruly and disruptive in those whose profession it is to help others in life's journey."

Besides giving the student in psychotherapy a sense of personal conviction about the efficacy of psychotherapy and the influence of the childhood nucleus on the adult personality, one of the central aspects of his therapy is that it should help the student focus on his own motivations for entering the field. Undoubtedly, a certain percentage of candidates will be weeded out by virtue of their own psychotherapy, not, hopefully, because they have been told that they are "no good," but because they have carefully examined their position. Some will discover in the course of therapy that their motivations for entering the field were primarily neurotic and that actually psychotherapy is not what they want to do at all. Unfortunately, there are a certain percentage of untrained psychotherapists floating around whose major motivation in doing treatment is to find help for themselves. When these therapists get involved with patients they put a totally unreasonable burden on the patient and pose a great danger.

87

People who are seeking to become psychotherapists for such primary motivations can hopefully be made, through their own personal therapy, to see that the solution to their problems cannot come by acting out with patients.

I cannot emphasize enough how important it is for both the integrity and health of the psychotherapist, the protection of the patient, and a vital matter for whoever is training psychotherapists to see to it that no one is allowed to be given any kind of certificate that qualifies him to call himself a psychotherapist without having first undergone a thorough and successful personal psychotherapy.

The requirements a psychotherapist must meet in order to be able to deal with patients in an appropriate fashion are as follows:

1. He must have an awareness of his own interpersonal processes and behavior patterns through his personal psychotherapy.

2. He must have the ability to listen, and there must be sufficient satisfaction and security in his personal life so as not to impair this ability.

3. He must not use the narrative of the patient as a jumping-off place for his own daydreams. This requires a gratifying personal life.

4. He must have sufficient rest so he does not sit in the therapy and sleep with his eyes open.

5. There must be adequate financial remuneration, so that he feels his time has been well spent.

6. There must be a feeling of optimism about the outcome of therapy before assuming responsibility for the patient. This also reflects some confidence in his ability to deal with the patient.

7. He must have the ability to withstand the frustration and the prolonged time involved in the ups and downs of a long-term, intensive psychotherapy.

8. He must have the ability to tolerate hostility. This is probably the most difficult thing to adjust to—the day-in-day-out hostility toward himself that the psychotherapist will necessarily encounter in his private practice.

9. He must have the ability to shift between active and passive roles in psychotherapy. He must know when to sit back and listen and when to be active or interpretative. He must even be able to interfere directly with the patient's life, should that life itself be threatened (Voth, 1972).

10. He must have the capacity to identify with the patient, to put himself in the patient's shoes—the capacity for empathy. This is not sympathy. Neither is it experiencing the patient in an inferior position (see Chessick, 1969).

11. Finally, the therapist should be able to accomplish what is known as regression in the service of the ego; his ego should be able to shift back and forth from reality testing to the regressive level of the world of dreams in the service of better understanding and better empathy, as he listens to the patient.

The very office of the psychotherapist is an extension of his personality. This subject is important but infrequently discussed. There are certain obvious fundamentals that one would expect from the office of a psychotherapist, which in actual experience are not always present. For example, a patient sitting in the waiting room should not be able to hear what is going on in the consulting room. This may require an expensive soundproofing job. The best form of soundproofing, however, is not soundproof doors but some kind of a hallway between the waiting room and the therapist's office. If this can be arranged, it is of great benefit and it makes costly soundproofing unnecessary. It is further useful, especially in certain emergency situations, to have easy access to toilet facilities, washbowl, and a mirror. An office with such facilities is not difficult to obtain, given a little forethought on the therapist's part.

Some therapists like a fancy office with a secretary in the waiting room. However, patients generally prefer to sit by themselves in the waiting room and not be stared at by a secretary or receptionist. Therefore, if the therapist wishes to have a secretary, she should be appropriately placed out of the vision of the waiting patients, perhaps behind a glass sliding partition so that patients have at least a certain sense of privacy as they wait for the therapist. A receptionist who loves to chatter and gossip with patients can have a devastating effect!

The very position of the chair, couch, and desk in the office reflect the personality of the therapist. During my experience in training residents I have often visited their offices, and I have made it a point to revisit them after training is finished. I have been astounded at some of the arrangements they have developed. Some had large offices with a chair at each end so that the patient inevitably had a sense of having to shout across a wide chasm to reach the therapist. Others would have a desk—large and imposing—placed between the patient's chair and the therapist's chair. This carries a tremendous message with it and starts the whole therapy off on the wrong foot.

There are many other strange arrangements therapists manage to create, that reflect their regard for their patients.

Temperature is important, since a freezing office or a hot, stuffy office has a definite effect on the patient. The lighting in the office is also significant. A strong overhead ceiling light —surprisingly common—can give the impression of a "third-degree" room in a police station. Extremely dim light can be most upsetting to patients who are dealing with sexual, and especially homosexual, problems. The therapist must have a series of lights in his office so that he can keep control of the general amount of light regardless of the time of day or weather conditions outside.

The general decor of the office tells a great deal about the therapist. Offices furnished with file cabinets in a very businesslike manner communicate one kind of message. Offices with big overstuffed chairs, in which the female patient spends most of her time worrying about whether the therapist can see up her dress, relay a different kind of message. Everything should be arranged for the convenience of both the therapist and the patient. The underlying principle is to provide the same consideration for the patient as one would for a guest in one's own home. A telephone with a loud jangling bell that rings six or seven times in a forty-five-minute period can be terribly disconcerting, even if the therapist doesn't answer the phone. Loud buzzers or flashing lights that go on when the next patient comes in or when the secretary wants to give a message can be very destructive. If the patient has a signaling system that he uses when he comes into the waiting room, such as pushing a button or flipping a switch, it should not make a noticeable disturbance in the therapist's office, if a patient is in there. There is nothing more disconcerting to a patient in the middle of an emotional outburst or important thought near the end of an hour than

91

suddenly to have a red light go on in front of his face or a loud buzzer go off in his ear.

This is also true of all kinds of clock arrangements therapists use. The atmosphere of the therapist's office must not be that of a train station or an airport. Buzzers, clocks, and various signaling devices indicating the end of a forty-five-minute period give a loud and clear message of just how interested the therapist really is in the patient's problems.

The converse of this is also true, however, since permanence and consistency with regard to time are *very* important. A patient should not have an hour scheduled at a certain time and then have to wait an hour for the therapist. This should happen only in unusual emergencies and should be discussed immediately in that therapy hour. The patient deserves a certain promptness on the part of the therapist and must also consequently expect that his hour will end with a certain promptness. Consistently starting late with a patient and consistently running late with a patient are evidences of countertransference. They are not demonstrations of affection for the patient or proof of being an extra-good therapist; patients soon catch on to this. The therapist's office should have a clock in it that is clearly visible from all chairs and couches, so that the patient doesn't have to keep stealing glances at his wristwatch and the therapist isn't burdened with that either. A therapist, sincerely concerned with his patient's welfare, will carefully consider the total arrangement of his office.

The humaneness of the psychotherapist is expressed in his compassion, concern, and therapeutic intent toward his patient. He is a treater of the sick and suffering, and his aim is to help the patient to get well. The humaneness is expressed in an attitude that clearly shows that the patient has rights and is respected as an individual. He is to be treated with ordinary courtesy. Rudeness has no place in psychotherapy. If we want the patient to work with us as a co-worker on the material he produces, we must take care that the mature aspects of the patient are consistently nurtured in the course of our work. Imagine a therapist who does not greet his patients in the waiting room with a "hello," but simply opens the door with a stony face and lets the patient walk in, sit or lie down, and begin working. Many other examples of this kind of behavior, sometimes of an even grosser type exist and should, of course, be avoided.

Stone (1961) is convinced that the nuances of the therapist's attitude can determine the difference between a lonely vacuum and a controlled, but warm and human, situation. He talks about the "physicianly vocation"—a kindly and helpful, broadly tolerant and friendly interest in one's patients. This is an example of maturity on the part of the therapist, of the sense of identity, of a life-long vocation, of a commitment and a real relationship to another individual. It is not role playing. If there are excessively severe deficits in human response on the part of the therapist, responses that the patient may reasonably expect or require, there are going to be very serious transference distortions and the therapy will flounder. Greenson (1968) echoes this thought, when he writes: "The patient will be influenced not only by the content of our work but by how we work."

The attitude, manner, mood, and atmosphere in which we work greatly affects the patient whether we like it or not. He may react to and identify with precisely those aspects of us that are not necessarily conscious to us. For example, if a

93

patient's child is seriously ill and she comes in crying and worrying about it, and the therapist insists on continuing without discussing the matter at all and shows no concern, this will have a profound effect because it represents a lack of normal human response. It will insure a deleterious and destructive reaction sooner or later in the therapy situation.

A very important part of therapy consists of establishing the initial "contract" with the patient. The subject of payment and missed hours is often a good demonstration of how the therapist and patient are going to relate to each other throughout the entire treatment. The therapist has to decide what he will do about hours that are missed and what his fee is going to be. (This is discussed further in the next chapter.) The particular decision he makes will be a function of his own personality and his own needs, as well as his assessment of what the patient can afford and what is best for the patient. Discussion of this must take place at the beginning of the therapy. If it doesn't, the following kind of situation can easily occur. The patient begins treatment, comes for two or three months, then one day calls up that he is sick and has to miss the hour. At the end of that particular month the patient gets a bill in which there is a charge for the missed hour. At this point the patient comes in and says: "Oh doctor, I think you made an error on my bill, you charged me for one extra hour." Thus begins a vitriolic and unpleasant confrontation between the patient and the therapist, in which the therapist insists that he must be paid for his time, and the patient feels cheated and taken advantage of because no explanation was ever made as to what the arrangement would be for missed hours. In that kind of a mood and atmosphere no kind of alliance can develop between the patient and therapist.

A working alliance is mandatory for any therapy to be successful. The concept of a working alliance or a therapeutic alliance was introduced by Zetzel (1956) and brought to the general attention of the psychiatric community by Greenson (1965). Very often the key to understanding therapeutic stalemate is found in the failure of the patient to develop a reliable working relationship with the psychotherapist. This working relationship depends both on the patient and the therapist. No matter what the patient is like, if the therapist does not meet the requirements we have discussed, a good sound working alliance cannot develop. In that case the therapy is doomed from the very beginning.

The patient must, of course, also make a contribution. He must have the capacity to form a working alliance. Some patients simply cannot do it, and such patients will not respond to psychotherapy. The best definition of a working alliance is that it is an alliance between the patient's reasonable, or conscious or mature, ego and the therapist's working, or therapeutic or analytic, ego. What makes this possible, claims Greenson, is the patient's partial identification with the therapist's approach as he attempts to understand the patient's behavior. In simpler terminology, if the therapist is genuinely interested in the patient and genuinely concerned with understanding the patient—rather than with using the patient to relieve some of his own ungratified needs—and if the patient has the ego capacity to develop a working alliance, then the patient will develop and exercise one of the unique functions of a human being—the capacity to stand off and observe one's self. Psychologically speaking, the patient will come over and sit in the therapist's chair and identify with the therapist's approach of nonanxious investigation. Hopefully, the patient will even identify with the therapist's tolerance towards himself. If this can be accomplished, the emergence of material otherwise threatening and guilt-producing will be feasible.

It is possible to train the patient's ego in the therapy situation to the point where the working alliance can be formed, maintained, and improved. This is done by consistently focusing on the alliance in such a way as to reinforce those ego functions in the patient that contribute to the alliance and by attempting to stimulate the necessary ego functions that are inadequate. A mutual concern with the working alliance tends to enhance it.

Parallel to the old rule that one must interpret resistance before content, one must also form a good working alliance with the patient before *any* interpretations will have the desired therapeutic impact. Any number of examples could be given of psychotherapies that have failed because of insufficient attention to the working alliance. This represents one of the most common beginner's mistakes.

Patients give all kinds of signals that the experienced therapist can pick up which indicate that the working alliance has not been properly formed. A good example comes from the kinds of questions patients ask. If a patient must repeatedly ask a question—for example, is he allowed to smoke, or is he allowed to read something he wrote down, or do you want to hear about a certain subject—one can be sure that there is something wrong with the working alliance. Similarly, if a patient comes late consistently, this must be understood as resistance, and it could be a sign again that the working alliance has not been properly formed.

One of the typical examples of a failure in the working

96

alliance is when the patient insists on seeing the psychotherapy as a seminar or classroom situation. He listens to the interpretations of the therapist and tries to fit them into what he is doing in a very intellectual way and then turns to the therapist for what could be called a "grade" or approval. As this example demonstrates, sometimes it is very difficult to separate the conditions of the working alliance from the conditions of the transference. There is probably a borderline area in which these two overlap.

The attitude of the patient toward the therapist in terms of how he perceives the treatment itself is often a good reflection of the condition of the working alliance at any given time. The best way to test this out is simply to ask the patient how he thinks the therapy is going. It is also useful at the beginning of psychotherapy to ask the patient what he knows or what he has read about psychotherapy. The ideas of how a patient and therapist work together brought in by patients from what they have read or seen on television or in the movies can be absolutely fantastic. The therapist has to be prepared to find out about these things and, if necessary, to correct them.

Not all bizarre attitudes that patients have about psychotherapy are manifestations of transference. They can be a function of what the patient has come to expect from experiences with other therapists. One patient of mine had previously been in "psychotherapy" with a neurologist. This neurologist had an hourglass that he would turn over at the beginning of each session, and as soon as the sand had run out of the glass he would terminate the treatment session. However, during the sessions the neurologist answered a number of telephone calls. Thus, because there was no opportunity to

97

increase the length of the sessions and to make up for time lost due to the telephone call interruptions, the patient was made to sacrifice his time to the hourglass. It is not difficult to see what kind of subliminal irritation such conduct could provoke in the working alliance. With such examples the poignant truth of Jaspers' maxim, "The therapist is the patient's fate," becomes all too clear.

CHAPTER 5 *Beginning the Treatment*

*M*ANY of the details concerned with the subject of beginning treatment are overlooked. Some of these details may seem self-evident when actually pinpointed, yet in my supervisory experience it became clear how often they were neglected, much to the detriment of subsequent therapy. When the details of the initial interviews and the therapeutic contract are poorly handled, it has a very destructive effect on the atmosphere of the psychotherapy, and it makes the formation of a therapeutic alliance almost impossible. Therefore, attention to these apparently banal details is extremely important.

It is poor technique to cover the entire work of beginning the treatment in one interview. This is because of the tremendous anxiety that most patients bring to their first experience of psychotherapy. It is most useful to have at least two and sometimes three to five intitial interviews with the patient before any decisions are made regarding treatability, goals of treatment, and so on. Furthermore, these interviews should be spaced apart in time. The use of a double slot of time for the initial interview—that is, two hours where there would generally be one—is, I believe, an inferior method. It is best, except in emergency or obviously acute situations, to give the patient a one-hour interview and then, if possible, within several days—sometimes even a week—give the patient a second interview. It should be explained to the patient at the end of the first interview that all questions and issues that he has in mind regarding his treatment and so forth will be answered, but that another interview or two is needed before any rational discussion can take place. Patients usually accept this very well.

The great advantage of this approach is that patients almost invariably show their worst side in the opening interview. The anxiety is often so tremendous that the patient may appear far sicker and far more incapacitated than he actually is. There are so many social pressures on people regarding the subject of psychiatrists and psychotherapy, that they have often built up all kinds of imaginative terror before they walk into the therapist's office. Sometimes just being in the office for an hour has a tremendously relaxing effect, as they recognize that the therapist is not a devil, a trickster, a charlatan, or a "creep," and they develop some feeling for him as a reasonable human being.

Psychotherapy begins at the very first contact with the patient. This usually takes the form of a telephone call in which the patient asks for an appointment. Most therapists

100

take such phone calls themselves, although some have a secretary or nurse who schedules the patient. If possible it is best to respond to phone calls oneself, because the encounter between the therapist and the patient will occur from the very first moment of that telephone call. In fact, some patients are actually rejected on the basis of the opening request for psychotherapy over the telephone and others reject the therapist at this point.

Sullivan (1954) paid special attention to the very first few moments of the initial interview. He calls this phase the formal inception and notes some of its central aspects. It is important that the therapist does not greet his patient with what Sullivan calls "a lot of social hocum that might be all right in meeting aged maternal relatives." "I think that the social manners of some doctors have antagonized a larger portion of their really life-size patients than have their failures and skills and their obvious stupidities of judgment." Sullivan points out the foolishness of such astonished greetings as "Oh, hello, come in!" which might be all right with a person recently returned from London but not very useful in the opening of the first psychiatric interview. Sullivan states that, although he doesn't show a great welcome to the patient, he does try to act as if the patient were respected. He tries to know the patient's name before the first interview, and greets him with it, thereby relieving the patient of any morbid anxiety as to whether he came on the wrong day and so on. He asks the patient to come in, a form of ordinary hospitality.

At this point it might be worth repeating again that the general behavior of the psychotherapist should be somewhat parallel to the consideration that he would show a guest in his home or anywhere else. So for example, Sullivan points out

101

THE TECHNIQUE AND PRACTICE OF INTENSIVE PSYCHOTHERAPY

that he takes a good look at the patient when the patient is first met at the door, but he does not then sit down and stare at the patient. Once the patient enters the office, it is indicated to him where he should sit. Sullivan brings up an experience (which I have also had) where a "great man" invited him to confer about a paper, asked him in, and then sat down and stared at Sullivan for a long time without asking him to be seated. Sullivan, in his inimitable way, writes: "I decided that that was a poor way to treat a stranger."

Seating accomplished, Sullivan then tells the patient what he knows so far as to why he is there. If the patient has telephoned to make an appointment, a slight summary of the telephone conversation is presented in a very straightforward fashion. If the referral is made from another physician and some information has been given, this is usually reported. It is most important to do this because sometimes there is a great discrepancy between why the therapist thinks the patient has come and why the patient himself thinks he has come. For example, a patient may come with the idea of helping a spouse or a child, whereas the therapist may have the idea that the patient has required or requested or been referred for treatment, himself. Confusions like this should be quickly cleared up at the beginning of the psychiatric interview, or the rest of the interview will never get off the ground.

The therapist then asks the patient in some fashion why he is there and what he hopes can be done for him and the interview has begun. There is a general purpose to these initial interviews. It is hoped that the climate for the entire therapy process is established. Diagnosis is reached if possible; some appraisal and formulation is thought of, and a disposition is planned. It is of fundamental value to try to assess as soon as possible some of the crucial dynamic problems of the patient, as well as the repetitive patterns in his life. One looks for immediate precipitating situations in the patient's illness and also for slightly more hidden situations.

The therapist tries to establish who are the significant others, as Sullivan calls them, in the patient's life. One can often guess at the future transference manifestations in the first interview and how the patient will view the therapist as the transference develops. The first interviews can also present a total picture of the situation, which grows dimmer as the therapy proceeds and the therapist gets wrapped up in the small specific areas gradually brought up by the patient. In addition to this, the first interviews may work to orient the patient to the process of psychotherapy, which consist of mutual investigation rather than a friendly chitchat, a laying on of hands, or a giving of pills. The therapist tries to become aware of what is going on between himself and the patient as quickly as possible and to assess the motivation of the patient for therapy. As Menninger once put it: "Is the patient going to undergo treatment, undertake treatment, or undercut treatment?"

The initial interviews include making sure that you know such things as the patient's name, marital status, religion, address, home and business addresses and phone numbers, place of employment, the full name of the patient's wife, her religion, some information about the names and ages of the patient's family—sisters, brothers, parents—the place of work of the wife or husband, the names and ages of the children, their health and place of residence, who referred the patient, how the patient got to you, the status of the

103

patient's physical health, and drugs or medications that the patient may be taking.

The interviews usually begin with a discussion of the present illness. In most cases this is essentially a chronology of the appearance of symptoms because of which the patient has come. In general, it is best to let the patient tell his own story, except with very loquacious or circumlocutious patients. A little gentle encouragement will help the patient to tell in his own words and in his own way what has happened. It is important to begin with this question, rather than gathering data about family history or personal history, or the whole interview will make no sense to the patient. We then move on to getting the traditional family history. We want to know all about the parents and relatives, their ages, occupations, birthplace, personalities, medical, and psychiatric history. We want to know what the present family consists of and whether there were any other important relations living in the home at the time of the patient's childhood or at present.

We then gather a traditional personal history. We begin with the circumstance of the patient's birth and the pregnancy of the mother, asking whether there were any medical or social complications or emotional troubles at the time of pregnancy and birth. We want to know about the breast and bottle feeding and weaning problems, toilet training, when the patient walked, talked, and whether there were any problems that existed at these times. We ask carefully about any childhood neurotic problems such as sleep disturbances, nightmares, feeding problems, and so forth. We ask about the sleeping arrangements, whether the patient was brought up in a large home or tiny apartment, whether the crib was in the parent's bedroom, or whether the patient always had his own room.

In asking questions about sexual history, considerable discretion should be used. There is no hurry about gathering details about sexual history, and it makes no sense to a patient five minutes after you have met them, to ask what their masturbation fantasies are. Information of this nature can be gathered gradually in the initial interviews, and, if it seems to be an area of great anxiety, it can be postponed for a much later time.

It is very important to keep in mind the anxiety level of the patient in these initial interviews. If it is too great, questions should be kept on a factual level and focused on the areas where the patient can respond most easily. We must inquire about school history: the patient's attainments in school, how he socialized, at what age he went through school. A work history is extremely important. We must know what the career has been, how the patient has functioned on jobs, how long he has held jobs, and so forth.

A marital history is vital. We wish to know the age at which he married, the ages of the spouse or spouses, the length of the courtship, sexual adjustment (a question that sometimes must be postponed), experiences with contraception, and the attitude of the parents toward the marriage (which is important).

In addition, I always ask patients to tell me a dream or two and to recall for me the earliest memories of childhood that they can. I find the use of a dream told at the beginning of treatment along with the earliest memories of vital importance in making a psychodynamic formulation. The earliest memories either symbolize crucial past relationships or rep-

105

resent conflicts. The patient tends to insert things that did not happen until later and sometimes to insert fantasies. One does not get an accurate reproduction of an early memory but a conglomoration of early events, distortions, and sometimes untruths. These pseudomemories or fantasy memories can even have an active influence on the patient's adult behavior. Patients can be quite convinced that they remember certain traumatic things that happened to them when they were very little and can use these memories as reasons as to why they behave in a certain way.

While one is gathering this information formally, keep an eye out for the behavior of the patient. This is very important. Listen and pay attention to the way the information is given. Does the patient show despair or apathy? Does he speak diffidently? Does he display discomfort? Fear? Anxiety? Unhappiness? Grief? And so on? Pay attention to the way the patient behaves—the way he sits, whether he seems anxious, awkward, self-conscious, tearful, shaky—and his orientation, e.g., whether he seems dazed, confused, or responding to hallucinations. Even his gait, posture, general appearance, facial expression, type of clothes and grooming, and inadvertant motions are important. It is worth noting, too, whether the patient has arrived alone or accompanied and, if the latter, the behavior of the accompanying person.

This information, of course, is put together in a traditional mental-status evaluation, which can be found in any psychiatry textbook. We try to assess general appearance, manner, attitude, content of thought, memory, fund of information, intelligence, judgment, and insight, and it is best to try to do these things indirectly, rather than administering a series of formal tests, which often seem irrevelant to the patient and can be quite frightening if he cannot answer the questions. Usually it is possible to do this without administering any formal test. However, if there is any doubt, formal tests *must* be administered at the beginning of treatment. The therapist must be certain of the accuracy of the mental status.

The therapist should be alert to the couch diver. Occasionally one meets a patient in the initial interviews who walks into the office on request and immediately lies down on the couch before it can even be indicated where he should sit. Such patients are usually severely disturbed, unless they have previously been in formal psychoanalysis with an analyst who refused to take history. (Occasionally one finds a psychoanalyst who is against the whole idea of taking history and has the patient lie down on the couch and free-associate from the initial moment of the therapy.) As far as the practice of intensive psychotherapy is concerned, in my opinion, it is mandatory for the therapist to take a careful history in the first few interviews and not allow simply a rambling free association from the very beginning.

We attempt in the first interviews to make a diagnostic formulation. This should include understanding the nature of the current problem, *evaluation of the physical status by referral to appropriate physicians,* identifying the precipitating stresses, the patient's methods of solution or failure, the patient's predisposition for conflicts, and some of the past determinants in his life. We are interested in the nature of his personality, his methods of adjusting to reality, the kind of relationships he establishes, and his ways of handling basic feelings and drives such as anxiety, love, and aggression. We assess the balance of progressive and regressive trends in his personality, the degree of maturity, and capacity to tolerate frustration.

It is important to try to discover just what the patient

107

is reacting to. Are there external stresses? Is something of importance happening to the person or his loved ones? Has a change occurred in a significant relationship, and is this an extreme change, such as a loss through death or the birth of a sibling, or is it a slight change? Especially, has there been a wound to narcissism through a withdrawal of interest or lack of appreciation? Are there somatic diseases or injuries or a surgical operation past or pending? Is this an adjustment problem at a decisive area of life, such as going to school, adolescence, graduation, or birth of children, climacteric, aging, and various things involved in external stress. There are also clear internal stresses, such as increase in the feelings of guilt irrespective of their source, anniversary reactions, the attainment of a specific age, and other factors that can be pinned down as important to the patient's current complaints. Try to ascertain why the patient comes to see a therapist at this specific time.

It is necessary in the interviews to offer the patient some time for asking questions. At the end of the series of interviews the patient usually will have some questions, and these should be frankly answered, if at all possible. I also like to give the patient a few minutes late in the initial interviews during which I ask him to talk about anything that comes to him. This gives me some idea of how the patient will do with free association. If my request is followed by five or ten minutes of silence, then I know that the patient will have great difficulties with free association. Sometimes it is wise to try a minor trial interpretation to see how the patient reacts to it or to see if he can grasp it and deal with it. These are important ways of determining the patient's capacity to tolerate treatment.

Some assessment must also be made of the goals of treatment. A deliberate discussion of these is made with the patient. There may be a sharply circumscribed goal, attempts at superficial changes, or a setting up of more long-term goals.

The initial interviews must determine whether the patient is one the therapist can work with to any effect. This depends, as Saul (1958) indicates, on "the current balance of forces in the person, including his ego strengths and weaknesses and on how deep-seated these are, how ingrained, how early, and how thoroughly the injurious influences conditioned the growing infant and child." It does not make sense to sink limitless hours into working with patients who have little capacity and potential for therapy, when the same time could be spent working with patients who have a genuine capacity to tolerate psychotherapy and make gains in treatment. It is thus a primary responsibility of the therapist to determine in the initial interviews whether the patient's ego strength and his reality situation really make psychotherapy possible. It is pointless to begin with patients who cannot tolerate intensive psychotherapy either from a realistic, financial, or psychological point of view. Other arrangements must be made for such patients.

Thus, it is important in the initial interviews for the therapist to assess the ego strength of the patient. The concept of ego strength is not an easy one to discuss from a theoretical point of view. There are many objections to use of the term on a formal basis. However, for the purpose of clinical practice, there are certain indicators of ego strength that must be noted before a decision can be made about the psychotherapy of the patient. For example, the more that an individual has a general life pattern of persistent effort in a goal-directed

109

fashion, and of success in the various ventures that he has undertaken, the more likely it is that he will be able to sustain the course of treatment and ultimately achieve some measure of success. At the other end of the spectrum there are individuals whose life pattern has been one of repeated failures, ineffectual adaptation, or major disturbance and disruption even with hospitalization. Such patients, it is obvious, would have a poor prognosis for psychotherapy, although one cannot make any absolute predictions.

DeWald (1964) gives some specific indicators of ego strength that are clinically useful. The nature of the patient's object relationships is one of these. Since the therapist is going to be a significant object in the patient's life, it is important to assess what kind of relationships the patient has had with other people. DeWald points out that even if there has been a long-term but intensely hostile relationship with another person, this is more hopeful than when a patient has had no object relationships with anybody. There are many of the latter kind of people who come seeking treatment, and the prognosis for them is unfortunately, not good.

A second factor is the assessment of motivation. As DeWald points out, this is a function not only of what the patient consciously verbalizes but also of his unconscious attitudes, expectations, and implied motivation. A patient may say that he wants to get to the bottom of his problems but at the same time expresses an attitude of dissatisfaction if he does not get immediate advice or relief of symptoms, or if he is asked to talk about himself and his thoughts. In such situations it is this unconscious or nonverbalized motivation that will be significant. Patients who have been able to stick to and successfully accomplish long and difficult tasks in other areas such as school have a more favorable prognosis.

110

Another factor is called psychological-mindedness. Some individuals, by virtue of rigidly defensive psychological organizations, are unaware of their own emotional impulses, conflicts, reactions, and responses. They tend to focus almost exclusively on current external events. Such patients will generally have a difficult time in psychotherapy and are often more suitably treated by supportive techniques, unless psychological-mindedness can be developed. Alternately, patients who are extremely introspective to the point of excessive and continuous rumination, or who suffer from such internal awareness to the exclusion of reality and external life situations, will also have great difficulty in psychotherapy.

Another factor to assess is the use of defense mechanisms and the kind of mechanisms used. For example, intense reliance on projection, massive denial, or major withdrawal obviously precludes a good prognosis. Similarly, patients who act out in dealing with psychic conflict and combine this with projection would be very difficult patients indeed. It is reasonable to expect that the patient have at least average or better than average intelligence in psychotherapy and at least some capacity to tolerate the anxiety and frustration of psychotherapy without requiring recourse to psychotic breakdowns, addiction, acting out, and so forth.

DeWald mentions age as an important factor. It is clear that very old people or people with various degenerative diseases make generally poor patients for long-term psychotherapy. This does not mean, however, that all old people cannot be considered as candidates for long-term treatment. There are some exceptional old people who have psychologically remained young, and they can respond very well to a long-term psychotherapy, especially if there is a genuine reason for it and there is some use for it at the end of the treatment.

111

A patient in good health in the sixties, for example, may have twenty years of life ahead of him; by no means should the therapist ever make the tragic error of ruling out patients for psychotherapy on the basis of age alone. My oldest patient was seventy-eight years, and she was going strong ten years later!

Singer (1970) points out that the therapist must necessarily assume a somewhat authoritative role at the beginning of therapy, whether he likes it or not. It is pointless to pretend that he is an equal with the patient. On the other hand, in gathering relevant data, the therapist will define himself as a person genuinely interested in meeting the patient as a human being. Careful and sensitive diagnostic inquiry is important. Thus, the initial interviews set the tone for the psychotherapeutic process. They convey a sense of the importance, immediacy, directness, and seriousness of the psychotherapy. Through this behavior—and not through seductive or "palsy-walsy" behavior—the therapist expresses his respect for the patient. Furthermore, during the initial interviews, the patient's education for psychotherapeutic collaboration begins to take place. Careful inquiry by the therapist shows the patient the road to painstaking self-investigation.

The initial interview is also an experimental period, writes Singer, during which the patient and therapist have an opportunity to learn something about each other, so that they may come to a rational decision concerning the feasibility of working with each other. I often ask the patient after one or two interviews if he feels he can work with me. The answer is not always "yes" and reveals important further information about the patient—and sometimes the therapist.

The initial interviews are a time for arranging the formal

aspects of the patient–therapist collaboration, which is usually known as the therapeutic contract. Before setting up the therapeutic contract for the patient I ask whether the patient has any questions. These questions usually revolve around the cost, length of treatment, and the diagnosis. I try to discuss very frankly and invite collaboration from the patient regarding the goals of therapy and whether the patient should have intensive psychotherapy or not. If long-term psychotherapy is recommended, I frankly tell the patient that a long period of time is necessary, and it is difficult to predict exactly how long it will take, but I usually give an estimate of two years or more. The patient often asks about his diagnosis, and here I explore why he wishes to have a formal diagnosis, rather than quickly give anything out of the diagnostic manual that the patient will needlessly ruminate about.

The therapeutic contract establishes a certain setting and a certain atmosphere in which extraneous issues are kept to a minimum so that the therapist and patient may focus on the patient's internal processes and/or the transference reactions. This has been well described in the famous paper by Freud (1913a) "On the Beginning of Treatment," a classic in psychotherapeutic literature. Some of the points that Freud makes are (a) to avoid lengthy preliminary discussions before beginning the treatment, (b) to avoid a situation of previous treatment by the same doctor by another method (for example, one and the same doctor giving electric shock treatment and then taking the patient into long-term therapy), and (c) to mistrust all prospective patients who want to delay beginning their treatment. Freud writes, "Experience shows that when the time agreed upon has arrived, they fail to put in an appearance."

He points out that special difficulties arise when the therapist and his new patient are on terms of previous friendship or especially when their families are on terms of friendship and see each other socially. The therapist should not be in a socially friendly relationship with either the family of a patient or the patient himself. It is best to simply send such patients to another therapist, rather than needlessly tangle up the patient in a mixture of social reactions and transference phenomena. Taking on as patients those individuals with whom the therapist has or has had frequent social or professional contacts or members of the therapist's own family is almost invariably countertransference acting out, no matter how well rationalized. It is very unfair to the prospective patient. There are other therapists available.

Probably two of the most important aspects of the therapeutic contract are the issues that Freud calls "time and money." These issues will not require very much discussion with the patient and will not cause any trouble, providing the therapist has thought through in advance what his attitude is going to be to the questions of time and money. For example, a fee must be set that is reasonable. In general this fee should be the going rate in the community, and an effort should be made in the initial interviews to be sure that the patient can realistically afford the fee that is set. There is nothing wrong with investigating the patient's finances with the patient before an agreement is made about undergoing a long-term therapy. An un-self-conscious and frank approach to financial agreements is a very important indicator of what kind of approach is going to be taken by the therapist to various other so-called embarrassing or private matters in the psychotherapy. It is often the first indication that the patient

114

has of what kind of a person the therapist is and how he is going to deal with problems.

Under no circumstances at the beginning of psychotherapy should a bill be allowed to pile up. Patients should be billed monthly and should be expected to pay monthly; if the bill is not paid, this should be discussed, worked out, and rearrangements must be made. Most patients, if a reasonable fee is set and a correct investigation has been made of their capacity to pay, will pay their bill monthly without further ado, and the issue just doesn't come up. A small percentage of patients will make a big issue about the fee and about money, and this will obviously have to be dealt with as part of the psychodynamic material in the therapy. But it requires first a conviction on the part of the therapist that he is charging an honest fee from a patient who has the ability to pay him.

The whole question of payment can be used as a therapeutic tool (Allen, 1971), for it constitutes a significant aspect of the patient's experience of what kind of person the therapist really is. The therapeutic interaction at whatever level the therapy is geared, whether supportive or expressive, involves a relationship between patient and therapist in which the therapist's strengths and weaknesses are constantly being assessed, probed, and tested by the patient to see if they conform to past images and relationships. Foremost in all of this is a test of the therapist's integrity in conforming to, or being different from, corrupt parental figures with whom, or with some aspect of whom, the patient has often identified. The therapeutic interaction is, for some patients, their first life experience with someone who is careful to respect both the patient's and his own rights without dishonesty. One area in

115

which the therapist is often exposed to this type of testing is that of the patient's payment or nonpayment of his fee and the therapist's method of dealing with this problem.

A similar dynamic is involved in the problem of missed sessions and frequency of sessions. My clinical experience has been that the optimal beginning frequency of intensive psychotherapy sessions is twice a week, though some patients require three times a week. Alternately, some patients can only tolerate once a week. The major factor in this decision should not be the economics but the anxiety level of the patient. Certain patients need frequent contacts to reduce their anxiety level. Other patients, especially adolescents, become very anxious if seen too frequently and do better on a less-frequent basis. Unfortunately, the economic aspects almost always come into the situation. There has to be some discussion with the patient about frequency of sessions at the beginning and some exploration of what the patient can afford and what he expects.

Patients come in with strange conceptions about how often they are going to see a therapist. Some patients think that most people see a therapist once a month; others expect to be told to come in six times a week. Many of these misconceptions can be cleared up at the beginning of therapy and thus reduce a lot of potential anxiety.

If an error has to be made about frequency of sessions it is best to make the error in the direction of not enough sessions rather than too many. In general, it is easier to increase the number of sessions without disturbing the therapy than it is to decrease the number. Patients often experience this latter as a rejection.

One of the most knotty problems is the question of missed

sessions. The patient must be responsible for the payment for all sessions, but this cannot be made into too rigid a rule. The biggest mistake, of course, would be in not telling the patient that he is held responsible for all sessions. The therapist has the choice of either telling the patient at the beginning that he will have to pay for every session whether there is a legitimate reason for missing or not in his mind, or the therapist must put himself into a position of having to judge whether the missing of a session is legitimate or not. Some therapists advocate the former approach, and some advocate the latter. My experience has been that in intensive psychotherapy it is better to take a flexible approach.

I tell the patient at the beginning that he should try to schedule his vacations when I schedule my vacations and that if he has to cancel a session he should give me notice and I will try to fill the time. But he will have to pay for all sessions that are scheduled—unless something comes up that I agree is so serious that the therapy session would reasonably have to be missed. The most common example of this is a serious illness, but I leave the final judgment about whether a patient should pay for his session or not up to me, fully realizing that this will lead to considerable difficulty with a certain group of patients. The most important thing is to tell the patient at the beginning what kind of arrangement is going to be made.

Fromm-Reichmann (1950) presents a charming and humane attitude on the subject that deserves careful attention:

Some noted psychiatrists have advocated that interviews missed by the patient should be paid for, irrespective of frequency and validity of reasons. This has been explained on the basis of the fact that the doctor contracts for a certain part of his earning capacity in terms of time with the patient. This

117

is indeed true. Yet I feel that it is not the psychiatrist's privilege to be exempt from the generally accepted custom of our culture in which one is not paid for services not rendered. I realize, of course, that the unforseen loss of income-producing time is a handicap. I do not see any way in which this can be avoided in the above-mentioned incidents without interfering with the self-respect of the psychiatrist and the dignity of the profession. Moreover, to a productive personality, such free time may be of the essence.

In general, it has been my experience that it is best to err on the side of being liberal with excuses for missed appointments, rather than to be excessively rigid and strict. Careful attention must be paid by the psychotherapist to his reactions and attitudes toward missed appointments, as this affords an excellent opportunity to pick up manifestations of his countertransference, if he is honest with himself.

One of the questions often brought up at the beginning of therapy is the issue of hospitalization. The therapist must make a decision right away as to whether the patient will require hospitalization or not, and if this question is brought up this must be conveyed to the patient and his family. Appropriate action should then be taken at once.

Referrals should be acknowledged. The patient should be asked at the beginning of therapy if he has been referred by another physician or professional, and whether it is acceptable to him that a brief letter be written indicating that he has indeed made contact with the therapist and will begin treatment. This is especially important, because what the patient was told by the person making the referral is often vital. There is an unfortunate tendency, for example, of referring physicians who are not in the field of psychiatry to try to

118

soften the blow (as they see it) of referring the patient to a psychiatrist, by suggesting, that the patient needs a few sessions with a therapist to clear up his twenty years of chronic alcoholism, and so on. The patient then comes in expecting magic and is quite shocked and surprised when told about long-term psychotherapy or anything else. It is thus always worthwhile discussing details of the referral and why the referral was made and indicating back to the referral source that the patient has indeed made contact.

There are certain medical–legal aspects to psychotherapy that should be kept in mind. Some records should be made and kept in a private place as to the progress of the patient. I insist that every patient at the beginning of psychotherapy have a thorough physical examination. I do not do any physical examination myself, again to avoid needlessly complicating the treatment and also as part of educating the patient about the nature of psychotherapy. I refer the patient to a competent internist or general practitioner for such purposes.

I am against taking notes during a patient's session or the taping of sessions, as I think this again has a very harmful effect on the atmosphere of the psychotherapy. In the initial interviews I write down a few facts about names, dates, and ages that I cannot reasonably be expected to remember. If the therapist has to depend on tapes or notes of the process that is going on in the therapy, this indicates a countertransference difficulty.

Similarly, I do not take phone calls during a patient's therapy session unless it is a dire emergency. It ought to be kept in mind that a therapy session interrupted by a series of telephone calls produces a very disruptive atmosphere, and

119

the handling of telephone calls and letters from patients has an important effect on the therapeutic alliance. At the same time it is important to keep the door open for patients to mail letters or make phone calls to the therapist if they feel they must. A patient should know the therapist's home telephone number or know his answering service number, depending on the particular taste of the therapist. The patients should have the feeling that in an emergency they always can reach the therapist.

In the use of drugs, there is great variation among psychotherapists. My experience has been that the use of drugs in psychotherapy most often benefits the therapist's anxiety, not the patient's. Occasionally, when patients suffer from severe anxiety, I prescribe tranquilizers or even give them a few samples of tranquilizers from my drug cabinet, a technique I have found to be quite effective. I avoid the powerful tranquilizers in out-patient office psychotherapy, and I rarely use the so-called mood-elevating drugs. I have had poor results with the latter in office psychotherapy, and my impression is that they confuse the picture by the production of side effects rather than provide any definitive help. However, there is sharp disagreement about this among experienced clinicians. This may be due to differences in the type of patient referred to this or that psychotherapist, depending on reputation and interests. The most important factor is that if the psychotherapist is going to use drugs, he must use them judiciously and not as a way of avoiding the anxieties and emotions of the patient. Finally the psychotherapist must be able to withstand the incessant seductive advertising and expert salesmanship of the pharmaceutical houses.

The use of the sofa or couch in psychoanalysis was origi-

120

nated by Freud for two major purposes. He disliked having to be stared at for eight or more hours a day, and, as a technical motive, he wanted the expression of his face not to give the patient material for interpretations or to influence him in the choice of material to report. In general, it is an unwise procedure to use the couch in intensive psychotherapy unless the therapist is quite experienced, has had considerable training, and has definite reasons for doing so. Part of this is determined by what the goals of therapy are. The more extensive the goals and the better the ego strength of the patient, the more general indication there is to use the couch. But most patients in intensive psychotherapy should be started out on a face-to-face basis. There are some indications in borderline patients that make the use of a couch a reasonable technique. I have discussed this elsewhere (Chessick, 1971b), but I would urge the beginning psychotherapist simply not to place patients on the couch, because he will run into many difficulties that could be easily avoided otherwise.

Finally, a "Metapsychological Assessment Profile" has been introduced by Greenspan and Cullander (1973) for those who wish a systematic and formal outline for "scrutiny of personality functions relevant to analyzability." This has useful clinical and research potential, and may be helpful in deciding whether to send certain patients for a formal psychoanalysis.

CHAPTER 6   *The Opening Phase*

*A*FTER the therapeutic contract has been settled on
Freud (1913b) tells the patient:

"One more thing before you start. What you tell me must
differ in one respect from ordinary conversation. Ordinarily
you rightly try to keep a connecting thread running through
your remarks and you exclude any intrusive ideas that may
occur to you and any side-issues, so as not to wander too far
from the point, but in this case you must proceed differently.
You will notice that as you relate things various thoughts will
occur to you which you would like to put aside on the ground
of certain criticism and objections. You will be tempted to say
to yourself that this or that is irrelevant here or is quite unim-
portant or nonsensical, so there is no need to say it. You must
never give in to these criticisms but must say it in spite of

122

them—indeed you must say it precisely *because* you feel an aversion to doing so. Later on you will find out and learn to understand the reason for this injunction, which is really the only one you have to follow. So say whatever goes through your mind. Act as though, for instance, you were a traveler sitting next to the window of a railway carriage and describing to someone inside the carriage the changing views which you see outside. Finally, never forget that you have promised to be absolutely honest, and never leave anything out because for some reason or other, it is unpleasant to tell it."

I usually begin with some version of this statement to the patient. I also ask the patient to tell me if he has any dreams and to be sure to relate the dreams if he can remember them.

The presentation of this fundamental rule at the beginning of psychotherapy brings about a special problem in the opening phase of psychotherapy. One should never expect a systematic narrative, and this should not be encouraged. In fact if the patient from the very first minute carefully prepares everything he is going to communicate, ostensibly so as to make better use of the time devoted to the treatment, Freud points out this is really resistance. I have seen many forms of this preparation. Patients come in with notes, papers, and statements of every sort that they want to read and have obviously spent much time carefully preparing what they are going to present. The request that the patient report dreams can be used similarly in service of resistance. For example, the patient may come in with fourteen pages of notes on dreams he had all week long. It is incumbent on the therapist to realize what is going on.

Another problem that Freud mentions will be discussed

123

later in greater detail as part of acting out. The patient may carry everything outside from the sessions and talk over with some intimate friend (or spouse or parent) everything that has been said in the treatment. They may in this way drag a third person into the therapy. Care should be paid to what the patient is doing with the material of the therapy and recognizing this again as a primary responsibility of the therapist.

One of the most common problems to follow in the footsteps of Freud's fundamental rule occurs when the patient reports that he has simply nothing to say. Freud recommends energetic and repeated assurances to the patient that it is impossible for no ideas at all to occur to him at the beginning and that the silence in question is a resistance. Most of the time this works, and after a short period the patient begins talking. There are some patients, however, who either have to present a prolonged silence as a response to the request to free associate or will free associate with all kinds of rubbish and nonsense. They may take the idea of free association so seriously that they present actual gibberish to the therapist or they may react by presenting a high degree of intellectualized material, making themselves sound like professors giving a lecture to a class. These various ways of responding to the fundamental rule are all, of course, demonstrations of resistance, and the therapist must be aware they are such and not be trapped by them.

Probably the most serious problem occurs when the patient is chronically silent. Sometimes patients are silent for many sessions at the beginning of therapy because they have great difficulty in reporting what comes to their minds. In general, in psychotherapy, somewhat in contrast to formal psychoanalysis, it is unwise to permit long periods of silence if

124

they can possibly be avoided. Freud mentioned the idea of energetic statements, and I think this is what is needed. The patient may have to be asked many times what he is thinking about, how he is feeling, or what is coming to his mind. Active effort may be necessary, especially at the beginning of psychotherapy, to get the patient talking.

Of course, as the treatment progresses, if silences appear they take on a different meaning. They may very well be a response to what the therapist has said. In that case the therapist may have to interpret what he thinks the meaning of the silence is. It should also be pointed out that silence in the opening phases of therapy can indicate a faulty job of establishing the therapeutic contract. For example, if an adolescent patient is sent to therapy by a court and no serious effort is made to arrive at a therapeutic contract with the patient, the adolescent sits in glowering, defiant silence for session after session, unless something is done.

If the patient persists in silence for week after week, it does not always mean that therapy is failing. The therapist must try to understand what this silence means. For some patients the very act of frustrating the therapist has a therapeutic effect. Others have a need either to fail themselves in whatever they endeavor or a need to present a passive resistance to the therapist. These things must be worked through with the patient, and interpretations must be made. Sometimes a patient receives therapeutic benefit from observing the energetic efforts of the therapist to reach him, and this can be a more important experience for the patient than the interchange of information. Needless to say these are special situations, and they are undesirable in long-term therapy. They usually develop only with extremely sick patients.

Other major problems that sometimes accompany the

125

opening phase of therapy are the patient's complaint that his symptoms are worse and the dramatic appearance of psychosomatic symptoms. The worsening of symptoms at the beginning of treatment (or, alternately, the sudden disappearance of symptoms) is not an uncommon phenomenon. The intent here is obviously to badger the therapist into doing something and/or to demonstrate the therapist's incapacity to cure the patient. Another possible cause is the manifestation of increased anxiety at the beginning of treatment. Some patients have been holding everything in, until a therapeutic contract can be established. Once they feel that they are in therapy, they dump everything out. To the watching family it appears that their condition has suddenly become dramatically worse.

Occasionally, a situation arises in which the symptoms become so bad after the beginning of treatment that the patient has to be hospitalized. This should not be done unless it is absolutely necessary. It causes great perturbations in the process of therapy and focuses the treatment on the relief of symptoms rather than the understanding of them.

Psychosomatic symptoms manifest themselves most obviously as a development of aches and pains that make it impossible for the patient to get to the treatment sessions. This can be dealt with by interpretation, of course, although occasionally a patient literally drops out of treatment because these symptoms make it impossible for him to come. Some psychosomatic developments are much more subtle. For example, a patient of mine, threatened by treatment, spent the first month or two of her treatment insisting that she must be absolutely independent of every one. Yet a certain dependency is essential to the therapeutic contract. As we worked this through and attempted to get at the meaning of this patient's almost fanatical need for total independence, the patient began developing severe incapacitating stomach cramps. This forced further dependency in going to doctors, and having tests, and so forth. It took a lot of interpretive work and patience to help her through these psychosomatic symptoms.

The therapist should not lose heart if these appear or become severe. The symptoms should be understood as the result of something that is going on the treatment process. In the meantime, the patient should have the benefit of early medical treatment for whatever psychosomatic symptoms appear, and every therapist should have a good working relationship with one or two internists in order to deal with problems of this nature.

Another kind of problem that frequently arises at the beginning of treatment is the patient's complaint of so-called existential anxiety. It is very much in vogue these days to present one's complaints in an existential terminology popularized by Camus. In a series of literary essays, Camus (1955) argues that there is only one philosophical problem: whether or not one should commit suicide. Camus claims that judging whether life is or is not worth living amounts to answering the fundamental question of philosophy.

Many patients come in complaining that life is meaningless; they feel alienated, alone, they have no sense of identity, and so on, and so forth. The complaints are vague and difficult to pin down. It is an error to blame all of this so-called existential anxiety simply on psychopathology, but it is equally wrong to consider man's existential plight as being the basic cause for these anxiety complaints. In fact, it is very difficult to decide to what extent in modern life people can

127

be healthy as well as preoccupied with such ideas as the meaning of life and alienation. Freud felt that such preoccupations already constituted a sign of pathology. As a generalization this may be rather extreme.

In clinical experience, however, one finds that when there are many such complaints, it is usually a mask for pathology in interpersonal relations. In most cases it is fairly easy to see when existential complaints actually mask interpersonal pathology. The best way to approach these complaints is not to argue with them or engage in philosophical discussion with the patient about whether or not life is worth living but rather to get at the patient's object relations and developmental history and to see how such feelings came to be. This implies that, even in a successful psychotherapy, the patient may leave at the end of treatment with a certain sense of existential tragedy, and one can argue that this is an aspect of the human condition.

Another kind of problem that arises is the development of severe anxiety shortly after the beginning of treatment. This poses a serious threat, especially to the inexperienced therapist. Everything seems to be falling apart, the patient is terribly upset, he is having difficulty in functioning, and so on. It is a real challenge to the identity of the therapist, a test of his confidence, experience, self-esteem, and his own sense of integrity to cope with such situations. The most inadequate and insecure therapist immediately hospitalizes all such patients. This can lead to a farce, a revolving-door situation in which the patient goes in and out of the hospital every two weeks, suddenly getting better in the hospital, then coming out and deteriorating, and so on. A second amateur solution is to introduce powerful tranquilizing drugs at once. If this is done, the patient may either abuse the drugs, thus putting himself into a foggy daze and calling attention to the fact that something is severely wrong with him, or he may save up the drugs and take a lot in one dose, with all the dramatics this entails.

When severe anxiety appears in the psychotherapy process, the most important safeguard is for the patient to be able to reach the therapist and have a talk with him no matter when. There seems to be an inverse proportion between the number of telephone calls the therapist gets at home and the ease with which he can be reached! Those therapists who, in a matter-of-fact fashion, make it possible for a patient to get in touch with them whenever it is necessary get very few calls from the patients. Those therapists who make it very difficult for the patient to get in touch with them often get many hysterical telephone calls.

My general policy with telephone calls from anxious patients if the anxiety cannot quickly be allayed over the phone, is to schedule an extra session with the patient for early the next morning. I have found this to be a very effective technique in dealing with patients who call late in the evening or in the middle of the night and are very upset. First of all, it allays their anxiety and lets them get a night's sleep. Furthermore, knowing that first thing in the morning they will be coming in to an extra session, often has a tranquilizing effect of itself.

If one receives a series of such telephone calls, then it is often an indication that the patient is not being seen frequently enough. Patients get to know that if they call at night, they are bound to obtain an extra session. This should be discussed with the patient, and sometimes it is necessary for the frequency of sessions to be increased.

At times the therapy is *too* frequent, and the frequency

129

should be reduced. The anxiety level of the patient should always be kept at a certain optimal level (Chessick, 1969), so that he is not so comfortable that his motivation flags for treatment, but, on the other hand, he is not so anxious that he is paralyzed and unable to function.

At times it may actually be necessary to employ tranquilizing drugs, and I have found in my clinical experience the most effective of these drugs with the widest margin of safety to be Librium as far as out-patient therapy is concerned. The use of Valium is to be discouraged, as it occasionally causes urinary retention, leading to some bladder difficulties and even urethral constriction. The disadvantage of Miltown, my second choice, is its metabolic similarity to the barbiturates; in my experience Miltown has a fairly serious addiction potential.

Giving out Librium in situations where the patient's anxiety really seems to call for it is sometimes a reasonable technique, but it is rarely necessary. Even when these drugs are prescribed, they should be prescribed for short periods at a time, and then the need for them should be reassessed frequently. It must be made clear to the patient that the only purpose of these drugs is to bring discomfort to a level where he can work in therapy. In no sense do the drugs provide a cure. On the other hand, withholding of tranquilizers and even mild soporifics such as Doriden from severely anxious or insomniac patients can be a cruel form of countertransference acting out. The therapist must know himself.

This brings us to the subject of the expectation of magic in the opening phase of psychotherapy. A definite percentage of patients drop out of treatment in the opening phases of psychotherapy (see Chessick, 1971a). The reason for this is

130

that although an effort has been made to establish a good therapeutic contract, the patient secretly expects magic. He either wants immediate relief from symptoms or expects to be cured within three months. Sometimes it isn't the patient who expects this but the spouse. So, for example, if the husband is paying for treatment and after three months there has been no improvement in his wife or she seems worse, he refuses to pay for the treatment any more. This can sometimes, but not always, be helped by a consultation with the spouse.

As previously mentioned, an aggravating factor can be the referral source, and this is usually dealt with in the establishment of the therapeutic contract. One of the most effective ways of managing patients who have become worse shortly after the beginning of treatment is to suggest to them that if there is any doubt in their mind as to the efficacy or the usefulness of treatment, perhaps they would like to have a consultation. I have had several cases in which a real therapeutic alliance developed only after the patient went to someone else for a consultation to assure himself that all the time and money he was putting in was a reasonable investment.

A good therapist will never at any time in psychotherapy object to the patient's having consultation with another reputable psychotherapist and may even suggest some names if the patient wants them. The problem of the expectation of magic again underlines the great importance of establishing a proper therapeutic contract and thoroughly discussing with the patient the length of treatment at the beginning of the therapy.

Probably the most serious and difficult problem to come up in the opening phase of therapy is the one of suicide.

131

There are two articles that should not be missed on this subject (Havens, 1965; Hendon, 1963). Suicidal fantasies and wishes arise from several factors: using death as a retaliatory abandonment, gaining a feeling of omnipotent mastery through death, viewing death as a retroflex murder, hoping for death as a reunion with the mother or as a rebirth, seeking death as a self-punishment. All of these features can come up quite early in psychotherapy, and the patient emerges as a genuine suicide risk.

How do we assess this risk, and what do we do about it? Ask how deep and all-pervasive is the mood of the depression. Evaluate the patient's interest in the world, and interest in the therapy; investigate the patient's religious beliefs and interest in his family. Try to see to what extent there is a monotonous repetition of suicidal ideas. Seek out the vegetative symptoms of depression, depressive delusions, past history of other attempts at suicide, or other impulsive behavior. Ask the patient how he feels early in the morning when he has to awaken and face another day; look for brooding, lack of communication, lack of affect, increase in tension and hopelessness, patterns of insomnia and weight or appetite loss, unrealistic feelings that the world is flat and lifeless, anger at doctors, a feeling of helplessness, and a sense of having one's "back against the wall."

It is sometimes very difficult to assess whether or not the patient is a suicide risk. If one works with severely disturbed patients one will have to assume this suicide risk, and one will probably lose a certain small percentage of patients by suicide. If the patient seems definitely suicidal he must be hospitalized, but if there is a question, as there almost always is, one of the best protections is to bring a member of the family into the picture, sometimes even having a collaborative interview between a family member and the patient. The suicide risk then is frankly discussed, and it is made clear to a member of the family and to the patient that this risk must be shared by all. If the family insists, the patient should be hospitalized at once.

Most of the time the family is understanding, and, if there is a question about suicide, this discussion with the family in front of the patient will help the patient to see that his suicidal threats are a form of resistance and a way of getting the therapy into a terrible turmoil. It should be clearly understood that the *first* responsibility of the therapist is to assess the seriousness of the suicidal risk. If it is serious, it is absolutely mandatory to hospitalize the patient. The big problem, however, arises from threats and gestures, and every therapist will have to make certain decisions about whether to interrupt an out-patient psychotherapy and hospitalize patients whom they are not sure are actually suicidal.

It is especially important in the treatment of adolescents to bring the family in when these kinds of problems arise. It must be made clear to the patient that the ultimate decision whether to live or die belongs with him, and the therapist cannot make the decision for him. The therapist can do his best to attempt to preserve life, but he cannot live in a state of constant anxiety and guilt over the patient's threats of suicide. This must be worked through in the therapist before he can deal effectively with problems of this nature; if it is not worked through, it is going to pose a serious countertransference problem in treatment.

It is evident from this that the therapist must have a pretty clear idea, before he starts with a patient, of how he

133

will approach and handle problems involving the patient's family. If he does not, the family can form an extremely destructive influence on the psychotherapy and, in fact, in many instances can destroy the therapy process itself.

It is obvious that a therapist should never communicate with the family or anyone else without the patient's knowing about it. If a family member expresses a wish to communicate with me, I always get the patient's permission to accept this communication, and I discuss in advance with the patient what the communication might be about, what the family member may wish to know, and what I am permitted to tell. Furthermore, I discuss what it would be in the patient's best interest to tell the family. This problem becomes especially acute regarding telephone calls and letters. Before answering a letter received from a member of the patient's family, or writing to anybody else for that matter, regarding one's patient, one should always first have the patient's written permission, and there should always be a discussion of what the contents of the reply would be.

Many times there is a telephone call from an anxious family member. When this takes place, I allow the family member to talk as much as he wants to about anything he wants over the telephone. One should never turn off sources of information, no matter how one feels about these sources. When the family member begins to ask me about the patient I tell the family member that I thank him very much for the information he has presented, but that I cannot give any information without first getting the permission of the patient.

I then *begin* the next session with the patient by stating that I have received a phone call from the family member.

134

I think it is important to do this immediately in the next session for there may be suspicion in the patient's mind— should he happen to know that the family member called— that the therapist is not going to say anything about it. It should be kept in mind that even the most disturbed family members can sometimes come to the aid of a patient in an emergency, and one should never respond to the family, no matter how hostile or how destructive they have been to the patient, with countertransference rage.

Patients seem to get into the most fantastic sadomasochistic, mutually perverse and destructive marital relationships. This is frequently presented to the therapist as the patient's having made "a terrible mistake." It is a great error to become trapped and to work vigorously with the patient against the marital partner. Almost invariably, if the patient is involved in some weird marriage there is a reason for the patient's involvement in that marriage. Vigorous environmental manipulation to change the situation will most commonly result in the patient's soon becoming involved in a similar situation.

In general, marriages seem to involve a meshing of both adult mature needs and neurotic needs between partners. Marriages are usually multiply determined or overdetermined. Attempts to break up marriages by a therapist, or attempts to change the structure of marriages by marital counseling of couples seen together, often runs into this difficulty. The goals and the motivation (on an unconscious level) of the marriage precludes behavior change in many instances.

Of course, it is possible with effective marital counseling to render many improvements in a marriage, but the kinds of situations one usually encounters in intensive psychother-

135

apy rarely yield to marital counseling, although one or the other partner may clamor for it. Frequently, marital counseling has already been tried in one form or the other.

It should be kept in mind, on the other hand, that the psychotherapy of a marital partner places *great stress* on the other marital partner. The various mood changes and vicissitudes of psychotherapy in the patient in treatment have to be endured by the other partner. If there has been a meshing of neurotic patterns and one person begins changing this meshing and altering these patterns for the better, we know this will have a dramatic effect at times on the other partner.

It is quite common for one individual to begin psychotherapy and, as the psychotherapy progresses and the patient improves and matures, for the other partner to express a sincere wish to have treatment. This brings up a variety of problems. Who should do the treatment? If it is to be a different therapist, how should the patient be referred to therapy? I have found, in general, that the introduction (and referral) of a spouse to psychotherapy is most effective if the therapist of the other partner first sees the spouse. That is to say, if I am treating Mrs. A., and Mr. A. tells Mrs. A to tell me he wants treatment, I usually suggest that Mr. A. come in for an interview with me first. In the interview with Mr. A.—if he is willing to come in to see me, and he is usually quite eager to do so—I try to assess why he wants treatment and in what way his response to my therapy of Mrs. A. may have motivated this wish.

In most instances, if I feel that the motivation for treatment is genuine, I then refer Mr. A. to another therapist that I have confidence in, after getting his permission to discuss the interview with the other therapist. I also get Mrs. A's permission to bring up with the other therapist any pertinent factors that might help him in the treatment of her husband. I then prefer to have only occasional discussions with the spouse's therapist as the necessity arises. I think that a certain contamination occurs if there is too much communication between the two therapists of the two spouses. Above all, it must be made clear that the therapy of each person is for the individual benefit of that person—*not* for the primary purpose of saving the marriage. If the primary purpose is to treat the marriage, then it makes more sense to have marital counseling or marital therapy. It is very important that both therapists and both marital partners have a clear idea of the purpose of the therapy.

There have been a few instances where I have taken the patient's marital partner into psychotherapy on an individual basis. This has occurred when the spouse has been in treatment for a very considerable time, there is a good therapeutic alliance, and there are some indications in the psychodynamics that it would be valuable if the motivated partner was in treatment with the same therapist. In addition to that, it is a great learning experience for the psychotherapist. It is one of the best ways to realize what a completely distorted and one-sided picture every patient gives of his relationships with everybody else. Sometimes one wonders if one is talking with the patient about the same person. So, at times, having both marital partners in individual treatment is very beneficial, but almost always it is better to send the other partner to another therapist.

One of the greatest difficulties in the handling of the family is the problem of the paranoid husband. From time to time one encounters a female patient whose husband has

137

definite paranoid tendencies (and, less frequently, a male patient whose wife is paranoid). All patients' spouses fantasize about what is going on in the psychotherapy of their wife or husband. The paranoid husband often comes up with sexual fantasies that are allegedly occurring between his wife and the therapist. This can be extremely dangerous and lead to sudden psychotic explosions. The therapist must try to assess the general psychodynamics of the patient's spouse, even if it is only at second hand, from what he is told by the patient. Often remarks made by the patient's husband and reported to the therapist can help in recognizing the development of some kind of paranoid deterioration in the husband.

I have found that the best antidote for this kind of situation is to have a personal interview with the spouse. In general, there is a certain wisdom in long-term psychotherapy of giving the spouse of the patient a chance once or twice at least to have a look at the therapist. Many patients solve this for themselves by simply bringing their spouse along and parking him (or her) in the waiting room, so that when the therapist opens the door there is an introduction and each has a chance to look at the other.

In the situation of the paranoid husband, however, or if there is any suspicion that the husband is developing ideas of being persecuted or being taken advantage of by the therapist in any way, it is very wise for the therapist to insist on an interview with the husband. The same would be true of a female therapist seeing a male patient whose wife is developing certain delusional ideas. In a very short time during the interview with the husband, the air can usually be cleared. With a very matter-of-fact, firm, and authoritative approach, many delusional fantasies can be broken up by a direct

138

confrontation experience between the therapist and the spouse.

If it appears that the spouse is really psychotically paranoid and deteriorating, it may be necessary to insist that he have treatment. This is rarely successful, and such patients do not seek treatment. In one case that I treated a paranoid husband suddenly appeared in the waiting room of my office without an appointment, not long after the opening of his wife's psychotherapy. I invited him in and took up another patient's time to have an interview with him. I felt that it was an emergency, that unless this man was seen there was no telling what he might do. Several years later this man committed homicide and also killed himself, after being involved in a paranoid delusion involving his mistress. I feel that by seeing this man at the time I did I prevented a situation in which my patient, his wife, would probably have been killed —and perhaps avoided some serious danger to myself. The therapist must be alert and flexible in responding to these kinds of problems coming from the patient's family.

Serious problems can be involved with the family that is paying the therapist's bill, especially either the husband paying the wife's bill or the parents paying their child's bill. This can be a fertile field for acting out. The payment of the bill must not be allowed ever to constitute a threat to force the patient to do what the family wants. Under those circumstances, the therapist has the responsibility to call in the family and make clear what the situation is. If the family persists in this kind of behavior, the therapy should be terminated, provided the patient cannot find another way to pay for treatment.

Similarly, the charges should not be allowed to pile up

139

so that intense demands have to be made on a husband or family where much money is owed over months of bills. It is incumbent on the therapist to keep alert to this kind of behavior on the part of the family.

It must be kept in mind that the psychotherapy of the patient often threatens the family or the spouse in many ways. For example, very frequently, parents will trade delusions with the child. In one of my cases, a mutual bargain was struck between the teen-age child and the parents, although this was not stated on a conscious level. The parents agreed that the child would be the center of their universe; everything was given to the child and she was treated as somebody special. She was told that she could have anything she wanted and was superior to everyone. In exchange, it was agreed that the parents were wonderful, the raging, destructive mother was really a very good mother, and the passive, alcoholic father was a wonderful father.

This trading of delusions only broke up when the patient went out into the world and got married—and, of course, experienced the various blows of life. She couldn't have everything she wanted. When she came into treatment and started giving up her side of the bargain, the parents began vigorously attacking the psychiatrist and threatened, in every way they could, to break up the treatment. This put intense pressure on the patient and caused many anxious moments regarding the possibility of continuing treatment.

Fromm-Reichmann (1950) has pointed out the various factors that could cause relatives to be very hostile and uncooperative with the therapist. The therapist is supposed to be expert in handling interpersonal relations, and Fromm-Reichmann mentions that mistreatment of the relatives can

140

cause very unfavorable repercussions in the therapy and will work usually to the detriment of the patient.

The relatives often have to accept the idea that there is a psychiatric patient in the family and that all the family secrets are going to be told to a stranger and an outsider. They realize that their various blunders and mistakes will be revealed. There is no end to the cultural jokes and attacks on psychiatrists and psychotherapy they have read and heard. Most of the relatives are not sure whether the large therapy bill is being paid for any good reason. They feel uncertain, ashamed, and embarrassed and are never sure of whether they are being taken advantage of or not. The therapist must keep these things in mind when he receives hostile communications from the relatives and try to avoid a situation in which he is either fighting the patient's battle with the relatives or fighting directly with the relatives.

In general, my experience has been that the families of patients who require hospitalization have more disturbed relatives that one has to deal with than do the families of out-patients. It is often true with out-patients that sometimes the less emotionally sick spouse of a marital pair, or the relatively healthy child of a severely disturbed parent, will be the first one to seek therapy.

Special problems involving the family arise in the treatment of schizophrenics and in the treatment of adolescents. It is usually necessary in these instances for the family members to be interviewed individually at least once. Severely disturbed schizophrenics, for example, sometimes actually have to be brought to their therapy sessions. Usually they cannot work and earn the price of the therapy, so that the family is paying the bill.

Apart from seeing each family member separately, there is a value to seeing the family together, both to watch the family interaction and to announce the formal aspects of the therapeutic contract. If the parents are paying for the treatment or if the patient is unable to comprehend—for example, because of a psychotic daze—some of the basic factors of the therapeutic contract, it may be necessary to announce the terms of the contract in the presence of the patient to the members of the family. It goes without saying that at no time in interviews with the patient's family should any details or any information supplied by the patient be given out without the patient's advance permission.

Another great value in seeing the family of disturbed patients is to obtain what Fromm-Reichmann calls "collateral information." Often severely disturbed patients and adolescents do not give much in the way of history. Collateral information from relatives will help speed the therapeutic process and not obstruct it. The psychiatrist must be ever mindful of the unreliability of such information: The data may be distorted because the relatives are apt to be either very defensive or disturbed themselves, so the information may suffer from misrepresentation. But checking the data of the patient against that of the relatives is one way to counteract the danger of being misled by either the unreliability of the relatives or the unreliability of the patient.

In the situation with adolescents there is a certain sense of "loyalty." They don't like to say anything that might cast any aspersion on their parents. This often causes the adolescent patient not to give much of any history or discuss what is really bothering him as far as his parents are concerned.

The parents of adolescents in treatment also have serious

problems. An excellent beginning book on the treatment of the adolescent is by Sklansky *et al.* (1969). These authors point out that even the parents of normal adolescents feel bewildered, attacked, and rebelled against, insecure in their authority, worried about the present, and fearful of the future. Their image of the child is often rudely disturbed by the outbursts of adolescence. To see a previously dependent child, whose very dependency made him pliable and manageable, become suddenly rebellious and independent can be very painful for the parents.

It is especially very troubling to the parents because they want to be good parents and they often see that the patient's behavior is quickly bringing him into direct trouble with society. Thus, they have a sense of great urgency and a need for something to be done at once. They will put much pressure on the therapist. The adolescent now has the physical capacity to act out in all kinds of ways and can defy the parents in a way he never did before. He usually leaves the parents angry and confused, and both the adolescent and the parent feel misunderstood by each other, and quite bitter.

It is important in the therapy of adolescents to see members of the family individually at the beginning of the treatment. If possible, it is then wise to have further occasional visits with members of the patient's family, especially the parents, as the therapy progresses. This has to be set up at the beginning of the treatment and with the permission of the patient.

Some of these occasional visits take strange forms. For example, I had one patient whose father was a busy businessman always flying somewhere but who, about once a month, would call me long distance from someplace in the country

143

to talk for fifteen or twenty minutes about his feelings about his son. This turned out to be very useful in ventilating feelings and getting further information. Some parents of patients simply refuse to be involved in the therapy at all, and there is not much that can be done except to demand the minimum of having them bring the patient to treatment and seeing that the bills are paid.

In general, it is very difficult to get parents into formal therapy. They usually resist the idea and consider a suggestion for therapy as an indication that you feel that they are the cause of all the troubles. One must suggest therapy to the parents of the adolescent with great tact and only very carefully. One should not press this issue if the patient's parent shows an obvious rejection of the idea. Sometimes, after a therapeutic alliance has been established with the adolescent, it is then possible to move forward in getting a significant parent into therapy. It is obviously a tremendous advantage in the therapy of adolescents to have at least one of the parents in treatment. This treatment should always be with a different therapist than the therapist of the adolescent.

CHAPTER 7 *Transference and Countertransference*

*T*HE transference has a long history and there are many articles on the subject. Anyone wishing a detailed review of the background of this concept is referred to Orr (1954). The basic definition of transference is given by Fenichel (1945): "In the transference the patient misunderstands the present in terms of the past; and then instead of remembering the past, he strives, without recognizing the nature of his action, to relive the past and to live it more satisfactorily than he did in his childhood. He 'transfers' the past attitude to the present."

Fundamentally, transference is a form of resistance in which the patient defends himself against remembering and discussing his infantile conflicts by reliving them. It also offers us a vital and unique opportunity to observe the past *di-*

145

rectly and thereby to understand the development of the nuclear childhood conflicts in the patient. The importance of the concept of transference in any form of intensive psychotherapy should be clear from even this short discussion. In fact, many authors argue that the basic difference between intensive uncovering psychotherapy and supportive psychotherapy or conditioning therapies is in the way that the transference is recognized and dealt with.

Greenson (1968) points out that the term *transference* itself may be misleading. It is a singular noun, but transference phenomena are plural, multiple, and diversified. The term *transferences* is grammatically more correct, but the phrase *transference reaction* or *transference* is customarily used. This is not to be understood as one specific transference only but rather a group of reactions and phenomena typically appearing in intensive psychotherapy. Greenson lists five important characteristics denoting a transference reaction. The outstanding trait that overrides all others and is included in all the others is inappropriateness: "It is inappropriateness, in terms of intensity, ambivalence, capriciousness, or tenacity which signals that the transference is at work."

A transference does not just arise in psychotherapy but can appear in many kinds of interpersonal situations and play a very important role. For the purpose of this work, however, we are interested mainly in the appearance of transference in psychotherapy. We usually speak of a positive transference and a negative transference. A positive transference implies reactions composed predominantly of love in any of its forms or in any of its forerunners or derivatives. Greenson writes: "We consider a positive transference to exist when the patient feels towards his analyst any of the following: Love, fondness, trust, amorousness, liking, concern, devotion, admiration, infatuation, passion, hunger, yearning, tenderness, or respect."

In the process of intensive psychotherapy we often do not worry as much about the appearance of positive transference as we do about the appearance of negative transference. In a negative transference we observe a series of reactions based on the various forms of hate. According to Greenson, "Negative transference may be expressed as hatred, anger, hostility, mistrust, abhorrence, aversion, loathing, resentment, bitterness, envy, dislike, contempt or annoyance, etc." It is always present, although it is often much more difficult to uncover negative transference than the manifestations of positive transference. There are many possible reasons for this clinical fact. The two most obvious are that patients don't like to become aware of transference hate and to express it and that therapists don't particularly enjoy being the object of transference hate and to have a deal with it or be exposed to it.

As a general rule of thumb one may say that for an uncovering psychotherapy to be successful there will have to be sharp manifestations of both positive and negative transference. To put it another way, if a person wishes to do psychotherapy he must be prepared to be exposed to powerful negative and positive emotional feelings coming from the patient, often on a highly irrational basis. This exposure to such powerful feelings can lead to many mistakes, retreats, and confusions in the psychotherapy if the therapist is either not prepared for them, not prepared to deal with them, or primarily preoccupied with his own needs and problems, so that he cannot clearly perceive what is going on.

147

Some other very important definitions are necessary at this point. One of the most difficult concepts is that of the transference neurosis. The original conception of the transference neurosis was designated as the situation in which the patient in psychoanalysis developed such intense transference feelings to the therapist that everything else in his life became of lesser importance. The classical conception of the transference neurosis has it that the infantile feelings and conflicts of the patient are projected *exclusively* onto the analyst, a situation that rarely occurs. Rather, the transference neurosis could be thought of as an extremely important or predominant object relationship that during a period in the therapy, supersedes all other relationships. Unfortunately, the concept of transference neurosis has run into difficulty, because very often, even in a formal psychoanalysis, the classical transference neurosis simply does not appear. One sees a great many varieties of transference phenomena, but a focal, sharply defined transference neurosis cannot always be expected to take place. The reasons for this are a matter of considerable debate.

A recent issue of the *Journal of American Psychoanalytic Association* (Calef, 1971) devotes almost the entire issue to the subject of the transference neurosis. At least certain basic premises can be agreed upon:

1. The transference neurosis revives the infantile neurosis.

2. It is created out of the *frustrated* demands for love that, in turn, arise out of the therapeutic situation as we structure it.

3. The symptoms of the transference neurosis are dynamic, shifting, and changing; it is not a static concept.

4. Important in the development of the transference

148

neurosis are the mechanisms of regression and repetition—indeed, the transference neurosis can be thought of as arising out of the repetition compulsion.

5. In the transference neurosis, the old symptoms of the adult neurosis that the patient has come to complain about "lose their libidinal force" and seem to be much improved, for the patient is preoccupied with the transference.

6. The transference neurosis is not identical to and does not describe in a one-to-one manner the nature of the infantile relationships that have been transferred.

7. Eventually, the transference neurosis itself becomes involved in a resistance to treatment.

The management of the transference neurosis, according to classical psychoanalysis, permits the undoing of repression and is the central issue of treatment. The concept of interpretation as resolving the transference neurosis differentiates psychoanalysis from other forms of treatment. It is important to clarify this issue a little more. According to classical psychoanalysis, a full-blown transference neurosis develops. This is then interpreted, and such interpretation permits an undoing of the transference neurosis, which, in turn, frees the patient from the nuclear infantile conflicts. It is the preoccupation with the transference neurosis that differentiates psychoanalysis from other forms of treatment; the efficacy of psychoanalysis is believed to be in the removal of the transference neurosis through interpretation, rather than through any other aspects of the treatment.

The transference neurosis may also appear in psychotherapy. It is not necessary for a patient to come in four or five times a week and lie on the couch for a transference neurosis to appear. On the other hand, it is much more likely that, if the transference neurosis is going to appear, it will appear under the conditions of formal psychoanalysis. But it is very important for anyone doing intensive psychotherapy to understand the concept of the transference neurosis and to be aware of its appearance, if it does appear in the psychotherapy.

The actual occurrence of a transference neurosis can be very dramatic. When all the factors I have described in transference and transference neurosis actually present themselves in psychotherapy, it is a remarkable experience for both the patient and the therapist. The sharp focusing of infantile demands and powerful emotions in a totally inappropriate manner on the therapist, when the patient and the therapist are actually both aware of the irrationality of this phenomenon and have both observed it to develop almost *de novo* out of the psychotherapy situation, can be the most crucial experience of the psychotherapy.

Unfortunately, the appearance of a transference neurosis is not always a reason to be jubilant. A transference neurosis can arise in situations where the patient has a very weak ego state and poor defenses. In such situations the patient cannot actually utilize the transference neurosis toward the working through of his problems. If a profound transference neurosis seems to be developing in a psychotherapy, the therapist must be careful to ascertain the ego state of the patient and to determine by the use of interpretation whether the patient is actually capable of utilizing the developing transference neurosis. If he cannot utilize it, efforts should be made to break up the transference neurosis by decreasing the frequency of the treatment, by active interpretation and support, and so on.

150

I am not advocating that the psychotherapist should become afraid when a transference neurosis appears and break up the therapy because he cannot stand the strength of the emotions that are aimed at him. He must be sufficiently mature and aware of himself that he can make a correct judgment as to whether a powerful transference neurosis appearing in psychotherapy is actually workable or not.

A transference psychosis sometimes appears. This is always a very undesirable situation that resembles the strong transference neurosis, but the patient has absolutely no insight into it and denies completely that the phenomena he is experiencing are transference at all. Such situations as falling desperately in love with the therapist can be understood as transference psychosis if this tremendous falling in love refuses to yield to any kind of interpretation, if the patient insists that the love is genuine and based on the marvelous qualities of the therapist, and definitely refuses to see any transference phenomena involved in it.

The transference often becomes a part of the patient's resistance maneuvers in a further effort to avoid undoing the forces of repression. This leads to terminological confusion because *all* transference can be thought of as a form of resistance to remembering. The difference is that transference as a resistance maneuver arises more specifically in certain situations in psychotherapy that call it forth and then functions as a resistance to further psychotherapy.

The most typical example of this situation occurs when patients wish for gratification in the transference. Quite frequently patients develop a strong wish for some kind of gratification from the psychotherapist at a point in the therapy; the patients may concentrate on that, refuse to coop-

151

erate with psychotherapy, and rage for hours because they are not getting the gratification they want. The kind of gratification demanded can be of all varieties. Sometimes it is a very minor thing, such as raging because the therapist won't help the patient with her coat. In other instances it can be major, such as demanding that the therapist marry them, go to bed with them, and so on.

The problem of how much gratification to give a patient in psychotherapy is a very thorny one, indeed. One general principle that can be kept in mind is: The more gratification the patient is given in the transference, the less uncovering is going to be possible, and the more difficult it is going to be to resolve the nuclear conflict. There are some situations where the transference demands become so overwhelming that the therapy cannot go on unless something is done. When this happens, it is often an indication that the patient cannot tolerate uncovering psychotherapy, and the therapy should be shifted to a more supportive and less frequent approach.

A different form of transference resistance is sometimes called a transference defense. In this situation, just as the patient would be expected to arrive at a certain insight out of the material that is being presented, there suddenly appears instead a powerful transference reaction, most typically a negative transference. For example, a patient who has been through an absolutely dreadful and frustrating childhood is beginning to arrive at the point where he is becoming aware of his tremendous yearnings for love and affection from one of the parents. This has only come about after a long working through of many defenses and resistances against anyone meaning anything to him, against needing anyone, even against forming a therapeutic alliance itself. At the point where one might expect the patient to show the first signs of some transference yearnings for the therapist, there appears suddenly, without any previous warning, the explosive feeling that everything that the therapist says is a form of hostile criticism. If it isn't in his actual words, it is in his tone of voice. The patient absolutely cannot shake off the feeling that everything the therapist is saying is hostile and critical.

An investigation of this reaction brings the patient to the realization that mother was a very hostile and critical person who was constantly making the patient an object of her criticism. The working through of this transference defense, which came up suddenly in the middle of a session when the patient was on the verge of feeling some positive feelings for the therapist, enables the patient later on to begin feeling those yearnings and permits the future development of more powerful transference phenomena.

The sudden and sometimes dramatic appearance of any transference manifestations at the very onset, in the middle, or at the close of a psychotherapy session gives rise to the possibility that the patient is using the transference to defend against feelings, memories, or emerging insight that must be denied at the time. The therapist must be vigilant and constantly aware of the appearance of transference manifestations that can show themselves either in small or subliminal ways, as well as in dramatic explosions.

Also, just as there are transference neuroses, there are character transference phenomena. These character transference phenomena can be thought of as hidden in more general behavior patterns. The term is somewhat misleading and confusing, but what distinguishes this form of transference from others is that the reaction to the therapist is part of the pa-

153

tient's habitual, representative, and typical responses to people at large, and the transference behavior is characteristic of the patient's relationships in general. It is this quality of nonspecific behavior that has led to the term *character transference*. The important point is that the patient may be reacting to the therapist with his habitual reactions *to a different kind of person than the therapist actually is*. This is what the therapist has to be aware of in watching for character transference phenomena.

Both character transference phenomena and transference neurotic phenomena are dealt with in a similar way in the process of psychotherapy, but the former is usually more subtle and tricky and more difficult to resolve.

One should be aware that patients have some foggy notions of what the transference is supposed to be or not supposed to be in psychotherapy. For example, some patients begin the psychotherapy by asking the therapist whether they are expected to fall in love. The kind of question, "Am I supposed to fall in love with you?" hides behind it a number of anxieties and concerns that should be dealt with in a very straightforward manner. The patient is told that he is supposed to report whatever thoughts and feelings come to his mind, but there is nothing that is *supposed* to happen. It is impossible to predict what kind of transference phenomena will occur, how intense they will be, or what their focus will be. We must deal with whatever arises in the therapy in a nonanxious interpretive manner.

The therapist must also be very carefully aware of the serious danger of the acting out of the transference outside of the therapist's office. I will discuss this later as part of the general phenomena of acting out. Another related aspect of transference problems is the negative therapeutic reaction. This, too, is a special area and will also be discussed later.

The greatest problem in the development of transference in psychotherapy occurs if the therapist misses what is going on. One of the most common causes of stalemate or failure in psychotherapy is when—due to various reasons in himself—the psychotherapist is unable to be aware of important manifestations of transference that are appearing in his patients. This leads us to a discussion of countertransference.

The most serious flaws in the handling of transference reactions are the subtle, chronic, unrecognized ones that can go on for years without being detected. These flaws usually stem from two main sources: countertransference reactions and incorrect understanding of the patient for reasons other than countertransference, for example, cultural differences and so on.

Countertransference reactions have a very important impact on the process of psychotherapy. The whole subject is poorly explored and poorly understood, and the student will have to be satisfied with a variety of definitions and conflicting attempts at clarification of the situation (Baum, 1969–1970). Singer (1970) points out that countertransference seems to appear "when the therapist is made anxious by the patient, when he fears feelings and ideas which therapeutic investigation may arouse in him, and when his desire to avoid anxiety and its dynamic roots force him into assuming defensive attitudes." These defensive attitudes interfere with his genuine therapeutic understanding of the patient.

In the broadest terms countertransference is thought of as a manifestation of the therapist's reluctance to know or learn something about himself. It is a reflection of his wish to remain oblivious of certain facets of himself and to allow unresolved conflicts in himself to remain buried. This powerful counterforce can move the therapist to quite hostile behavior against his patient. The hostility, which can be overt or covert, may be expressed in acts of omission or acts of comission or in irrational "friendliness" or irrational annoyance or anger.

Anyone who works with novice therapists will have a lot of experience with countertransference reactions, and a great deal of supervisory work consists of helping the beginning therapist to become aware of his countertransference reactions. Countertransference, according to Singer, can be grouped roughly into three categories:

1. Reactions of irrational "kindness" and "concern"
2. Reactions of irrational hostility toward the patient
3. Anxiety reactions by the therapist to his patient

All of these may occur in waking life or while dreaming.

Probably the most detailed study of countertransference has been made by Racker (1968), who has gone farther than anyone else in trying to understand the deep infantile and possible neurotic roots of countertransference reactions. There is certainly considerable room for debate and discussion on this subject, especially since Racker tends to explain these phenomena in some very controversial ways. Racker points out that the significance given to countertransference and the importance attached to it depends on two misfortunes that it generates. The immediate consequences of countertransference are: (a) It may distort or hinder the perception of unconscious processes in the patient by the therapist; (b) the countertransference may not interfere with the therapist's perception of what is going on, but it may impair the interpretive capacity of the therapist. Thus, for example, the manner, behavior, tone of voice, the form of the interpretations, and even the attitude toward the patient consciously or unconsciously may be vastly influenced by the countertransference. When a patient complains of the tone, manner, or voice of the therapist, it is not always a manifestation of transference to the therapist. It may instead represent the patient's perception of a countertransference problem in the therapist.

Obviously an understanding of the countertransference is vital to the successful carrying out of psychotherapy. I have not yet given a very specific definition of countertransference, since there is some disagreement on exactly what is meant by the term. It is usually defined in two limited ways or in one more general fashion. The most limited definition of countertransference is that it consists of a set of therapist transference reactions, in the form of fantasies, feelings, thoughts, and behavior, to the transference manifestations and the transference neurosis of the patient. The formal psychoanalytic definition in use today usually amends this to include therapist transference reactions—involving, of course, the significant persons in the therapist's childhood—to any aspect of the patient's personality, including the patient's transference (Reich, 1973). The most general definition of countertransference is to encompass the total reaction of the therapist, both transference or realistic reaction to all aspects of the patient's transference and general personality.

In all close human relations, some transference takes place. The nature of this transference in psychotherapy depends on the personality of the therapist, his various experiences in the past, and on the various characteristics of the patient, both physical and psychological, regardless of whether these are presented to the therapist as part of the patient's transference or as the patient's general personality. To be aware that countertransference is taking place is the crucial issue, for unanalyzed countertransference is most likely to be acted out and to present a barrier to understanding and interpreting. Conversely, to identify what aspects of the patient are producing countertransference gives us further valuable understanding of the patient. Thus, ideally, the therapist should be aware of his reactions to the realistic aspects of the patient's personality, and of his transference reactions to the patient, with focus on what aspects of the patient have stirred up his countertransference.

The purpose of this is neither to act out nor to share countertransference problems with the patient but to determine what aspects of the patient are producing the countertransference, for the purpose of further understanding. It is nonsense to burden the patient with our countertransference problems, especially those aspects of countertransference that are our transference to the patient. This is exploitation.

What is far more important is to be aware that countertransference is showing itself and to do something about that fact. Before we go into this in more detail, it should be pointed out that Racker and others have talked about a "countertransference structure," a "countertransference neurosis," and a "countertransference character disturbance." The countertransference structure is a consistent and relatively permanent aggregate of feelings, fantasies, and ways of reacting that develop in the therapist as a response to the transference and the personality of the patient over a long period of psychotherapy. Tower (1956) produced a very important paper, which has not received sufficient attention, on the subject of the countertransference structure and its importance in psychotherapy's ultimate healing.

A countertransference neurosis is said to occur when the patient becomes more important to the therapist than anyone else in his life. Except possibly in certain situations involving the psychotherapy of schizophrenics, as suggested by Searles (1965), the countertransference neurosis is almost always pathological and can be very dangerous. Racker interprets the countertransference neurosis mainly as an oedipal phenomenon, but this is subject to considerable debate.

Just as we differentiate among patients between neuroses and character disturbances and their various corresponding transferences, so we can differentiate countertransference neuroses and countertransference character distubances, although this rarely appears in the literature. Countertransference character disturbances involve the therapist's character. His countertransference character disturbance is analogous to the patient's character defenses. Thus the countertransference character disturbance in the therapist would involve certain forms of behavior and a general interpersonal approach to the patient, suggesting that the patient was someone significant in the therapist's past life who called forth this general character pattern in him. It is sometimes very difficult to spot this, but it is *very* important and does not get nearly the attention it deserves. Many failures in psychotherapy can be traced to unconscious countertransference character disturbances.

A variety of authors have discussed the signals that indicate a countertransference problem to be present. For example, Menninger (1958) can be paraphrased as noting the

159

following common ways in which countertransference makes its appearance:

1. The inability to understand certain kinds of material that touch on the therapist's personal problems;

2. Depressed and uneasy feelings during or after sessions with certain patients;

3. Carelessness with regard to certain arrangements for the patient's appointment, being late for it, letting the patient's hour run overtime for no special reason, and so on;

4. Persistent drowsiness of the therapist during the session or even falling asleep;

5. Over- or underassiduousness in financial arrangements with the patient or the same over- or underassiduousness regarding time arrangements and changes in appointment;

6. Repeatedly experiences of neurotic or unreasonable affectionate feelings toward the patient;

7. Permitting or encouraging acting out or acting in;

8. Trying to impress the patient or a colleague with the importance of the patient;

9. An overwhelming urge to publish, or give a lecture, about the patient;

10. Cultivation of the patient's dependency, praise, or affection;

11. Sadistic or unnecessary sharpness toward the patient in his behavior or the reverse of this;

12. Feeling that the patient must get well for the sake of the therapist's reputation or prestige, being too afraid of losing the patient;

13. Arguing with the patient or becoming too disturbed by the patient's reproaches or arguments;

14. Finding oneself unable to gauge the point of opti-

160

mum anxiety level for smooth operation of the therapeutic process, thus, alternation of therapy from one extreme of great patient anxiety to the other extreme where the patient is bored, disinterested, and shows no motivation;

15. Trying to help the patient in matters outside the session;

16. Getting involved in financial deals and arrangements with the patient on a personal or social level, recurring impulses to ask favors of the patient, with all kinds of rationalizations as to why one is asking the favor from that particular patient;

17. Sudden feelings of increased or decreased interest in certain cases;

18. Dreaming about the patient;

19. Much preoccupation with the patient or his problems during one's leisure time;

20. Finally, a compulsive tendency to hammer away at certain points.

This compulsive tendency to hammer away at certain points may not necessarily show itself in the emphasis of interpretations. Such hammering away, of course, would involve countertransference, but another, more subtle, kind of hammering away that we frequently see in countertransference problems is in trying to force a patient into a regressive transference. Some novice therapists, for example, feel that the patient *must* develop a transference neurosis in intensive psychotherapy, and they try to force this on the patient by a variety of maneuvers. This has been discussed by DeWald (1964). Such forcing of transference is always to be considered as a countertransference problem in the therapist.

After the therapist has established a particular structure and routine of procedure with each patient, he should carefully examine any departures from the structure and routine that he introduces because they may well be related to countertransference.

What does one do when a serious countertransference occurs? It must be made clear that the difference between a novice therapist and an expert therapist is *not* that the novice has lots of countertransference and the expert therapist has none. It is true that the expert psychotherapist, who has gone through a thorough and extensive psychotherapy or psychoanalysis of his own, will tend to have less fractious and less unruly countertransference reactions than the novice therapist who is unaware of his own problems. However, even the most mature and well-analyzed psychotherapist is going to have important countertransference reactions to his patients over a period of time (Reich, 1973). A countertransference structure, as defined above, *always* appears in long-term intensive psychotherapy.

The difference between the novice and the experienced psychotherapist is that the experienced psychotherapist is constantly on the lookout for the countertransference and the countertransference structure, becomes aware of it when it occurs, keeps it in check in terms of not permitting the acting out of countertransference feelings, and holds it in abeyance or even utilizes it for the purpose of the psychotherapy.

If the therapist is aware of a persistent countertransference attitude, it is sometimes possible to compensate for this by conscious decision and control. DeWald (1964) writes that

the emphasis must be on the therapist's willingness to accept the occurence of countertransference without undue guilt or shame, and on his honesty and self appraisal in attempting to

162

identify and understand such reactions. As with the patient in treatment, the therapist then must attempt to use such newly gained understanding and awareness to change his reactions and behavior in the current situation. Unless the therapist is willing to face issues of psychological truth within himself, he is hardly in a position to request or require this from his patients.

In attempting to identify a countertransference the therapist must apply the same standards of honest and forthright self-appraisal to himself that he expects of the patient. When a countertransference problem is severe, the therapist may have to use at least one of three alternatives. The first of these, and the simplest, is to keep one's therapeutic interventions and activity at a minimum for a short period of time, while the therapist is busy working through his own countertransference problems. A general rule of thumb is that if one feels anxious with the patient, that is a good time *not* to make interpretations or therapeutic interventions, because they will almost invariably be meant to allay the therapist's own anxiety.

If the therapist feels chronically anxious with a patient, a situation has been reached in which he, himself should seek personal help. Assuming that the therapist has already had his own intensive psychotherapy, he must deliberately and meticulously investigate himself and see where the problem is coming from. If this is not successful he ought to consult a colleague. *My experience has been that a consultation is extremely helpful and important in dealing with countertransference.* A great many cases of personal disaster, suicide, sexual acting out, failure, and stalemate in psychotherapy could have been prevented if the therapist would have had the courage to get a consultation from a respected colleague at a point where he had some awareness of the countertransference manifestations that were appearing. I insist on two maxims regarding behavior toward one's patients as the "categorical imperative" of psychotherapy. These serve as a check on countertransference acting out: Never be either exploitative or retaliative toward one's patients and always behave as you would toward a guest in your home, with your wife (or husband) present.

There is a strange aspect of countertransference that is not much discussed in the literature and that tends to develop in a covert and subliminal way. Even though the therapist has been well analyzed, there is a possibility that certain vague countertransference feelings and even behavior will be allowed to creep into the therapy in a clandestine fashion. If the therapist has even a dim or fleeting awareness that countertransference problems are developing in therapy, he should go to an experienced colleague and present the case. The countertransference aspects will then appear and can be discussed. As soon as light is focused on them, they will very often be removed as an interfering force in therapy. I have seen many cases where the famous maxim of Benjamin Franklin's *Poor Richard's Almanac,* had it been followed, would have saved a disaster in the psychotherapy: "Do not do that which you would not have known"—that is to say, do not behave with the patient in psychotherapy in such a way that you would be unwilling to have it generally broadcast and known to your colleagues. Here lies a third important check on countertransference acting out in psychotherapy.

The countertransference should not be thought of as an intrinsically negative thing. It only becomes negative and interferes in psychotherapy when it is not correctly recognized and handled. A discussion of countertransference is not complete unless it is also pointed out that the aim of the therapy of the therapist is not to remove the possibiliy of all countertransference reactions but to make him capable of being aware of these reactions.

Sometimes these reactions, if studied objectively, can lead to further information and data about the patient. If the therapist notices that he is having a countertransference reaction and analyzes this in himself, he may become aware that something the patient is doing or something the patient is saying is producing countertransference. He may not have been aware previously of the message or communication the patient was trying to send. Instead of listening, he has been reacting—suffering from a countertransference reaction. In this sense countertransference, just like transference, can be thought of as a resistance to uncovering and remembering. The analysis of countertransference in the therapy brings the reward of knowing and understanding new material that was previously not in the awareness of the therapist.

The interaction of the transference of the patient and the countertransference structure of the therapist is probably one of the basic and most important factors in healing through intensive psychotherapy. I will discuss this in more detail in a later chapter. Racker (1968) writes,

The struggle with the resistances for the sake of the patient's health thus acquires a certain similarity to the famous wrestling of the Biblical patriarch Jacob with the Angel. This continued undecided the whole night through, but Jacob would not yield and said to the Angel: "I won't let you go unless you

165

bless me." And finally the Angel had no choice but to do so. Perhaps we shall also finish the struggle, as Jacob did, somewhat lame-legged, but if we fight as manfully as he, we shall no less enjoy from our own inner being a blessing of a sort; and the patient will as well.

In less poetic terms I suggest that a parallel struggle goes on throughout the process of psychotherapy in both patient and psychotherapist. In the patient there is a struggle between the forces of resistance and the innate biological and psychological forces toward health and toward mastering of his conflicts. In the therapist there is a struggle arising from the stimulus of the personality and transference of the patient. A struggle occurs between the desire, on the one hand, to understand and interpret the transference properly and the tendency to misunderstand and misinterpret the transference out of countertransference problems, on the other. The patient must fight within himself to overcome the forces of resistance. The therapist must systematically struggle within himself to understand and master the forces of the countertransference structure, which always interfere with his correct understanding and interpretations to the patient.

These co-existing struggles are central in determining the outcome of psychotherapy. They also explain the oft-repeated remark by experienced therapists: In every psychotherapy the therapist "learns" from his patients. He expands his boundaries of human understanding, increases his maturity, and achieves further ego integration. Conversely, unanalyzed negative countertransference experiences over a prolonged period can produce what Wile (1972) calls "therapist discouragement," an irrational pessimism regarding his

166

therapeutic work and his personal life. This leads to premature termination of therapy cases, and even the abandonment of the profession itself, the susceptibility to new fads and short-cut active techniques, or an irrational overoptimism and overconfidence in one's powers of healing. Perhaps worst of all, "Deprived of his sense of purpose and value in what he is doing, the therapist may turn to his patient for compensatory reassurance and affirmation."

CHAPTER 8   *Acting Out and*
Acting In

RESISTANCE, and intervention designed to deal with resistance, have come to be recognized as the core of the therapeutic process. Freud (1900) defined resistance in *The Interpretation of Dreams* as anything that "interrupts the progress of analytic work," a definition, he cautioned, that could easily be misunderstood.

Even once a patient has agreed to the basic contract and has attempted to express whatever comes to mind, certain phenomena soon appear that interrupt and interfere with the steady, smooth flow of thoughts, associations, feelings, and memories. These various phenomena are collectively termed *resistance*. Acting out is known as a particularly pernicious form of resistance because it can break up the therapy entirely, if it is not correctly recognized and dealt with.

I have already mentioned the occurrence of transference as a resistance in Chapter 7. The case of Dora, which Freud described in 1905, is a famous example of an analysis disrupted by the acting out that developed out of the transference. Freud (1905) writes,

> But I was deaf to this first note of warning, thinking I had ample time before me, since no further stages of transference developed and the material for the analysis had not yet run dry. In this way the transference took me unawares and because of the unknown quantity in me which reminded Dora of Herr K., she took her revenge on me as she wanted to take her revenge on him, and deserted me as she believed herself to have been deceived and deserted by him. Thus she *acted out* an essential part of her recollections and fantasies instead of reproducing it in the treatment.

I cannot recommend strongly enough that the reader study this case in detail.

Freud returned to the subject of acting out and resistance in a very important paper entitled, "Remembering, Repeating and Working-Through." This paper is the second in a series of papers on "technique" by Freud. It was written in 1913. For those who are seriously interested in doing intensive psychotherapy, the whole series of papers on technique by Freud found in Volume 12 of the *Standard Edition* are mandatory reading. Freud (1913b) writes,

> . . . the patient does not *remember* anything of what he has forgotten or repressed, but *acts* it out. He reproduces it not as memory but as an action; he *repeats* it, without of course, knowing that he is repeating it."

For instance, the patient does not say that he remembers that he used to be defiant and critical towards his parents' authority; instead, he behaves in that way to the doctor. He does not remember how he came to a helpless and hopeless deadlock in his infantile sexual researches; but he produces a mass of confused dreams and associations, complains that he cannot succeed in anything and asserts that he is fated never to carry through what he undertakes. He does not remember having been intensely ashamed of certain sexual activities and afraid of their being found out; but he makes it clear that he is ashamed of the treatment on which he is now embarked and tries to keep it a secret from everybody. And so on.

Above all the patient will *begin* his treatment with a repetition of this kind. When one has announced the fundamental rule of psychoanalysis to a patient with an eventful life-history and a long story of illness and then has asked him to say what occurs to his mind, one expects him to pour out a flood of information; but often the first thing that happens is that he has nothing to say. He is silent and declares that nothing occurs to him.

Freud goes on to connect this phenomena with what he calls "the compulsion to repeat," an issue that became extremely important in Freud's later theoretical considerations. This compulsion to repeat becomes the patient's way of remembering, according to Freud, and he emphasizes that what interests us most of all is the relationship of this compulsion to repeat to the transference and to resistance.

We soon perceive that the transference is itself only a piece of repetition, and that the repetition is a transference of the forgotten past not only on to the doctor but also on to all the other aspects of the current situation. We must be prepared to find therefore, that the patient yields to the compulsion to repeat, which now replaces the impulsion to remember, not only in his personal attitude to his doctor but also in every activity and relationship which may occupy his life at the time—if, for instance, he falls in love or undertakes a task or starts an enterprise during the treatment. The part played by resistance, too, is easily recognized. The greater the resistance, the more extensively will acting out (repetition) replace remembering.

It is essential that the therapist have a clear grasp of acting out, because, as already mentioned, this type of resistance probably represents the clearest danger to any psychotherapy and can easily break up a treatment. In the interest of getting a true idea of this type of resistance, there are certain phrases or terms that the therapist should be familiar with. The extreme acting-out patient can be called a sociopath or even a delinquent. Such a patient represents a special problem and does not epitomize the ordinary, everyday case in which acting out occurs. Bird (1957) presents an excellent article on the acting-out patient. The acting-out patient, he states, does not confine his conflicts within himself: "He externalizes his conflicts; he always involves others, he does so rather directly. Furthermore, his behavior is highly susceptible to outside influence. What this means theoretically is that the acting-out patient has failed to establish within himself the internal structure which is necessary to enable him to struggle with himself."

This inability to internalize and to confine his conflicts is what Bird calls the "pathogonomic functional defect" distinguishing the acting-out patient from all other people. This developmental defect comes out of a failure of the ego of the

171

child and of the mother to move apart; it has important oral roots as pointed out by Altman (1957).

At this point, however, we are not concerned primarily with the acting-out patient but rather with acting out as it occurs as resistance during the process of the psychotherapy of a patient who does not significantly and continuously act out. These are the conditions under which a psychotherapy can suddenly and unexpectedly be threatened with destruction. The predominantly acting-out patient does not pose as much of a threat to the therapy as this latter type of patient. In the taking of a history it is usually clear when a patient is in an acting-out type, so the therapist expects and is prepared for acting out and deals with it from the very beginning. Acting out as an unexpected resistance in psychotherapy is more difficult to handle. As in the case of Dora, it is usually rooted in the transference. If a transference neurosis—which is very painful and involves strong feelings that threaten to emerge to the consciousness—begins to form, it tends to be countered by acting out rather than remembering. In the case of Dora, the patient acted out by simply leaving treatment in order to gain her revenge in the transference on Freud, who represented important males in the patient's past.

Acting out may also constitute a resistance in psychotherapy and occur as a response to an interpretation. This is especially true regarding a wild interpretation or an intepretation that has been made prematurely or without sufficient preparation. An example of this can be found in any supervisory experience with neophyte therapists. For instance, a therapist who deals too quickly and vigorously with interpretations of a schizophrenic patient's affect hunger or starvation for love and affection may find the patient responding by a sudden hyperphagia: he begins to eat voraciously day and night or alternately, he may suddenly refuse to eat and actually go into a state of starvation and anorexia. What has happened is that rather than having to deal with the unbearably painful feelings of starvation for love and loneliness, the patient switches the whole arena to the gastrointestinal tract and then acts out either the starvation or intense defenses against the wish to take in, by dramatic behavior relating to the gastrointestinal tract. There are many examples of this.

A particularly important type of acting out in psychotherapy occurs with borderline patients. Borderline patients, when they act out, tend to act out very dramatically and can often get themselves into a great deal of difficulty before the therapist is even aware of it. Lipschutz (1955) described two important manifestations that the transference can take in borderline patients. These involve the intense and uninhibited expression of transference wishes early in the therapy and the common appearance of a third person toward whom these transference feelings are later transmitted. Lipschutz points out that in the borderline schizophrenic these qualities in the transference become more apparent immediately and are unhesitatingly expressed: "The borderline patient shows very little inhibition upon the first contact with the physician. The patient will express open feelings for the person of the doctor, either love or hate, accompanied by actual verbalization of the sexual act with him."

One should always be suspicious, if a patient shows obvious and frank transference manifestations very quickly, that one is dealing not with an excellent and analyzable patient but with a weak and beleaguered ego. In such cases the transference may later suddenly or gradually fit the clinical picture

173

of a neurotic patient. At the same time a transition is made from the therapist to a stranger or a third person. This third person is endowed with the same qualities and power that were originally attributed to the parents and early in therapy to the therapist. Exaggerated feelings of love and hostility are then brought to sessions, with as much fervor, and accompanied by the same uncensored fantasies, as the patient heretofore experienced about the therapist, but they are now connected to the third person. Very little insight accompanies this, and it represents a dangerous situation. For example, caught in the "love" aspects, the patient may actually marry the third person or get involved in an affair with the third person. The hate aspects may drive the patient to do actual physical harm or violence to this third person. Since there is little insight present, the situation poses a great problem. If the third person transference is challenged too directly or too aggressively, this may lead to a frankly psychotic or a depressed picture with strong risk of suicide.

The therapist must be very alert to third-person types of relationships that occur in the course of psychotherapy. Considerable acting out with this third person may occur before the patient can finally be persuaded that this is really a shift of fantasies away from the therapy and a draining of affects that belong in the therapy situation. Thus, as Freud pointed out, the occurrence of the transference produces a tremendous source of resistance, because the flood of strong and painful feelings and affects, which really belong to the transference, are unacceptable and have to be acted out in this case with a third person rather than remembered and reported in the psychotherapy.

The highly erotized transference that borderline patients

174

form also holds grave dangers. Such transference may appear as a stormy demand for genital contact with the therapist from patients of either sex. If this is rejected, the patient claims deep hurt and humiliation. Repeated interpretations are not accepted, and the patient keeps insisting that his love for the therapist is real. Freud (1915b) was aware of this phenomenon in his paper on "transference love," and he gave this kind of patient a gloomy prognosis. He suggested that when the patient stubbornly insists on and persists in transference love, "the best thing to do is to acknowledge failure and withdraw."

Rapaport (1956) was less gloomy and suggested managing this problem in the following way:

> Erotization is what the patient wants to make of (the analytic situation) under pressure of the repetition compulsion, while a corrective emotional experience is what the analyst tries to give to the patient by acting differently from the pathogenic parent. This is accomplished by constant reality testing and keeping the tenuous balance between allowing the patient to believe that one is sincerely interested in him and has full confidence in his capacity to act effectively and in a mature manner, and at the same time discouraging any assumption that one has a stake in his therapeutic success.

This quotation is highly debatable because of Rapaport's concept of what goes on in therapy. The important point is that one should not acknowledge failure and withdrawal unless one *absolutely has to* in the therapy, when confronted with such erotized transference in borderline patients. The achievement is to recognize that this kind of transference has developed and to deal with it. If the therapist, out of his own

175

problems, is unable to recognize what has developed, disasterous things can occur. In a number of instances this happens when the therapist, because of his own narcissistic needs, accepts the patient's highly erotized transference as representing a genuine falling in love with him. In some cases the therapist actually has divorced his wife and married the patient out of the idea that at last he has found someone who really loves him and cares for him. I am not sure whether this is a more disasterous termination to a therapy than one in which the therapist has resolutely refused to notice that the patient is declaring an undying love for him, until one day the therapist discovers that the patient has bought a house right next to his, has moved in, and is monitoring the therapist's every move—practically living on the therapist's doorstep.

How disasterous acting out can be in psychotherapy if it is not properly recognized! Even after the therapist has become aware of the dangers of gross acting out, a far more subtle variation can occur that has been given the title of acting in by Zeligs (1957). He describes acting in as, "a middle phase in a genetic continuum in which acting out, *without verbalizing or remembering,* is at one end—acting in lying somewhere in between—and verbalizing and remembering without *action* is at the end. Acting in is a compromise phase between id impulse and ego defense."

Zeligs concentrates mainly on postural acts and other kinds of body movements on the couch, but it should be pointed out that postural acting in is only one form of acting in. It should be clear that remembering and verbalizing are closest to secondary process behavior and represent the dominance of the ego over the id. Postural acting in or any kind

176

of an acting in is a sort of compromise between secondary-process behavior and primary-process behavior; the latter would be represented by gross acting out.

Acting in is much more subtle, and it is *very* important that the therapist r cognize it. Besides the various postural and body movements that the patient shows, acting in may be understood as behavior by the patient in psychotherapy that represents manifestations of the patient's conflicts that are not at the same time presented in remembering and verbalizing. I shall give some examples of acting in very shortly, but I would like to comment first on the fact that acting in *by the therapist* is an equally important and dangerous matter. Most therapists do not grossly act out in psychotherapy with their patients. When that happens it is usually easy to recognize and disasterous consequences occur rather rapidly. But it is far more widespread to find acting in by the therapist.

One of the most typical types of acting in we see in the neophyte is the need to mother and feed the patient. This may arise out of the countertransference problem the therapist has to the patient himself or may represent a neurotic character problem of the therapist. At any rate, it is most important to understand that any kind of acting in by the therapist, whether it be a subtle maternal, loving, overly gratifying type, a sexual or erotic type, or a hostile type, works in an antitherapeutic direction and tends to encourage gross acting out by the patient.

It is perfectly possible for the patient and therapist to be having a verbal exchange and to seem to be discussing the material of the psychotherapy, while at the very same time significant acting in is taking place. Usually in gross

177

acting out it is almost impossible to maintain the facade that psychotherapy is going on at the same time, unless an actually delusional presentation is made to the patient: for example, stating that having intercourse with the patient is for the benefit of the therapy. Most patients are not so psychotic as to go along with this kind of gross acting out. On the other hand, most patients will eagerly lap up acting-in behavior. Furthermore, it should not be conceived that only one or the other of these various types of acting out occur at a time. Much more typically, we see a whole variety of resistances working at once, and it is often very difficult to separate out one from the other. It can only be done in a theoretical fashion. To illustrate, I would like briefly and sketchily to describe a case from my own practice in which five varieties of resistances appeared rather quickly within the first year of therapy of a borderline patient.

Genevieve, a thirty-year-old nurse, came from an incredibly unhappy childhood, where the mother was extremely cold, rigid, and superreligious and the father was an alcoholic, subject to tempers in which he beat the mother and the children. During his alcoholic binges, he would pursue them all over the house until he found them in their hiding places. Then he would beat them. Essentially, the patient had no object relationships with anybody at the time she came into treatment, but she expressed a strong wish to begin forming relationships with people and to overcome her illness. The first defense that appeared was in the variety of ways in which she attempted to manipulate the premature termination of therapy. Either she felt she did not want to come or she felt that perhaps she was being cheated in the therapy. She talked over the therapy with other doctors at the hospital where she worked; she collected all kinds of objections to psychiatry and psychotherapy from these doctors; and finally when we had worked through all of these, she discovered that she could not afford psychotherapy. She then attempted to change jobs and found a position in which she could not get the time off for psychotherapy.

Accompanying all this were frequent bouts during the psychotherapy, and especially before and after the sessions, in which she would be angry and curse herself. This could be thought of as a form of resistance by the displacement of the hostility in the transference. It was also a way of discharging the positive affects by turning them into their opposite and discharging them on herself, rather than in the therapy and on me in the transference.

Interpretation and working through of this led to some hysterical feelings about sexuality. The patient had many dreams and fantasies of sexuality involving torture and dismemberment, cruelty and sadism, although she could not recover any memories in her childhood in which she experienced parental sexuality or any kind of sexuality in this fashion. Her thoughts and dreams read like concentration camp experiences and certain types of pornographic novels in which sex and sadism are constantly put together. I felt that this was again a form of resistance to her own sexual impulses by hysterically overemphasizing and overdramatizing the sadistic aspects of sexuality in an attempt to make the whole subject of sexuality look as horrible as possible and thus create reasons for powerful repression.

Simultaneously, the patient took part in some gross acting out. She got some dates with boyfriends, apparently gave them the impression that she was interested in sexual relations, invited them into her apartment, and then, when they attempted to make a pass at her, suddenly became horrified. The relationship was dramatically transformed from a seductive one between her and the boyfriend into a wrestling match in which the man was shocked, felt like a rapist, apologized profusely, and left. This acting out, besides serving as a disguised expression of her sexuality, contained another way of reassuring herself of the horror of sexuality, the danger and untrustworthiness of men, and so forth.

Besides this gross acting out, much more subtle forms of acting in took place in the psychotherapy of great theoretical interest. The patient manifested considerable silence, and she finally gave away the meaning of this by saying that she felt herself making an effort to keep anything from coming to her mind because she did not want to let anything out. It suddenly became clear that the patient was acting in a toilet training situation, in which she was hiding something from the hated father. This led to interesting memories from childhood, when the father would barge in drunk while she was sitting on the toilet, tear her off the pot, and use the toilet himself. Her hatred of him for this was expressed in childhood by her refusing to use the toilet, refusing to go when the parents wanted her to go, and going in the bushes outside of the house instead. Here was a subtle form of acting in as we have described it, which, when interpreted, resulted in the recovery of certain memories about her relationship with her father. The purpose of this brief case presentation is to show the extreme complexity and the variety of acting-out and acting-in defenses that can appear often in one chaotic bundle during the course of a psychotherapy and that must be recognized and interpreted.

180

This kind of complex combination of acting out, acting in, and a variety of other resistances can prove lethal to a psychotherapy, if it is not thoroughly understood. Another combination of these factors is especially evident today in patients who suffer from so-called existential despair. This type of patient—suffering from a combination of projecting and acting out that we call "externalization"—maintains his own level of despair and defeats his life and the psychotherapy.

In order to understand this lethal combination of circumstances better, let me begin with a review of Winnicott's (1958, 1965) notion of "maternal function." Winnicott points out that the function of the "good-enough mother" in the early phases of life can be boiled down to *holding, handling,* and *object presenting.* He writes (1965),

> Holding is very much related to the mother's capacity to identify with her infant. Satisfactory holding is a basic ration of care, only experienced in the reactions to faulty holding. Faulty holding produces an extreme distress in the infant, giving a basis for:
>
>> the sense of going to pieces,
>> the sense of falling forever,
>> the feeling that external reality cannot be used for reassurance, and other anxieties that are usually described as "psychotic."

Winnicott also points out that handling facilitates the formation of a psychosomatic partnership in the infant. This contributes to the sense of "real" as opposed to "unreal." "Faulty handling militates against the development of muscle

181

tone, and that which is called 'coordination', and against the capacity of the infant to enjoy the experience of body functioning, and of BEING." Object presenting is also important, in that faulty object presenting blocks the way for the development of the "infant's capacity to feel real in relating to the actual world of objects and phenomena." In addition, Winnicott feels that the development is a matter of maturational process, the accumulation of living experiences, and must take place in a "facilitating environment."

Winnicott has a tendency to write in a very terse style, and it is necessary to reread his phrases again and again to get a real appreciation of the depth of his experience and understanding. From his point of view, with which I entirely agree, defective holding and defective handling of the infant in the early stages of development will produce extreme distress, which results later on in a profound sense of unreality, the inability to have a sense of identity, disturbances of body functioning, and a lack of the experience of being— a concept that philosophers recently have written a great deal about. He points out (1965) that, "Young people can be seen searching for a form of identification which does not let them down in their struggle, *the struggle to feel real*, the struggle to establish a personal identity, not to fit into an assigned role, but to go through whatever has to be gone through."

Beginning with selected aspects of the unconscious phenomena that result as a consequence of defective maternal functioning or defective holding and handling in infancy, let me review briefly Freud's famous concept of the repetition compulsion. This consists of the tendency in waking life, to relive—dramatize, restage—in different settings an earlier emotional experience, relationship, or atmosphere that has made a deep impression, or in dream life to reenact it with often much the same setting. Healy *et al.* (1930) point out that Freud found in the transference neurosis phenomenon his main argument for postulating the existence of a repetition-compulsion principle in psychic life. Thus the repetition compulsion is based primarily on clinical data from psycho-analytic psychotherapy, and it is not simply a metaphysical presupposition.

The same authors review Franz Alexander's concept of the repetition compulsion as founded on "the principle of inertia." This "inertia"—which could be defined as the avoidance of change and active psychic effort—and its replacement by automatism "seems to be the fundamental fact underlying all biological processes."

The universal tendency to repeat earlier, often unpleasant or even disastrous emotional experiences, usually involving one or the other of the parents, is a remarkable clinical fact that is illustrated again and again in the practice of intensive psychotherapy. The main demonstration of the repetition compulsion in psychotherapy occurs in the classic transference neurosis. But experience with borderline patients has called the attention of clinicians to another related and dramatic aspect of the repetition compulsion as it appears both in the psychotherapy situation and in the patient's general relationships to other people. This is called externalization.

Credit for coining the term *externalization* is usually given to Anna Freud (1965). She describes externalization as a subspecies of transference and separates it from the transference. In her description of externalization in adults she depicts, for example, severe obsessional neurotics staging quarrels between themselves and their analysts about minor matters in order to escape from inward indecisions caused by ambivalence. As another example she writes, "In the analysis of drug addicts, the analyst represents at the same time or in quick alternation either the object of the craving, i.e. the drug itself, or an auxiliary ego called upon to help him to fight against the drug." Her main experience with externalization is, of course, in the analysis of children, and she sees externalization in child analysis as a process in which the person of the analyst is used to represent some part of the patient's personality structure.

The concept of externalization was clarified with respect to the psychotherapy of borderline patients suffering from deep narcissistic problems in a paper by Brodey (1965). Brodey points out that in his experience with family units, externalization appeared as a mechanism of defense defined by the following characteristics:

1. Projection is combined with the manipulation of reality selected for the purpose of verifying the projection.

2. The reality that cannot be used to verify the projection is not perceived.

3. Information known by the externalizing person is not transmitted to others, except as it is useful to train or manipulate them into validating what will then become the realization of the projection. In other words, externalization makes possible

a way of life based on relationships with unseparated but distant aspects of the self. What is perceived as reality is an *as-if*

184

reality, a projection of inner expectation. The senses are trained to validate; the intense searching for what is expected dominates and enforces validation. It is difficult not to validate an unquestionable conclusion. Each validation makes the conclusion even less questionable. The restricted reality perceived is experienced as if it were the total world.

The psychotherapist senses the intensity of his patient's effort to manipulate him into validating projections. He experiences conflict as he struggles against this manipulation, but behavior that will be used as validation seems the only way to gain a relationship with the patient.

Thus, the manipulation of the therapist into behavior that is symmetrical with the projection is different from the simple transfer of feelings to a therapist. "Even if the therapist does not wish to conform, he still finds himself conforming to the narcissistic image. For no matter what he does, pieces of the therapist's actual behavior irrelevant to the therapist's self-identity are seized on by the patient, to whom they are predominant *as-if* characteristics. The identity that the patient sees may be unknown to the therapist (although it holds a kernel of truth which usually is disturbing to the therapist)." Even the therapist's active denial of the patient's presumption is used by the patient in the service of proving to the patient that the therapist is actually congruent with his projective image.

Brodey points out that the therapist of the ego-disturbed patient must become skilled at managing his congruence with the patient's projected image. This management is often intuitive and emotionally demanding. "Being a distorted object is much easier than being nonexistent."

185

Fundamentally, externalization is a combination of projection followed by selective perception and manipulation of other people for the purpose of verifying the initial projection. Other people are experienced wholly in terms of their value in verifying the initial projection. Only those aspects of other people that have this value are perceived at all. Thus, the most benign therapist approaching the borderline patient finds himself quickly transformed into a horrible monster by the patient's selective perception. Unless he is aware of this danger, he is inclined either to retaliate or quarrel with the patient's extremely unflattering image of him. This image, however, usually contains a kernel of truth. Hence, it functions as a direct assault on the therapist's narcissistic conception of himself as a benevolent physician.

Giovacchini (1967a) has carried the concept of frustration and externalization even further. He discusses that type of behavior that is intended to be defensive but is paradoxically self-defeating. This kind of behavior is usually the result of externalization and must be distinguished from self-defeating behavior resulting from a breakdown of the personality. Patients of this nature cannot cope with a warm and nonthreatening environment. "They react to a benign situation as if it were beyond their level of comprehension. These patients do not have the adjustive techniques to interact with a reasonable environment. Their formative years were irrational and violent. They internalize this chaos, and their inner excitement clashes with their surroundings. When the world becomes benign and generous, the patient withdraws in panic and confusion." Giovacchini points out that the patient expects and brings about his failure and adapts himself to life by feeling beaten in an unpredictable and ungiving world. He distinguishes this from a masochistic adjustment and points out the relationship of externalization to the repetition compulsion, upon which it is based.

Thus when the therapist presents this kind of patient with a consistently benign environment—which Winnicott (1958) has described as parallel to the healthy maternal environment—the patient cannot trust the lack of frustration. Instead of risking the inevitable disappointment that he expects, the patient prefers relating "in a setting in which he has learned to adjust. If the analyst does not frustrate him the patient's psychic balance is upset. To reinstitute ego equilibrium the patient attempts to make the analyst representative of the world that is familiar to him."

Externalization is not simply a projection of internal aspects of the personality onto the therapist. It also contains a mode of adaptation or adjustment that makes interaction between the ego and the outer world possible. As Giovacchini points out, "Externalization provides the patient with a setting that enables him to use adjustive techniques that he has acquired during his early development.

Conversing with a patient who utilizes externalization as a significant ego defense and as a method of adaptation to a reality of which his experience is repeated failure gives us an insight into the concepts of existential anguish and subsequent existential despair. The credit for introducing the concept of existential anguish into Western thought belongs to Kierkegaard, although the concept itself is implicit in much earlier literature, such as the Book of Job. Kierkegaard (1946), however, based his entire philosophical inquiry on the concept of existential anguish and made it central to modern thinking.

187

A distinction must be made here between anxiety as it is used in the clinical, psychotherapeutic sense and the "anxiety" or "dread" that Kierkegaard * speaks of, which I call existential anguish. The technical meaning of the two terms is really rather different, and it confuses matters considerably to include both under the term *anxiety*. May (1950) and others have reviewed Kierkegaard's concept, and I will not spend much time on the subject. It is sufficient to point out that Kierkegaard also views existential anguish developmentally, beginning with the original state of the child. He does not, in my opinion, however, really pin down the source of existential anguish, since he considers it to be a universal condition related to freedom and the possibilities of human decisions and choices.

Kierkegaard and many philosophers who followed him have overemphasized the importance of existential anguish in the life of the ordinary human being (Chessick, 1969). However, existential anguish unquestionably becomes an important concept in dealing with people who suffer from emotional difficulties. Investigation in psychotherapy repeatedly shows it to emerge as the consequence of disturbance in holding and handling in the early stages of infancy. This disturbance can leave the individual, as Winnicott suggests, with a defective sense of being (see Chessick, 1973a), a preoccupation with the meaning of life, confusion over his own identity, and lack of a place in the panorama of human events. Together, these factors constitute existential anguish, and often a deep yearning for physical holding and caressing accompanies this condition.

* Kierkegaard's term *Angst* is usually translated as "dread," although May uses "anxiety." Unamuno rendered it as *agonie* and Sartre by *angoisse*.

Existential anguish, if prolonged, can lead to an increasing sense of hopelessness, despair, and meaninglessness of life. Kierkegaard gives an excellent description of his sense of "melancholy" in his journal (Jones, 1969). This "melancholy" is not to be confused with the psychiatric term and is better designated as existential despair.

> I feel so dull and so completely without joy, my soul is so dull and so completely without joy, my soul is so empty and void that I cannot even conceive what could satisfy it—oh, not even the blessedness of heaven.
> It is terrible when I think even for a single moment, over the dark background which, from the very earliest time, was part of my life. The dread with which my father filled my soul, his own frightful melancholy, and all the things in this connection which I do not even note down.
> From a child I was under the sway of prodigious melancholy, the depth of which finds its only adequate measure in the equally prodigious dexterity I possessed of hiding it under an apparent gayety and *joie de vivre*.

One of the most fascinating features of philosophers who are preoccupied with the concepts of existence and being is that their lives are so deeply intertwined with their philosophy. There are no better examples of this than the dramatic lives of Kierkegaard and Nietzsche. Both of these thinkers illustrate in different ways that combination of an unconscious need for the use of externalization as an adaptative defense and a conscious preoccupation with existential anguish and existential despair.

There is a self-reinforcing pattern in this type of situation. The person who is using externalization may often ex-

189

perience repeated failure in interpersonal relations and a sense of persecution, rejection, or abandonment by his fellows. Such a person will find ample evidence in his life for a morbid preoccupation with the meaninglessness of existence. His profound sense of despair and his deep inner need to find some way out of his dilemma—often manifested by agitated chaotic behavior—will make him perceive himself as trapped in a universal, existential agony. Without therapy, this type of person runs the risk of becoming an impulsive suicide. Even with therapy a certain percentage of patients, who have repeatedly experienced rejection, abandonment, and failure —which they attribute to a variety of external causes, from the wrath of God to a general human malevolence—reach a point where suicide seems preferable to continued suffering.

Aside from therapy and attempted suicide, there are often characteristic ways in which people suffering from existential despair can react. They may develop megalomania or become totally insane. More commonly, their despair may become chronic and be linked with a clinical depression that leads to permanent constriction of their creative potential. Self-destructive escapes such as drugs and alcohol are also frequent.

There are, however, possible constructive solutions to existential despair. Kierkegaard gives us a lead when he urges man to form a passionate commitment to a creed or ethic (Copleston, 1965). Indeed, his own despair, like Tolstoy's, led to a deep commitment to a personalized form of religion. Many psychotherapy patients, less remarkable in all ways than these notable men, similarly resolve their reality problems by passionate commitment to some cause, some philosophical or religious system. The best-known example of this is Breuer's patient Anna O., who became passionately committed to social work on the European continent.

From this discussion, the variety of difficulties that patients immersed in a combination of unconscious externalization and conscious suffering from extential despair can present become obvious. For those who are particularly interested I have gone into this subject more deeply in another publication (Chessick, 1972b).

CHAPTER 9   *Resistance and*
Interpretation

*N*O fully satisfactory classification of resistances exists in psychotherapeutic literature. The classification generally used was first presented by Freud (1926) in his book *Inhibitions, Symptoms and Anxiety*. He distinguished five kinds of resistance and classified them according to their source:

1. The resistance of repression (the resistance of the ego's defenses).

2. Resistance of the transference. "Since transference is a substitute for memory and is based on a displacement from past objects onto present objects, Freud classified this resistance too as derived from the ego" (Greenson, 1968).

3. The gain from illness, or secondary gain, also placed by Freud under ego resistance.

4. The repetition compulsion, (see Chapter 8) or what

192

Freud called the "adhesiveness of the libido"—a rather difficult phrase. He considered this resistance to stem from the id.

5. Those resistances that arise from unconscious guilt and a need for punishment. These, of course, originate in the superego.

One can find elements of almost all of these types of resistance in the resistance that one encounters clinically. Hence, the classification is not particularly helpful. Greenson (1968) has presented the problem in another way. What are the forces within the patient opposing the analytic processes and procedures?

(1) The unconscious ego's defensive maneuvers, which provide the models for the resistance operations. (2) The fear of change and the search for security, which impel the infantile ego to cling to the familiar neurotic patterns. (3) The irrational superego, which demands suffering in order to atone for unconscious guilt. (4) The hostile transference, which motivates the patient to defeat the psychoanalyst. (5) The sexual and romantic transference, which leads to jealousy and frustration and ultimately to a hostile transference. (6) Masochistic and sadistic impulses, which drive the patient to provoke a variety of painful pleasures. (7) Impulsivity and acting out tendencies, which impel the patient in the direction of quick gratifications and against insight. (8) The secondary gains from the neurotic illness, which tempt the patient to cling to his neurosis.

I think this is a clinically more useful classification of the forces of resistance and that any practicing therapist will be well advised to keep it in mind.

Another way to approach this problem, as Greenson also

193

suggests, is to divide resistances into ego-alien resistances and ego-syntonic resistances. The ego-alien resistances appear foreign, extraneous, and strange to the patient's reasonable ego, and, as a consequence, such resistances are relatively easy to recognize and to work with. The patient will readily form a working alliance with the therapist in his attempt to analyze such resistances. In contrast to this, the ego-syntonic resistances are characterized by their seeming familiarity, rationality, and purposefulness to the patient. He does not sense the resistance function of the activity under scrutiny. Such resistances are harder to recognize and more difficult to work with. Greenson (1968) feels that they usually represent well-established habitual patterns of behavior of the patient, and character traits, sometimes of social value. He places reaction formations, acting out, character resistances, counterphobic attitudes, and screen defenses in this category.

The working through of ego-syntonic resistances is difficult. Such resistances have first to be made ego-alien for the patient, before they can be dealt with. Thus, our task, writes Greenson (1968), "will be first to help the patient establish a reasonable ego in regard to the particular resistance. Only if this is accomplished will the resistance emerge as an ego-alien resistance. Then one can hope to attain a history of the particular resistance and analyze it. When the patient can understand the historical reasons for the origin of the resistance defense, he will be able to differentiate his past needs for that defense and the present inappropriateness of the defense."

What becomes clear from this material is that psychotherapy must always deal first with the patient's resistances, and only secondly with content. It is surprising how frequently this well-known shibboleth is violated by young therapists. It is often very tempting for narcissistic reasons to

194

do wild analysis—to reveal to the patient how brilliant the therapist's knowledge of content is. However, unless resistances are removed first, such interpretations of content will lead, at best, to nothing.

It is usual in therapy to begin by dealing with the ego-alien resistances. After the patient has been able to form a reliable working alliance, then it is possible to start working on ego-syntonic resistances. These ego-syntonic resistances are, of course, present from the beginning, but it is pointless to start by attacking them. The patient will simply deny their significance or merely give lip service to understanding.

The problem of dealing with resistance is the central problem of the technique of psychotherapy. *How* does one deal with resistances? What does one do? What did Freud say about the subject? In one of his earliest books (with Breuer), *Studies On Hysteria* (1893), written before the discovery of transference, Freud made his important basic statement about resistance and the process of psychotherapy.

> What means have we at our disposal for overcoming this continual resistance? Few, but they include almost all those by which one man can ordinarily exert a psychical influence on another. In the first place, we must reflect that psychical resistance, especially one that has been in force for a long time, can only be resolved slowly and by degrees, and we must wait patiently. In the next place, we may reckon on intellectual interest which the patient begins to feel after working for a short time. . . . But lastly—and this remains the strongest lever—we must endeavor, after we have discovered the motives for his defence, to deprive them of their value or even replace them by more powerful ones. . . . One works to the best of one's power as an elucidator (where ignorance has

195

given rise to fear), as a teacher, as the representative of a freer or superior view of the world, as a father confessor who gives absolution, as it were, by a continuance of his sympathy and respect after the confession has been made. One tries to give the patient human assistance, so far as this is allowed by the capacity of one's own personality and by the amount of sympathy that one can feel for the particular case.

There are a series of specific clinical procedures that are best used to approach the problem of resistance. The first thing the therapist must do is listen. If the therapist has the capacity to listen, and is not immersed in his own counter-transference problems, sooner or later he will recognize the particular resistances at hand. In the process of recognition he will engage in the two types of intervention that usually precede interpretation: clarification and confrontation. So the therapist listens, recognizes, and then shares the processes of clarification and confrontation with the patient.

Clarification focuses on conscious and preconscious mental processes. It is an intervention that presumes that the patient has access to the material, although he may not have expressed it for himself or have been fully aware of it. DeWald (1964) points out that clarification cannot be effective in those instances, "where the material is unconscious, since those processes are not available easily to the patient's conscious attention." He continues,

The purpose of clarification is to give the therapist a more clear and focused idea of what is being presented. However, at other times the therapist may have a reasonably complete understanding of the process, but he may feel that the patient needs more clearly to recognize what he is expressing. Some-

196

times this involves rephrasing of what the patient has already said, but from a slightly different point of view in order that it may become more clear or precise. At other times it may involve asking the patient himself to rephrase some idea, so that in the process of doing this the patient becomes more explicitly aware of what has been going on in his own mind. Such interventions by the therapist may also include a request for greater detail, for further elaboration or for the patient to fill in with material that he omitted or has partly expressed.

The next form of intervention is confrontation, by which the therapist directs the patient's attention to something conscious or preconscious that has already been expressed but on which the patient's attention is not focused at the moment. "At times this involves pointing out similarities and differences in certain bodies of material, or showing the patient repetitive patterns derived from the experiences, feelings and thoughts already presented. It may involve calling the patient's attention to behavior or responses of which he can easily become conscious, or it may at times involve reminding the patient of previously expressed material or experience" (DeWald, 1964). In every instance confrontation involves directing the patient's attention to elements of experience or behavior observed in him by the therapist but without drawing any inferences as to the possible meanings *behind* them.

After the therapist has listened and recognized the resistances and followed through the processes of clarification and confrontation with the patient, he has prepared the atmosphere for interpretation. Interpretation, working through and after-education provide the major techniques by which resistances are dealt with and removed.

Before demonstrating a resistance to a patient, the ther-

197

apist should wait for it to recur several times. A typical be-ginner's mistake is to demonstrate resistance after just one instance, out of an eagerness to get the therapy moving. It is only often a resistance has presented itself repeatedly that it is possible to clarify and confront and get the patient to treat the resistance as ego-alien.

Sometimes the therapist must intervene in such a way as to actually increase the resistance and thus help it become demonstrable. An attempt is then made to clarify the "mo-tives and modes of resistance" (Greenson, 1968). We attempt to find out what specific painful affect is making the patient resistant, what particular instinctual impulses are causing the painful affect at this moment, and what precise mode and method the patient uses to express his resistance. This is followed by interpretation, in which we ask what fantasies or memories are causing the affects and impulses behind the resistance. We pursue both the history and unconscious pur-poses of these affects and the type or mode of resistance in order to see what similar modes have appeared in the patient's history. Finally, we investigate the unconscious purposes of this particular type of resistance.

Then we take part in a working-through process in which we repeat and elaborate these steps over and over again in various contexts. It should not be assumed that this is always a simple and methodical process. The therapist is often con-fronted with difficult decisions. Freud was aware of this. He pointed out that certain patients confront the therapist with difficult decisions regarding gratification in the transference. I have referred to this (Chessick, 1968) as the crucial dilemma that the therapist must face, at least in the treatment of borderline patients. When we ask the patient to become in-

198

volved in therapy with us, we automatically mobilize his deep anxieties regarding penetration and annihilation. Strange reactions occur (see, for example, Chessick, 1972a). Sometimes the patient becomes locked in a neurosis of abandonment, as described by Odier (1956). Sometimes the patient already suffers from this before coming to therapy, and the process of therapy, itself threatens those neurotic but vital binds that have been formed to protect him from unbearable anxiety. There is no time to work through this situation, and the maintenance of the therapy itself can be a touch-and-go problem from session to session. In such cases the therapist has to determine to what extent he must offer himself as a real object to the patient and at times even to intrude himself as a real object into the life of the patient. Obviously, the more we are dealing with psychotherapy and the less we are dealing with formal psychoanalysis, the more indications exist for such intrusion into the life of the patient.

It must be admitted that many patients cannot tolerate the abstinence and isolation that a formal psychoanalysis brings. They simply will not stay in therapy. Here is the perplexing situation as Freud (1905) conceived of it:

> No one who, like me, conjures up the most evil of those half-tamed demons that inhabit the human breast, and seeks to wrestle with them, can except to come through the struggle unscathed. Might I perhaps have kept the girl under my treatment, if I myself had acted a part, if I had exaggerated the importance to me of her staying on and had shown a warm personal interest in her—a course which even after allowing for my position as her physician, would have been tantamount to providing her with a substitute for the affection she longed for? I do not know. Since in every case a portion of the factors

199

that are encountered under the form of resistance remains unknown, I have always avoided acting a part, and have contented myself with practicing the humbler arts of psychology. In spite of every theoretical interest and of every endeavor to be of assistance as a physician, I keep the fact in mind that there must be some limits set to the extent to which psychological influence may be used, and I respect as one of these limits the patient's own will and understanding.

The dilemma of the proper proportion of gratification and abstinence in the transference is a serious one. It accounts for the many failures in psychotherapy with patients who simply cannot stand the abstinence demanded by the usual psychotherapy process. However, any therapist who makes a deliberate attempt to give some kind of gratification in the transference must be aware, above all, that he runs an extremely dangerous risk of countertransference acting out or acting in. Even assuming that he knows himself well and is taking part in such gratifications for purposes that are not neurotic—a highly questionable assumption—he must also be aware that *any form of primary-process gratification as an attempt to remove resistance* (or for any other rationalization) *inevitably has a counterproductive effect*. It tends to strengthen primary-process thinking and behavior in the patient, to fix the patient on the gratification and on primary-process behavior, and to move the patient away from the essence of psychotherapy. The aim of the therapeutic process —which is to get the patient to remember and to verbalize what is going on in his mind in order to understand himself, mature, and find an increased capacity for conflict-free ego functions—must never be forgotten. The pathetic experiences of Ferenczi near the end of his life, even when viewed sym-

200

pathetically (Balint, 1968), form a poignant demonstration of what happens when these principles are ignored.

INTERPRETATION

The tactical goal of an interpretation is to help the patient become consciously aware of the meaning of some element in his own mental life. Strategically, this involves the patient's recognizing mental contents that were previously unconscious and defended against. Interpretation, therefore, acts as a tool chiefly in an insight-directed treatment stiuation; it is less commonly used in supportive treatment. Only some of the highlights of the technique of interpretation can be brought out here. It is, after all, both a skill and a delicate art that develops gradually as the therapist's self-knowledge, clinical experience, and maturity increase.

Every other procedure prepares for interpertation, amplifies the intepretation, or makes an interpretation effective. To interpret is to make an unconscious or preconscious psychic event conscious, to give it meaning and causality. The reasonable and conscious ego is made aware of something it had been oblivious to. By interpretation the therapist makes the patient conscious of the history, source, mode, cause, or meaning of a given psychic event. This usually requires more than a single intervention. Hence, the need for working through.

The therapist must use his own conscious mind, empathy, intuition, and fantasy life, as well as his intellectual and theoretical knowledge, in arriving at an interpretation. By interpreting we go beyond what is understandable and observable by ordinary conscious and logical thinking, and the patient's responses are necessary in order to determine whether the interpretation is valid or not.

The fact that this technique of interpretation is partly an art is brought into sharper focus by French and Fromm (1964), who designate the language of the unconscious as an "evocative language. . . . It differs from the language of the artist only in the fact that its meaning has been disguised by the psychic censor." Since artists often take delight in disguising their meaning, this does not constitute an absolute difference. Dreams and other irrational products of the mind can express a patient's unconscious feelings and thoughts with a vividness and accuracy that a more technical language cannot even approximate. French and Fromm remind us that this kind of communication is what Freud had in mind when he compared the analyst's unconscious to a telephone receiver. The patient cannot describe or explain to the therapist what he is unconsciously feeling or fantasying. Nevertheless, the patient's words are able to evoke in the therapist an empathic sense of what is going on in his unconscious. This evocation in the therapist of feelings or fantasies associated to the patient's own unconscious is what Freud calls *resonance* between the therapist's unconscious and the patient's unconscious.

This evocative effect of the patient's words makes it possible for the therapist to "understand" the language of the unconscious. It follows that, at least to some extent, interpretation is an intuitive art. No claims are usually made for it as a rigorous scientific procedure. "Direct, intuitive interpretation is like understanding a foreign language," write French and Fromm (1964). "We cannot really understand another language by translating it word for word into a language with which we are familiar. We must first catch the spirit of the strange language, so that we can understand it directly."

Resonance is what is necessary to produce an empathic understanding: the spirit of the patient's unconscious is then caught by the therapist (see also Chessick, 1965). Empathic understanding, however, should be based on some evidence. Since we usually do not stop to think how we arrive at a direct intuitive interpretation—and sometimes don't even know on what evidence or impressions we have based such interpretations—direct intuitive interpretations are very difficult to check and can be erroneous. Thus, French and Fromm suggest that interpretations be double-checked and the evidence and reasoning on which they are based be conscientiously examined. Often initial and intuitive impressions are based on only part of the evidence. In such cases the therapist should check whether the rest of the evidence supports his interpretation. Our initial intuitive interpretation may appear to be in conflict with part of the evidence, and, if so, we should revise our initial interpretation or look for a better one to replace it.

All successful interpretaton is based on adequate listening. The psychotherapist must be able to listen. If he cannot listen in every sense of the word, he cannot possibly arrive at correct interpretations, DeWald (1964) approaches this subject by discussing the therapist's activity in listening, which is, of course, a good deal more than a passive recording of the material verbalized by the patient. The therapist takes note of the pattern and the sequence of the material presented, the "temporal juxtaposition" of the material. He takes note of material that has been omitted by the patient. He tries to observe, while listening, his own personal reactions to the patient and to the patient's material. He uses himself as an exploring instrument, on the basis that his own personal reactions to the patient may indicate some of the effects that the patient produces in other people with whom he interacts. This gives the therapist a better understanding of the patient's interrelationship to his environment outside of the treatment.

In many ways the therapist has to use himself as a stethoscope. At the same time, he has to adopt an attitude of "evenly-suspended attention" (Freud, 1912), in which he doesn't limit himself to specific ideas, thoughts, or feelings produced by the patient at that particular moment but rather attempts to let his thoughts and associations range freely over the material. As he listens and observes, he may be reminded at times of similar phenomena—general patterns or particular instances of human behavior and experience—that he has encountered in himself or others. This may enable him to bring in new ideas and new understanding of the material that would not be noted if he adhered to rigid listening and recording of the exact data from the patient.

It follows that the skilled therapist must have a superior capacity to listen with an evenly suspended attention. A certain lack of rigidity, a sensitivity and empathy with the patient as he presents his thoughts and describes his experiences are necessary. This empathy involves the therapist in making a partial and transient identification with the patient, putting himself into the patient's shoes (Chessick, 1965). If the therapist does not have the capacity to listen with evenly suspended attention or to empathize with the patient—or, in more technical terms, to regress in the service of the ego and oscillate back and forth between such a regression and the secondary-process capacities of putting the information received in this regression into terminology that can then be expressed to the patient—the therapist will fail.

The material presented by the patient produces in the therapist an empathic identification and understanding. Then the therapist must rationally understand and organize the material in a way that makes it comprehensible to the patient. The therapist must also decide how and when to present what he has understood to the patient. For example, if the therapeutic session is almost over, it may be tactically wiser to wait for another time, since the end of a session is not the best time to present the patient with new ideas.

It is clear from this that listening, in a therapeutic sense, is an extremely active process. It occurs silently within the therapist and permits him fully to observe the patient's behavior, as well as his own association and emotional responses to the material presented by the patient. DeWald (1964) points out that the therapist,

> induces in himself a partial regression in the service of the ego, thereby searching for connections, associations, meanings and an empathic understanding through a partial and reversible identification with the patient. Having arrived at such an understanding the therapist then reverses his own regressive ego processes, and returns to the objective position and secondary process thought of a therapist interacting with a patient. He then evaluates and organizes the understanding so achieved in the light of his overall theoretical and clinical knowledge and also in the light of the strategy and immediate tactics of the particular treatment process. How such understanding and awareness are used by the therapist is a function of the therapeutic strategy and goals.

Another way of approaching the problem of the taxing and difficult procedure of listening is to attempt to set out a series of rules that the therapist can use to help himself in understanding unconscious material. Saul (1958) gives

205

a series of such rules that I have found very useful in my own clinical work and teaching. I would like to paraphrase and expand these:

1. Keep very close to the material; do not introduce your own associations, do not swing wide and far away from the material in your ideas about it.

2. Look for the big major central themes first, what Saul calls the "headlines," as compared with the subsidiary themes and the details.

3. Keep to the level of consciousness of the material. Do not mix levels. This is extremely important in the art of interpretation. If a patient is dealing with material in the area of resistance it is very important to keep interpretation in the area of resistance and not interpret content when the patient isn't ready for it. Or, if the patient is presenting deep, pregenital, unconscious material in sexual genital form, it is important not to make probing interpretations of the pregenital material before the patient is ready for it. This is a common example of wild analysis and is a grave mistake because it simply mobilizes defenses.

4. Distinguish dynamics from content. No matter how unintelligible associations and dreams may be, at least the main topics and tendencies, the emotional forces, and something of their interplay are usually discernible. If the therapist finds himself throughout even a single session totally lost and with no understanding of the material at all, this represents either a lack of training or a countertransference problem or both. The only solution is consultation. For a therapist of any integrity this will come as a command, self-instigated. In general, there are far too few consultations. Many disasters could be avoided by this simple device.

206

5. Keep separate what is current in the present life situation from the transference and from the past or childhood. It is important to get these aspects clearly differentiated in our thinking about the material the patient presents to us.

6. Be alert to the effects on the material of current stimuli in the patient's life and also from the transference. In psychotherapy one always has to keep a sharp eye on what is going on in the reality situation of the patient at any given time. Ignoring the reality situation soon makes of therapy a sterile intellectual process that gets nowhere and usually causes the patient to feel rejected and, correctly, misunderstood.

7. Review the material both in terms of the libidinal motivations directed towards self and others and the hostile motivations. Look for manifestations of fight and flight. Try to understand material in terms of the ego, id, and the superego, rather than emphasizing any one of these three realms of mental functioning and ignoring the others. All material contains ego motivations and sexual as well as aggressive motivations.

8. Pay close attention to the *sequence* of associations and dream elements. The beginning of the hour often expresses the theme of the hour; the end of a dream represents solutions, or lack of them, to conflicts.

9. In the study of the hours, watch for those associations and that material connected with the greatest emotional response and just what the affects are. One of the ways to avoid getting bogged down in a great deal of apparently incomprehensible patient material is to concentrate on those areas of the material that seem to be associated with the most feeling and those that seem to be associated with the least feeling. Sometimes the patient isolates the material from the affect,

207

and material that seems to be presented in the coldest and least feeling manner can be the most important, if the therapist is alert.

10. Look for the positive progressive forces in the patient as well as the regressive ones. In our eagerness to understand unconscious material, we sometimes forget that the patient is changing and improving. We lose sight of the fact that the patient has within him a progressive force toward health and this can also be influencing the material and communications we are receiving.

11. Study the interpersonal relations of the patient for his object relations—persons whom he loves, hates, is dependent on, and so on—and for identifications and projections. This is obviously very important.

12. Finally, be very cautious about interpreting symbols, slips, errors, and so on, on an *ex cathedra* basis. Look for what the patient himself accepts and acts upon in the material. Saul calls this "a prognostic guide" to what the person is really capable of accepting and acting on in real life. One of the most common beginner's errors is to attempt to impress the patient or bowl the patient over by wild *ex cathedra* analysis of slips of the tongue, errors, or dream symbols. This almost invariably has a paradoxical effect, and represents a countertransference problem in the therapist.

Alexander (1956) points out that the supreme requirement for the correct handling of interpretations, more important than any principles or rules, is the precise understanding in detail of what is going on at every moment in the patient. If we have this precise understanding, then in analytic therapy our main allies are the striving of unconscious forces for expression and the integrating tendency of the conscious ego.

208

Alexander points out that even if we do nothing else but not interfere with these two forces, we will be able to help many patients.

He describes the "total interpretation." We should, if possible, make our interpretations total or approaching totality when we can: "Interpretations which connect the *actual life situation* with *past experiences* and with the *transference situation*—since the latter is always the axis around which such connections can best be made—are called *total interpretations*. The more that interpretations approximate this principle of totality, the more they fulfill their double purpose: they accelerate the assimilation of new material by the ego and mobilize further unconscious material."

There are certain factors that can be kept in mind that will help one in developing the art of interpretation. First of all, the patient must be ready to receive an interpretation, and there must be preparation for interpretation by the understanding of unconscious material. I have already discussed this. Then, interpretation should be as total as possible, and it should refer to major emotional forces and not bog down in too many intricate masses of detail. Interpretation should be realistic and in the clear, simple, and everyday language of the patient. It should never be wild. It should be presented in a matter-of-fact way, in a friendly and practical manner, and should be brought out almost casually so that the patient can accept and think about it without feeling put upon or forced into a situation where something is being rammed down his throat.

Correct interpretations obviously also help the therapeutic alliance. They assume an ability on the therapist's part to understand accurately the patient's unconscious and the

209

central emotional forces in the material at hand. The correct interpretation is based on a great deal of evidence, focuses on main issues and not side issues; is presented in a direct, non-technical fashion, and is narrowed down to the presenting material. The therapist should wait until he has enough material and information so that the patient is almost making the interpretation by himself. The only exceptions to this are emergency situations where the therapist feels that the whole therapy is in danger unless some form of resistance is stopped. He may then have to interpret widely and deeply in an attempt to put a stop to therapy-threatening or even life-threatening behavior, for example, in the emergency psychotherapy of depression (Bychowski and Despart, 1961).

No discussion of interpretation would be complete without discussion of the inexact interpretation. This concept was formalized by Glover (1955). He distinguished between the "incomplete" and "inexact" interpretation. An incomplete interpretation is simply a step in technique in which the therapist gets the patient to move closer to the unconscious material, but the interpretation is not total. It is based on lack of sufficient clinical material and problems with resistance.

An inexact interpretation has a different purpose, although at a given moment it might on the surface seem to be the same. An inexact interpretation is deliberately offered as providing a definitive meaning to a certain arrangement of material, a meaning that, in the unstated opinion of the therapist, actually falls short of the truth. The therapist has judged that the complete truth would be dangerous or intolerable to the patient. The patient seizes the inexact interpretation eagerly, because it helps him to continue to repress the truth. He can turn his back on the truth and, with the newly offered

210

belief, form a new symptom. The process at work here is, effectively, one of displacement. It is fostered by the therapist to bolster the patient's defences when uncovering psychotherapy is contraindicated.

Tarachow (1963) has discussed this in some detail. It also is important, he notes, for the therapist to realize the difference between an inexact interpretation and a wrong interpretation. An inexact interpretation is deliberately handed to a patient to enable the patient to shore up his ego structure and to maintain stability of his defenses. A wrong interpretation is simply a mistake by the therapist that the patient eagerly jumps upon to shore up the forces of resistance. This will generally cause some difficulty in the progress of the therapy, unless the therapist is alert to the patient's responses and realizes that he has made a mistake.

The best test of an interpretation is in the response that it receives from a patient. If the interpretation is utilized in making a psychic change—such as the removal of a resistance or in the service of improved life adaptation—it is meaningful and useful. It is obvious that an important measure of the therapist's success in the technique and practice of psychotherapy is in his capacity to produce meaningful and useful interpretations. This capacity is partly intuitive and partly developed by study and clinical experience. Above all, it is enhanced by the personal integrity of the therapist, his genuine dedication to understanding himself and the patient.

CHAPTER 10 *Dreams*

*B*ONINE'S book (1962) on dreams opens with a quotation from the Talmud: "A dream which is not explained is like a letter which has not been read." However, there is a surprising paucity of material about dreams and dream interpretation in the standard textbooks on psychotherapy. Little teaching is done in the subject within ordinary training programs for psychotherapists. Only the psychoanalytic institutes delve into the subject in detail. Nevertheless, a tremendous amount of published material on dreams can be brought together in a way that would be understandable and useful to the psychotherapist.

Dreams are the royal road not only to the unconscious, as Freud said, but to an understanding of the psychotherapy process and also to an understanding of the psychotherapist!

They are vital to an evaluation of the psychotherapist: a key to how well he is doing and what his countertransference problems are in any given psychotherapy.

I will not engage in any theoretical discussion on the meaning of dreams here. There is no substitute for Freud's magnificent book on *The Interpretation of Dreams* (1900) and his series of lectures, constituting Part II of *Introductory Lectures on Psychoanalysis* (1915a). These works of Freud, and a study of dreams should form an important part of the curriculum in any psychotherapy training program.

Special attention, however, must be given here to the problem of dream interpretation, since there is not much agreement on how dreams should be handled in psychotherapy. Some therapists avoid them altogether, while others seem to be so fascinated by them that their patients feed them endless streams of dreams. The decision about what to do with a patient's dream in psychotherapy must be tailored to the patient and the nature of the treatment siuation. There can be no easy generalizations on this subject. The therapist has to make a judgment as to what he will do with dreams just as about what kind of interpretations he will offer to the patient and whether they will be exact or inexact.

Some patients bring in very few dreams, and some bring in many dreams indeed. A general rule of thumb is to focus more on dreams when they occur few and far between and focus away from them when they occur in great abundance. One should always ask the patient to tell one or two of his dreams, as well as recount his earliest memories, at the beginning of every psychotherapy. It is part of the initial history. Taken together with carefully assembled historical material, the initial dreams and the earliest memories should almost always enable one to construct an initial genetic dynamic formulation of the patient. This is formulated as an hypothesis in one's mind and is of infinitely more value in psychotherapy than a formal diagnosis.

Some authors advocate passing this initial genetic–dynamic picture over to the patient, but I think this is a great mistake and can cause difficulty in the therapeutic alliance. The initial dynamic formulation, in my opinion, should be used as a *working hypothesis* for the therapist in evaluating and pursuing material. It should always be subject to change, depending on the material that emerges. The therapist, when the patient presents dreams, should try, after eliciting associations carefully, to fit the dreams into the genetic–dynamic formulation he has already made and if necessary alter this formulation. In discussion with the patient he should try to concentrate on the relationship of the dream to what is being discussed in therapy at that time. Dream interpretation follows the rules I have mentioned for all interpretations: It must be kept in the focus of the therapy at the time and at the level of therapy. It is absolutely mandatory to avoid clichés and wild symbol interpretation and to stay away from textbook language and attempts to impress the patient with one's brilliance. This always backfires.

Probably the earliest classic on dream analysis in the Freudian tradition is Sharpe's (1951) book that deals with the formation and interpretation of dreams in clinical practice. This work is of considerable historical interest. Chapter VIII in it refers to changes in the technique of dream interpretation that have come about with the evolution of psychotherapy. Dream interpretation has shifted from analyzing dreams as simply manifestations of infantile sexual wishes, to analyzing dreams in terms of understanding the status of ego function. Sharpe also describes dreams illustrating the progress being made in the therapy. She makes deductions concerning psychic change over a period of therapy and presents dreams indicating sexual development, indicating modification of the superego, and indicating the patient's ability to deal effectively with his psychic problems.

This trend is brought to fruition in a newer book by French and Fromm (1964). Their approach is a controversial one. They believe that the dream, like the dreamer's waking behavior, has a cognitive structure. The purpose of interpretation is to get an increasingly comprehensive grasp of this structure, which is a constellation of related problems, usually involved with fitting into interpersonal groups or pairs. Identifying these problems is made more difficult by the defensive dream work. Sometimes the therapist cannot find the problem in the dream, only a wish. When he finds out why the dreamer reacted against the wish, he may identify the problem. Once one problem is found, a constellation of related problems may be reconstructed and a focal conflict identified and traced to its sources in the patient's past.

Dream interpretation has shifted (along with psychotherapy in general) from a simple reading of the unconscious, an attempt to find infantile wishes, to an attempt to understand the patient's problem-solving processes or ego functions: "By focusing our interest on the ego's problem of protecting itself against premature commitment to disturbing conflicts, we have brought the dreamer's defenses into much simpler and more intelligible relationship to the problem-solving function of the dreamer's ego" (French and Fromm, 1964).

The important question is obviously *how* to go about spotting these problem-solving functions or, in general, how to understand unconscious material. This brings us back to the whole subject of developing the art of interpretation. It is obvious that the crux of the problem is in developing a therapist who is capable of an empathic, imaginative, and intuitive grasp of the language of the unconscious (see Chessick, 1971a). French and Fromm are rather vague in this particular area.

If I had to recommend one book on the subject of the dream besides Freud's (1915a) *Introductory Lectures on Psychoanalysis* or his *Interpretation of Dreams* (1900) I would recommend the book by Altman (1969). In the first part of his book Altman reviews the sources of the dream, dream work, symbols, and so forth. In the second part he brings up various important aspects of the dream in clinical practice: for example, the problem of the initial dreams in therapy.

I have already mentioned that initial dreams are central in early genetic–dynamic formulations, but it is also important not to make premature interpretations of initial dreams. This merely fortifies anxiety and multiplies defenses; vigorous interpretation of a dream presented early in therapy may interfere with the therapeutic alliance and the formation of the therapeutic alliance must precede any successful interpretation. In many ways the first dream expresses the patient's central problem in a nutshell (Fromm-Reichmann, 1950), and after the therapist has become acquainted with the dreamer and the genetics and dynamics of his difficulties, the therapist then may be able to make sense of the initial dream in a new and significant way.

Altman points out that clinically we see dreams as expressing resistance, as well as transference, anxiety, suppression, and infantile sexuality. Dreams can also be an expression of how the ego is functioning and of what progress is being made in the therapy. Thus, the dreams that the patient presents—if these are not presented for the purpose of resistance or if they are not primarily resistance dreams—provide a road to understanding what is going on in the patient, how the patient is functioning, what is going on in the therapy, and sometimes even what is going on in the therapist. That is why I wish to emphasize the importance of understanding dreams in intensive psychotherapy.

In clinical practice our choice of interpretation of dreams is based on the context in which the dream is given. When we single out one element of the dream to interpret among many we select, writes Altman (1969) "according to the relative weight and balance of the contents of the patient's mind, preconscious against unconscious, past against present, defense against drive (erotic as against aggressive). We select for emphasis that which will have the most meaning for the patient at that moment."

It is rare in psychotherapy to attempt to make as exhaustive an analysis of a patient's dream as is frequently done in classical psychoanalysis. We certainly attempt to do this in our own minds as the patient presents his dream along with the associations connected with the dream. But in interpreting dreams in psychotherapy it is almost invariable that we select out certain elements that seem relevant to what Saul calls "the red thread" or the focus of the material at the time in therapy. Sometimes we may go back to a dream later in therapy and pull out other elements that attain significance at a later time in therapy.

It is obvious that unconscious infantile drives are part of the motivating force if not *the* motivating force in dreams. These sexual drives and their derivatives, as well as the aggressive drives, constitute the very mainspring of the creation of a dream. Often in the patient's dreams we can quickly recognize sexual drive representations and be tempted to premature interpretation. In psychotherapy this should be avoided. A premature symbolic interpretation may be entirely unintelligible to the patient, and the therapy can degenerate into a debate between the patient and therapist as to the meaning of an umbrella in a dream. Obviously, this is senseless.

Dreams can provide the therapist with a reading of the progress of the patient's ego function. Often in psychotherapy there are no dramatic changes and shifts in the patient's equilibrium or in his symptoms or overt behavior. Usually growth and development of the ego and modifications in the superego are internal processes moving imperceptibly over extended periods of time without announcing their arrival. In some cases where certain kinds of defenses are used, the patient may show much more improvement outside of the therapy than inside of the therapy. In all of these situations dreams can be used to see where we are and what is going on. "Dreams often herald the growing capacity for the recognition of reality, for containment of impulse, and for the formation of fresh identifications. Their interpretation thereby gives us insight into the pending change of function brought about by the modification in the nature and distribution of unconscious forces through the psychotherapy before we see any changes in the clinical picture."

Altman (1969) points out that if you plot a graph of

activity for any therapy, the results show peaks and valleys and long plateaus. These long plateaus, difficult for the therapist, consume most of the graph, but it would be incorrect to interpret them as registering a total absence of development. In fact, these plateaus can be concerned as much with the internal processes of growth, integration, and intrapsychic realignment as with resistance. They are constructive and often understanding the dream material helps the therapist get over these long plateaus and keeps him in constant touch with the patient's intrapsychic forces. Dreams enable him to distinguish between a stalemate and a long period of working through in which changes are actually taking place. Thus, dreams are the key to understanding not only the unconscious material of the patient but the psychotherapy itself.

Another and different approach to dreams has been presented by Bonine (1962). Problems that in the classical approach would be dealt with as fundamentally sexual are treated by Bonine as aspects of the total personality. All dreams, all feelings in dreams, all dream symbols, sexual or otherwise, ultimately refer to aspects of the total personality functioning of the patient as it operates through the broad range of interpersonal relations. According to Bonine, the basic cause of anxiety in dreams or waking life is the feeling of impending failure of functioning in interpersonal relations. When this functioning is threatened, the sense of self is threatened. Sources of these anxieties are frequently brought into focus by dreams. In addition to that, they bring resistance behavior into focus. Patients may not recognize the existence or nature of the intensity of their resistance until they can identify it through dreams of resistance.

Thus, the appropriate interpretation of dreams requires the collaboration of patient and therapist. The dream role of the therapist, "reflects the patient's relationship with the analyst himself, not with the analyst as a surrogate for somebody else," according to Bonine.

This is a rather extreme view, but it has its usefulness in the clinical practice of psychotherapy. As a simple example, I might mention the case of a priest, who, after three years of psychotherapy and obviously in need of more treatment, was transferred to another country, forcing a premature termination of the treatment. The patient accepted the transfer without showing much feeling or complaint. He came rather passively to therapy and made considerable gains in his interpersonal relations, but he had meticulously kept from getting at his deeper problems involving sexual functioning. His passive acceptance of the transfer and termination of psychotherapy at the time it came up indicated a further attempt to keep repressed his obvious conflicts about sexual functioning. The patient refused to acknowledge any such difficulties, until nearly at the very end of the treatment he reported the following dream: "I was taking a bath naked in the river. It seemed all right but there was a thermometer there. I read the thermometer and it said that the water was hot and polluted. At that point I decided I better get out of the river and began worrying about the pollution."

The interpretation of this dream, as it was eventually presented to the patient after suitable associations were gathered, turned out to be one of the actual associations of the patient: "I am in hot water and I don't know it." This was a quite useful interpretation of the dream, because it indicated that the patient had unfinished business that he was leaving by the transfer. This kind of interpretation was rewarded a few days later when the patient came in horrified; he dreamed that he was having some kind of sexual relations with his sister. This led to discussion of the whole problem of the physical plan of the house in which he lived as a child, in which there was an atmosphere of great repression of any kind of sexuality and in which the patient indulged in a great deal of sexual peeking and secretive masturbation. This illustrates how the prematureness of a termination of therapy can be discovered by a patient through the proper interpretation and understanding of dreams.

The greatest source of help to understanding a dream is the patient's own associations to the dream. Before making any attempt to interpret a dream, the patient should be asked for his associations to the dream as a whole, to its various parts, and to the single items in it that seem to warrant special attention. The patient should then give his own viewpoint as to the meaning of the dream. Only when all that the patient has to offer is exhausted should the therapist step in with his attempts at interpretation.

It follows that a therapist must know the person whose dream he is to interpret and that he must be well acquainted with the person's history and life experience. The idea of interpreting dreams at a cocktail party or just "reading" a dream, through symbols, in order to show one's brilliance is utterly ridiculous. Furthermore, the therapist must know the reality setting in which the dreamer lives at the time of dreaming and presenting the dream. This holds true for all problems of interpretation. We must know as much as possible about the patient, about what is going on in the therapy at any given time, and, of course, we must have the capacity to

221

understand the language of the unconscious, if we are to be able to make any interpretations properly—especially interpretations of dreams.

Every psychotherapist must have techniques of evaluating any given psychotherapy, or even specific psychotherapy situations, by which he can understand what is going on and perhaps what has gone wrong. I will now discuss the use of dreams in understanding a psychotherapy and give a number of examples of dreams that have been very important in evaluating the psychotherapy of my patients.

A patient's dream may be viewed as a means of conveying information to the therapist that the patient has been unable to convey while he was awake. All implications of the doctor–patient relationship are reflected or represented in the dreams of the patient during treatment. Probably the most important type of dreams in this context is the dream in which a direct, uncensored representation of the therapist appears. According to Gitelson (1949) this may indicate the dreamer's realization of the therapist's countertransference difficulties. There are, of course, other possibilities.

In my experience the person of the therapist appearing in a patient's dream may represent a reaction to a wrong interpretation (which, of course, could be wrong due to the therapist's countertransference distortion). For example, if the patient dreams, after a session in which an interpretation has been made, that the therapist trips in the mud on his face, this can often be understood as the patient's way of telling the therapist he has made a blunder. Alternately, a dream of this kind can have a defensive or resistance function and protect the patient from dreaming about someone whom he is actually much more anxious or in conflict about. Such dreams are always important.

222

Fromm-Reichmann (1950) spends considerable time on the means of expression characteristic of dream processes. The dreamer, she points out, uses imagery rather than spoken words. For example, a writer finds himself faced with seemingly insuperable obstacles in the formulation of a difficult philosophical problem. He may express this experience in a dream by seeing himself on the bank of a wide river with swift currents that he must cross in order to complete a difficult journey. The dreamer may also express himself by symbols and pictures, and, as I have already pointed out, such material must be interpreted with great care by the therapist.

Even delusional material appears in dreams; smells are very important in this context. The language and logic of a dream may be irrational, regressive, and autistic. Dream material may be presented that is diametrically opposed to what is actually meant. Crowds may signify privacy, for instance. It is then necessary for the therapist to translate from this primitive and metamorphic kind of childhood logic back to secondary-process logic. Similarly, the sequence of various dream parts may be distorted as compared with their sequence in waking life, for there is no logical sense of time and space in the dream world. The therapist must have the capacity to translate back into waking sense. Often the focal core of the dream material makes itself known by the repetition of certain contents in various contexts and connections.

Fromm-Reichmann (1950) suggests two excellent extraneous ways of becoming acquainted with and sensitized to the language of dreams in the unconscious. One is furnished by "studying the means of expression as they are used in the productions of psychotics." The other source is from the study of "folklore, fairy tales, and legends, in which dreams are recorded which people have had in common

223

throughout the centuries." I have found it extremely useful to have a knowledge of folklore and fairy tales because their themes appear again and again in patients' dreams. Another and analogous source from which the therapist increases his familiarity with the language of the unconscious—in addition to studying his own dreams and those of his patients—is through dreams and their interpretations in the Bible, drama, poetry, and fiction from ancient times to the present. The classic Greek dramatic literature and the plays of Shakespeare are especially fine sources for this material. It is obvious from this alone that the training of the psychotherapist must be aimed among other things, at providing a maximum possible capacity for understanding the imaginative language of the unconscious.

If the patient is not progressing well enough, or if the dynamics or nuclear emotional constellation are difficult to understand, then Saul (1958) suggests that the focus and perspective can often be clarified by reviewing the first ten dreams of the therapy, isolated from the other material, and then also reviewing a series of current dreams. Every therapist, no matter how experienced, obtains fresh insight, focus, and perspective, if he takes time to review a patient's dreams, even isolated from the mass of other material. Saul contends that it is rarely advisable for students to study ponderous verbatim notes of therapy sessions or even to keep any. It is, however, worthwhile to record dreams over a series of six to ten sessions, for the central dynamics that shape the person's life are usually disclosed in the early dreams of the therapy, and progress in treatment is usually shown in dream samples taken at intervals. The dreams at the end of treatment are especially revealing, as are samples taken long after therapy is over. This review of dream series acts as an important tool in enabling the therapist to assess his own work, especially in situations where he is worried about the progress of the therapy or where the therapy seems actually to be failing.

The technique for approaching a dream series is the same as that for any unconscious material. Very briefly, in reviewing a series of dreams (after one has also included carefully elicited associations):

1. Keep close to the material.

2. Look for the major central themes first.

3. Keep to the level of consciousness and repression in the material.

4. Try to distinguish the dynamics behind the material from the content.

5. Try to separate the present life situation from the transference and the childhood patterns.

6. Look for effects of current stimuli on the dreams and associations.

7. Review the material for libidinal and hostile motivations.

8. Review the material for the ego aspects—that is, aspects of ego functioning and sexual motivations.

9. Pay close attention to the sequence of the dream elements.

10. Watch for the material connected with the greatest emotional response.

11. Watch for positive progressive forces as well as for regressive ones.

12. Examine object relationships, identifications, and projections.

13. Be very cautious about interpreting symbols.

14. Try to stay with what the dreamer's ego accepts and acts on.

This is an important guide to what the patient will accept in the way of interpretations in the therapy, as well as in his general behavior. In fact, in some situations of dream interpretation, I have actually asked the patient what he would do if the situation he dreamed about was a reality situation and noted how he answered this kind of question to get an idea of his ego functioning.

Let us now turn to some clinical examples to illustrate the various ways that dreams can be important in the process of intensive psychotherapy. The case readiest at hand is that of Genevieve, which I presented in Chapter 8 and which is worth rereading at this juncture. My whole review of her variety of defenses was touched off by a dream. This is the kind of dream I call a *trigger dream;* in other words, the discussion of a dream triggered a whole variety of important material that the patient had kept just below the surface but had not been quite ready to discuss up to that time. The dream follows: "I was at a birthday party for a doctor; it was pleasant, but I knew I had to be tortured after the party, and I was trying to run away." The discussion of this dream and its associations led to associations of sex with torture, with associating torture from childhood with a sadistic attacking father, and to the hysterical defense of trying to relate all sexual feelings to a dangerous situation in which the patient would be tortured. This led to a discussion of Genevieve's attempts to run away from treatment, to discharge her feelings about the therapist through anger at herself. It further led to an understanding of her resistance to the treatment by over-emphasizing the sexual aspects of it, and of her defense through insisting that the treatment was like toilet training. This was an important trigger dream and was, indeed, fertile and productive.

Some dreams are simply resistance dreams and are not quite so productive. For example, a patient dreams "I was in a store with my boss who is also my psychiatrist. I didn't want to see him for a session—he would just talk about another patient, which won't help me." The association to this dream led to an understanding that the patient did not want to come to the therapy session. She considered it a nuisance. It emerged that this was due to the fact she was too embarrassed to discuss what was really bothering her. There was anxiety about the therapist's asking about some of this material. Then came associations to a previous therapist who talked a lot about other patients. These associations were in the service of resistance, the assumption being that if the patient really brought up what was bothering her no privacy would be insured, and it would be chattered about to other patients, and so forth. This is a relatively simple dream in which the resistance aspects were predominant and could be taken up with the patient on a one-by-one basis.

One can also trace the existence of important anxiety by means of dreams. For example, "I was in a room with a tiger. It was a pet tiger and had been left with me. It was playful, and it just gnawed on me, but I was scared. I shut it in my mother's room. I said to myself, 'Let him eat her.' Then I felt guilty. Then the next thing I knew the tiger was with me again." This dream has many elements of anxiety in it, and the patient, who was a passive–aggressive personality, had a tremendous problem with his highly aggressive mother. The dream led to considerable discussion about the patient's feelings toward his mother, his fear of his own aggression, and his way of retaliating by being passive, thereby not allowing himself to make any progress in psychotherapy for the sake of anyone, and punishing the therapist by frustrating his efforts. This is what I would call a rather typical dream in psychotherapy, in which the emphasis and interpretation is more on ego functioning than on any oral, cannibalistic or incorporative instinctual drives. The patient is also obviously hiding that in the dream but is not at all ready to deal with it.

One can see from this how the psychotherapist must make a *choice* in dealing with dreams, depending on his assessment of what the patient is ready to hear in the way of interpretations. In general, the choices should be in the direction of interpretations dealing with resistance and ego function, rather than direct interpretations of infantile sexual material. Such material should only be interpreted when the patient seems ready to receive it, and this is measured by the patient's capacity for ego function.

Below is an example of a dream that followed an interpretation and indicated a favorable response, in terms of improved ego functioning, to the interpretation. At a previous session it had been interpreted that the patient was motivated not to understand herself but to manipulate the therapist— whom she saw as a great magician possessing wondrous powers—to give her all the things that she did not have and that she wanted in life. Fortunately, enough material was available to show her in many little ways how she had been attempting this manipulation. The following hour the patient reported this dream: "I was at a cafeteria and I was surprised and rather pleased to see that the big shots in the corporation were also at the cafeteria, and they had to wait in line for

228

their food just like the rest of us. The scene shifted, and I was with a man who had a hand on my breast. I was feeling guilt about that and not much sexual arousal." The associations to this dream and the interpretation led to the understanding that the dream represented, first of all, some recognition that the therapist did not have magical powers. Therefore, the patient would have to deal with her own problems by working these through and understanding herself, not by manipulating the therapist. This led to the second scene of the dream, which represented the beginning of a serious attempt on the part of the patient to understand some of her difficulties, which were actually not sexual but pregenital. However, they first appeared in this dream material as a combination of the sexual and pregenital, and, indeed, in her clinical behavior the patient showed a lot of sexual material that had an underlying pregenital cast to it. In this case a correct interpretation enhanced the ego's function of reality testing, led to more integration on the part of the patient, and to the production of new psychic material and better motivation to understand that material.

A much more difficult problem of dream interpretation arises in the psychotherapy of borderline patients and in schizophrenic patients. In these patients dreams are often fraught with raw and direct pregenital and instinctual material, and it is almost impossible to avoid this. As a matter of fact, avoiding it is often interpreted by the patient as an attempt at flight from material. The therapist appears to be just as frightened of the material as the patient. In such cases the therapist must have a very considerable understanding of himself and of his own reactions to deep, uncensored, unconscious material. The following dream came from a patient who might be called a borderline case or hysterical psychotic and who had been hospitalized with the complaint that her father was poisoning her food: "My husband is abandoning me saying he doesn't love me. Second scene. I am eating worms. My husband wants me to move away, far away from Dr. Chessick. He says no, it is not too far away, and I try to prove to my husband by taking a ride on the train that it is too far." The associations and interpretation of this relatively brief dream brought out a plethora of material. The patient began to talk about her mother's great coldness, and then she began talking about her father's behavior when she was a child. He would eat with her and criticize her about eating. She reminded herself about the time when she thought that having his penis in her mouth would swell her up with a baby, and she offered spontaneously the association that the worms in the dream represented her father's penis. She shifted back and forth in this very emotional therapy session between feelings of great rage at her mother and great rage at her father for "poisoning" her, and efforts to make up for her mother's coldness by using her father for what she missed from her mother.

The important question is how did the patient respond after she presented the dream, went on at length with her associations, and listened to the interpretation of the situation: that is, her great need for feeding from her mother and some attempt to shift efforts to her father for what she couldn't get from her mother. The response lay in the dream she presented the next time she came in: "A child was caught in a clothes dryer and then in another scene somebody had his head caught in a stereo cabinet." Her associations to this dream were that as a child she had to get into some dramatic mess—this was a patient who mutilated herself—so that her mother would see how sick she was; she noted her mother was upset one time when a neighborhood child was caught in a clothes dryer. Another association was her hatred of people who taunted her about the way she dressed and looked and her hatred of her compulsive need to eat. Thus, the material from the first dream was followed by dream material indicating many pregenital fantasies in which the patient was attempting to stuff herself with food and dramatically bring herself to the attention of her mother. Getting into the clothes dryer or stereo cabinet also must be understood as part of Lewin's (1950) "oral triad." What I have tried to demonstrate with this dream material is how very complicated dreams can become, especially in borderline or psychotic patients, and how important it is that the therapist be comfortable with all kinds of pregenital and sexual material and have the capacity to deal with it as it appears in the psychotherapy.

If one wishes to distinguish between a beginning psychotherapist and an experienced psychotherapist, or determine whether a psychotherapist is talented or not, or decide whether a psychotherapist is truly proceeding with a psychoanalytic orientation or just paying lip service to it and going on secretly with a dogmatic or authoritative kind of treatment, the easiest and simplest way to analyze the psychotherapy is to look at the dream material and the way the therapist handles the material as it appears.

Another way to make this evaluation is to ask whether any dreams have occurred at all. If no dreams whatever appear in an uncovering psychotherapy, something has gone seriously wrong. This may not necessarily be a function of the therapist. It is not uncommon to run across some people with

231

such rigid ego structure that they cannot even for a moment report a dream. Such patients, needless to say, are extremely poor candidates for intensive uncovering psychotherapy and do better with a supportive approach. Here again, one of the ways of assessing the ego functioning of a patient at any given time is not only by looking at his dreams but by looking at how much he dreams or at least how much he can remember of his dreams, associate to them, and present them to his therapist. At the same time it must be kept in mind that presenting the therapist with a plethora of florid dreams and wild associations can easily be used in the service of defense!

The dreams the psychotherapist has about his patients are most valuable. These must invariably represent countertransference. It is incumbent on the psychotherapist to keep careful watch on his own dreams; any dreams or recurrent fantasies about a patient demand understanding and will always provide new insight into the patient. In case the therapist, on the basis of his personal therapy and self-understanding, finds himself unable to analyze his dream about a patient, he should feel obliged to seek a consultation. Integrity is again the issue. The therapist is failing in his obligation toward his patient if he refuses for any reason whatever to demand from himself a thorough understanding of his own reactions involving his patient. One can hardly expect patients to be motivated to understand themselves, if the therapist does not possess a similar determination.

CHAPTER 11 *Primary Love or Primary Narcissism?*

THE metapsychological aspects of narcissism, especially as these fit into the remainder of metapsychological theory, was left in an unfinished and unsatisfactory state at the time of Freud's death. It remains even today a very controversial issue. The purpose of this chapter is to clarify frequently confusing terminology, to bring the reader up to date on some very new aspects of the debate over metapsychological aspects of narcissism, and to focus primarily on those features of current thinking on narcissism that are pertinent to the practicing, psychoanalytically oriented psychotherapist. This leads to direct crucial, clinical considerations in the psychotherapy of patients suffering from narcissistic disorders and so-called ego defects.

The standard psychoanalytic references admit that the

present status of the concept of narcissism in psychoanalytic theory is somewhat uncertain. Brenner (1955) explains that this is because the concept was developed by Freud before the dual theory of instincts had been formulated. In spite of this, the concept of narcissism, according to Brenner. ". . . remains a useful and necessary working hypothesis in psychoanalytic theory." The term is used to indicate at least three different, though related, concepts when applied to an adult: (a) a hypercathexis of the self (b) a hypocathexis of the objects of the environment, and (c) a pathologically immature relationship to these objects.

Brenner points out that Freud believed the major portion of libido remains narcissistic, that is, self-directed, throughout life. This is usually referred to as "normal" or "healthy" narcissism. Brenner explains, "He also believed that those libidinal forces which cathected the psychic representatives of the objects of the outer world bore the same relationship to the main body of narcissitic libido as do the pseudopodia of an amoeba to its body. That is to say, object libido derives from narcissistic libido and may return to it if the object is later relinquished for any reason."

The standard teaching on the subject is presented by Nagera (1969). The concept of autoeroticism is used by Freud to describe a specific type of sexual activity and gratification that is characteristic of the very earliest phase of life. During the autoerotic phase each component instinct or erotogenic zone that is aroused presses for gratification independently of others. In 1909 Freud had already introduced an intermediary stage between autoerotism and object-love. In this intermediary stage, narcissism, the different component instincts are somehow unified and take the self as a love object. Nagera states,

Consequently the type of sexual gratification during the phase of primary narcissism is autoerotic as well, the object being one's own body and not an external one as in the following phase of object love. The difference between the autoerotic activities of the phase of primary narcissism and those of autoerotism appears to be that those corresponding to primary narcissism are less close to the biological realm of phenomena than those belonging to the phase of autoerotism in which there is no awareness of the self as in primary narcissism.

Freud contends that the ego cannot exist in the individual from the start; it must be developed. The autoerotic instincts, however, are there from the beginning, so new physical action must be added to autoerotism in order to bring about narcissism. This is elaborated in Freud's (1914b) famous paper on narcissism. Thus, *narcissism* is the term used to describe a libidinal position intermediate between autoerotism and object relations (or alloerotism). Later, withdrawal of cathexis from objects gives rise to what is called secondary narcissism.

Freud's (1914b) paper "On Narcissism" may be regarded as pivotal in the evolution of his views. Strachey (Freud, 1914a) explains,

> It sums up his earlier discussions on the subject of narcissism and considers the place taken by narcissism in sexual development; but it goes far beyond this. For it enters into the deeper problems of the relations between the ego and external objects, and it draws a new distinction between "ego-libido" and "object-libido". Furthermore—most important of all, perhaps —it introduces the concepts of the "ego-ideal" and of the observing agency related to it, which were the basis of what was ultimately to be described as the "superego" in *The Ego and the Id.*

This very difficult, overcompressed paper demands and repays prolonged study and forms the starting point of many later lines of thought. The paper on narcissism is one of the most difficult that Freud ever wrote, and, in contrast to many of his writings, it is not quite clear in places just what Freud meant. He himself was unsatisfied with it and soon went on to newer theories of the instincts and newer, never quite satisfactory, elaborations of his theory of narcissism.

In order to understand some of the clinical aspects of the treatment of patients with narcissistic disorders and ego defects, and for a better perspective on later elaboration by other authors, at least some examination of Freud's paper on narcissism is necessary. In it we see Freud's answer to the question of the relationship of autoerotism and primary narcissism: Autoerotism is a primordial attribute of an instinct and cannot be considered narcissism, since the latter requires an ego. Autoerotism becomes narcissism when the ego develops to the point of reality testing and when the ego can distinguish between the self and the object.

Freud establishes the antithesis between ego-libido and object-libido: The more one is employed, the more the other becomes depleted. Thus, the highest phase of development of which object-libido is capable is the state of being in love, when the subject seems to give up its own personality in favor of an object cathexis. Freud feels the opposite condition to be true in the paranoid states.

Because autoerotism exists from the start, the autoerotic instincts are also there from the beginning; when the ego develops, a new set of ego instincts have to be differentiated. Thus, in this early alteration of his instinct theory, Freud distinguishes between ego instincts and sexual instincts; this is the only one of Freud's four instinct theories that might be labeled nonpolarized. Thus, certain, but not all, ego instincts are seen as nonlibidinal, "ego interest," for example. The ego's integrity depends on how much ego-libido is available, for this is what holds the ego together.

Freud writes, "We say that a human being has originally two sexual objects—himself and the woman who nurses him —and in doing so we are postulating a primary narcissism in everyone, which may in some cases manifest itself in a dominating fashion in his object choice." Moving on to disturbances of this development, Freud honestly explains, "The disturbances to which a child's original narcissism is exposed, the reactions with which he seeks to protect himself from them and the paths onto which he is forced in doing so—these are themes which I propose to leave on one side, as an important field of work which still awaits exploration." He instead discusses the transformations of ego-libido in normal adults and outlines the concept of the ego-ideal.

In normal development the ego-ideal is set up and becomes the target of self-love, which was enjoyed in childhood by the actual ego: "The subject's narcissism makes its appearance displaced on to this new ideal ego, which, like the infantile ego, finds itself possessed of every perfection that is of value." What is projected in the ego-ideal is "the substitute for the lost narcissism of his childhood in which he was his own ideal." This differs substantially from the concept of sublimation (see Chapter 2): "A man who has exchanged his narcissism for homage to a high ego ideal has not necessarily on that account succeeded in sublimating his libidinal instincts." One can see hints, even in this early paper, that a *parallel development* takes place in the formation of the ego-ideal and the vicissitudes of narcissism or ego-libido, on the one hand, and in the development of mechanisms of defense

237

and sublimation involving the libidinal (sexual) instincts, on the other. This is *not* developed at length by Freud.

One of the most interesting clinical descriptions in Freud's paper is of the neurotic who is impoverished in his ego and incapable of fulfilling his ego-ideal. This type of patient seeks a return to narcissism by choosing a sexual ideal after the narcissistic type, which possesses the excellences to which he cannot attain. Freud writes, "This is the cure by love, which he generally prefers to cure by analysis. Indeed he cannot believe in any other mechanism of cure; he usually brings expectations of this sort with him to the treatment and directs them towards the person of the physician. The patient's incapacity for love, resulting from his extensive repressions, naturally stands in the way of a therapeutic plan of this kind." The unintended result of this is that when the patient becomes partially freed from repressions, he withdraws from treatment in order to choose a love object, leaving his cure to be continued by life with someone he loves. The trouble with this solution is that it carries all the dangers of a crippling dependence on the helper.

The final major consideration in Freud's paper is the introduction of the concept of the self and self-regard. Self-regard is an expression of the size of the ego, and everything a person possesses or achieves, every remnant of the primitive feeling of omnipotence that his experience has confirmed, helps to increase his self-regard. The relationship between primary narcissism, the development of the ego, and the development of the concept of self remained unclear and required further working out in metapsychological theory.

Jacobsen (1964) carefully makes the distinction—which is vital to any understanding of patient material—between the concept of self, self-representations, and the system ego.

Hartmann uses the concept of "self"—a descriptive term to distinguish the person from the surrounding world of objects —to refer to the whole person of an individual, mind and body.

The self-representations are mental representations of the bodily and mental self in the system ego that may or may not become cathected with libido and aggression. Thus, according to Jacobsen, it is not the ego but the self-representations that become cathected with libido in secondary narcissism, leading to inadequacies in Freud's theory.

These preliminary considerations give an idea of the great complexity of this subject. The main justification for examining the matter at such length is the increased emphasis in modern clinical practice on patients with so-called ego defects and narcissistic disorders. Before approaching the clinical aspects of this problem it is important to note that *a fundamental parting of ways* is implied in Freud's statement that the ego is not there from the beginning or, to put it another way, that object relations of the type that we could call object-love are not there from the beginning. Thus, it is possible for the infant or small child to have a relationship to objects in the environment but only, or at least primarily, for the purpose of narcissistic gratification. The gratification is still autoerotic, whereas in true object-love, which comes later, part of the libidinal cathexis of the self is transferred onto external objects.

A diametrically opposite viewpoint to this is taken in the work of Balint (1953, 1968) reviewed by Kahn (1969). We are now in a position to understand what Balint means by his concept of primary object-love. He believes that primary object-love is present from the beginning, and it may be described as the demand to be loved and satisfied without being under any obligation to give anything in return. This is an archaic way of loving the mother and is directed at an object. According to Balint, primary narcissism is a detour or deflection that occurs when primary object-love is frustrated. Balint insists that what is primary is in object relations, and, thus, primary love is object-love and not narcissism; all narcissism is secondary, according to Balint.

This leads Balint to distinguish among three levels of psychotherapeutic work. One of these rests in the area of the Oedipus complex, which is the usual classical case, and the second lies in what he calls the area of basic fault. The third is in the "area of creation," even more primitive, with no outside object involved and not amenable to analytic methods.

In the area of the basic fault, there has been a disaster in the early mother–child symbiosis, leading to a profound frustration and hunger for primary object-love. Balint (1968) argues, "I should like to submit that the theory of primary narcissism has proved self-contradicting and unproductive. It created more problems than it helped to solve; more than fifty years of hard thinking and critical observations have not been able to resolve the internal contradictions inherent in it."

Balint concludes that from the clinical point of view, interpretations given to patients who are starving for primary love are, by themselves, useless; what is necessary is to permit a therapeutic regression in an appropriate holding environment, somewhat akin to Winnicott's (1958, 1966) concept of "management" that somehow replenishes the patient's lack of primary love supply. He feels that the traditional psychoanalytic treatment is not sufficient, and "a new regime must be established by doing something more, over and above the traditional passivity."

Freud consistently advised that in the treatment of regression, even when it is structured as part of the treatment

240

process, the therapist maintains his normal, sympathetic, passive objectivity and should not respond to the patient's longings or cravings except by interpreting them. Freud (1915b) even argued in his paper "Observations on Transference Love" that it is inadvisable to go beyond this, because cases in which this policy fails will prove, as a rule, unsuitable for analysis. Thus, the treatment *must* be carried out in this kind of abstinence or privation.

Although Balint certainly does *not* in any way advocate the direct massive attempt to satisfy the patient's cravings à la Ferenczi—and indeed rules out gratification for the patient that might excite tension of any sort, such as sexual excitement—he does insist that there is a healing power in the relationship between the patient and therapist, especially for those patients who are working in the area of the basic fault.

Balint is not really able to describe in detail what such a healing relationship would be. He (1968) writes,

> It is difficult to find words to describe what it is that is created. We talk about behavior, climate, atmosphere, etc. all of which are vague and hazy words, referring to something with no firm boundaries and thus reminiscent of those describing primary substances. In spite of the fact that the various forms of object relationship cannot be described by concise and unequivocal words . . . the atmosphere, the climate, is there, is felt to be there, and more often than not there is even no need to express it in words—although words may be an important contributory factor both to its creation and maintenance.

The question of how far the therapist should go in response to the demand or need for a particular form of object relationship from a patient is crucial (see Chessick 1968, 1969) and also discussed in Chapter 9. Some analysts firmly believe that only those forms of object relationships are permissible that allow the analyst to retain the passive, sympathetic, objective role described by Freud. Balint feels that such analysts insist this to be an absolute parameter. If the analyst abandons it for any reason, the treatment is no longer called psychoanalysis. Thus, differentiation between patients who are working in the area of the basic fault and those in the area of the Oedipus complex is irrelevant, if the therapist works in this manner.

On the other hand, Balint insists that in some cases in which words—that is, associations followed by interpretations—do not seem to be able to induce or maintain the necessary changes, additional therapeutic agents should be considered: "In my opinion, the most important of these is to help the patient to develop a primitive relationship in the analytic situation corresponding to his compulsive pattern and maintain it in undisturbed peace til he can discover the possibility of new forms of object relationship, experience them, and experiment with them."

Balint gives a few examples of how the "unobtrusive analyst" can foster this process. For example, the more the analyst can reduce the inequality between his patient and himself, the better are the chances of a benign form of regression. The analyst also, provides time and a milieu that has a holding or therapeutic function. The environment "should be quiet, peaceful, safe, and unobtrusive; that it should be there and that it should be favorable to the subject, but that the subject should be in no way obliged to take notice, to acknowledge, or to be concerned about it."

Again Balint warns us that by providing this special therapeutic relationship the analyst must avoid becoming an omniscient and omnipotent object, and he must be sure that the gratification will result not in a further increase of excitement in the patient but will lead to the establishment of a tranquil, quiet, well-being and to "a better safer understanding between the patient and himself." He adds, "None of the details of the therapeutic attitude outlined here are essentially different from what the analyst adopts when dealing wih patients at the Oedipal level, and even the topics worked with are usually the same; but there *is* a difference, which is more a difference of atmosphere, of mood."

Fundamentally, I do not think that there is any necessary connection between Balint's theoretical conceptions and what he is advising the clinical therapist to do. If one carefully followed his recommendations, one is not carrying out an active therapy, in the sense of Ferenczi, at all,but simply permitting and tolerating a controlled regression of importance during the psychotherapeutic process. The therapist is simply being a decent human being who understands when to push the patient with interpretations and when to allow the patient some time for peace, quiet, and working through. I do not think that this differs in clinical practice from how any sensitive, humane, and feeling physician would act with his patient. Thus, there is a substantial gap between Balint's highly controversial theoretical considerations and the general office practice of psychoanalytically oriented psychotherapy. The difference seems to be more an emphasis on a theoretical explanation of what is and is not important in therapeutic process, rather than any fundamentally different approach to the patient.

In order to understand this more clearly it is necessary to focus on an unusually important book by Kohut (1971). This book is of major significance both because of its extension of the whole concept of narcissism and its suggestions regarding the formal psychoanalysis of narcissistic personality disorders, and because of the clear picture it gives of a formal psychoanalysis carried out by an individual with firm mature identification as a psychoanalytic psychotherapist.

The material in the book, which is extremely difficult and merits a lot of attention, is almost entirely based on the formal psychoanalysis of a small group of patients. It is not easy to generalize from this material to the problems of the psychotherapy of patients of this nature.

Kohut attempts to separate two categories of patients: those with narcissistic personality disorders, on the one hand, and those with psychotic disorders—or the milder or disguised forms of the psychoses that he refers to as borderline states—on the other. Thus, for Kohut the borderline patient is the borderline schizophrenic or the borderline psychotic patient.

The patient with the narcissistic personality disorder, as Kohut points out in the footnote on the first page, is usually active, socially comparatively well adjusted, and reasonably well functioning, although his personality disturbance interferes more or less seriously with his capacity to work, to be productive, and above all with happiness and inner peace.

The immediate question is: "How is one to differentiate the psychopathology of the analyzable narcissistic personality disturbances from the psychoses and borderline states?" For Kohut the answer seems to rest almost entirely on the type of transference that is formed when the patient is taken into a formal psychoanalysis. Thus, a differential diagnosis on the basis of initial interviews or symptomatology is almost impossible, if I understand Kohut correctly. He writes, ". . . the spontaneous establishment of one of the stable narcissistic transferences is the best and most reliable diagnostic sign which differentiates these patients from psychotic or borderline cases on the one hand, and from ordinary transference neuroses, on the other. The evaluation of a trial analysis is, in other words, of greater diagnostic and prognostic value than are conclusions derived from scrutiny of behavioral manifestations and symptoms."

Thus, Kohut places the unanalyzable psychoses or borderline states on the one hand and the analyzable cases of narcissistic personality disturbances on the other. The former tend toward the chronic abandonment of narcissitic configurations and toward their replacement by delusions; the latter show only minor and temporary oscillations, usually toward partial fragmentation.

The schizoid patient, whom Kohut includes among the borderline cases, keeps his involvement with others at a minimum as the outgrowth of a correct assessment of his regression propensity and narcissistic vulnerability. Such patients correctly evaluate their assets and weaknesses. "The therapist should thus not be a bull in the china shop of the delicate psychic balance of a valuable, and perhaps creative individual, but should focus his attention on the imperfections in the defense structures." To put it another way, the appropriate therapy for schizoid or borderline patients is not formal psychoanalysis, because a transference regression will take place that will lead to a severe fragmentation of the self. Instead, a psychoanalytically sophisticated form of insight thereapy is called for that does not require the therapeutic mobilization of the self-fragmenting regression.

In this manner Kohut distinguishes among three groups of patients:

1. The ordinary psychoanalytic treatment case that forms a transference neurosis,

2. The borderline or schizoid or schizophrenic patient

245

who is an unsuitable candidate for psychoanalysis and for whom a regression will lead to self-fragmentation and

3. The narcissistic personality disorder, who forms certain definitive types of stable transference in a formal psychoanalysis and, thus, is analyzable.

In his theoretical orientation Kohut, in direct contrast to Balint, stays with the classical psychoanalytic viewpoint, postulating a first phase of autoerotism followed by primary narcissism. In normal development "The equilibrium of primary narcissism is disturbed by unavoidable shortcomings of maternal care, but the child replaces the previous perfection (a) by establishing a grandiose and exhibitionistic image of the self: *the grandiose self;* and (b) by giving over the previous perfection to an admired, omnipotent (transitional) self object: *the idealized parent imago.*" Kohut elaborates and distinguishes the vicissitudes as the equilibrium of primary narcissism is inevitably disturbed, with much greater care and attention than any author has previously paid to this subject.

Under ordinary circumstances, the grandiose self and the idealized parent imago—important for ambition, enjoyment, and self-esteem—become integrated into the adult personality. With each of the mother's inevitable minor empathic failures, misunderstandings, and delays the infant withdraws narcissistic libido from the archaic imago of unconditional perfection (primary narcissism) and acquires in its stead a particle of inner psychological structure that takes over the mother's functions in the service of the maintenance of narcissistic equilibrium. Thus, tolerable disappointments in the primary narcissistic equilibrium lead to the establishment of internal structures that provide the ability for self-soothing and the acquisition of basic tension tolerance. If severe nar-

246

cissistic traumas are suffered by the child, then the grandiose self and the idealized parent imago are retained in unaltered form, *not* transformed into the adult personality, and exert a pressure of their own.

From this theoretical structure it follows that the transferences that arise from the formal psychoanalysis of the narcissistic personality disturbance will come from the mobilization of the idealized parent imago—an "idealizing transference"—and from the mobilization of the grandiose self—the "mirror transference." This depends, of course, on "the appropriately attentive but unobtrusive and noninterfering behavior of the analyst" that Kohut calls "the analyst's analytic attitude."

In the borderline patient and psychotic, the danger of regression to the stage of the fragmented self corresponding to the stage of autoerotism makes mandatory the maintenance of a realistic, friendly relationship with the therapist and the provision of psychotherapeutic support, since a workable transference for a psychoanalysis cannot take place. But for the narcissistic personality disorder, Kohut writes,

> To assign to the patient's nonspecific, nontransference rapport with the analyst a position of primary significance in the analysis of these forms of psychopathology would, thus, in my opinion, be erroneous. Such an error would rest on an insufficient appreciation of the metapsychologically definable difference between unanalyzable disorders (psychoses and borderline states) and analyzable forms of psychopathology (transference neuroses and narcissistic personality disorders).

Kohut describes the difficulties between the child and the parent that lead to disruption of the normal trend of

247

events in the vicissitudes of narcissism. Under optimal circumstances the child experiences gradual disappointments in the parent or idealized object; to put it another way, the child's evaluation of the idealized object becomes increasingly realistic, which leads to a "withdrawal of the narcissistic cathexes from the imago of the idealized self-object and to their gradual internalization."

If the child suffers traumatic loss of the idealized object or phase-inappropriate disappointment in it, then optimal internalization does not take place, and the psyche remains fixated on an archaic self-object:

> The personality throughout life will be dependent on certain objects in what seems to be an intense form of object hunger. The intensity of the search for and of the dependency on these objects is due to the fact that they are striven for as a substitute for the missing segments of the psychic structure. They are not objects . . . since they are not loved or admired for their attributes, and the actual features of their personalities, and their actions are only dimly recognized. They are needed to replace the functions of a segment of the mental apparatus which has not been established in childhood.

This viewpoint is clearly diametrically opposed to that of Balint and is of enormous clinical importance.

The trauma suffered most repeatedly is severe disappointment in the mother, who, because of her defective empathy with the child's needs, did not appropriately fulfill her functions as a stimulus barrier, an optimal provider of needed stimuli, a supplier of tension-relieving gratification, and so on, depriving the child of the gradual internalization of early experiences of being optimally soothed or aided in going to sleep. The mature psychic apparatus should later be able to perform these functions predominantly on its own.

The crucial differentiation among narcissistically experienced archaic self-objects; internalized psychological structures that perform drive-regulating, integrating, and adaptive functions previously performed by external objects; and "true objects" cathected with object-instinctual investments forms the foundation for recognizing the *profound distinction* between psychoanalytic metapsychology and *all other* points of view.

As an example, Kohut presents a patient in which, "the central defect of his personality was the insufficient idealization of his superego (an insufficient cathexis with idealizing libido of the values, standards, and functions of his superego) and, concomitantly, the strong cathexis of an externally experienced idealized parent imago in the late pre-oedipal and Oedipal stages." This led to a diffuse narcissistic vulnerability, the hypercathexis of his grandiose self occurring mainly in response to disappointments in the idealized parent imago, and the tendency toward the sexualization of the narcissistically cathected constellations. In such patients a hypersensitivity to disturbances in the narcissistic equilibrium takes place with a tendency to react to sources of narcissistic disturbance by a mixture of wholesale withdrawal and unforgiving rage, forming a very typical and frequent clinical picture.

In the working through of the idealizing transference, regressive swings take place after each inevitable disappointment in the idealized analyst, but the patient returns to the basic idealizing transference with the aid of the appropriate interpretation, providing these interpretations "are not given mechanically, but with correct empathy for the analysand's

249

feelings." This leads to the emergence of meaningful memories that concern the dynamic prototypes of the present experience. This is the essential paradigm of the working-through process in the narcissistic personality with the patient that forms an idealizing transference. It seems clear-cut and clinically useful.

The therapeutic activation of the grandiose self occurs in the appearance of the mirror transference, which is more complicated because it is divided into several types. In its most archaic form the analyst is experienced as an extension of the grandiose self. In a less archaic form there is an alter-ego twinship transference in which the analyst is experienced as being very similar to the patient. In the most mature and more common form, the analyst is experienced as a separate person but important to the patient and accepted by him only in the framework of the grandiose needs.

Thus, "the mirror transference is the therapeutic reinstatement of that normal phase of the development of the grandiose self in which the gleam in the mother's eye, which mirrors the child's exhibitionistic display, and other forms of maternal participation in and response to the child's narcissistic exhibitionistic enjoyment confirm the child's self-esteem and, by a gradually increasing selectivity of these responses, begins to channel it into realistic directions."

Which *type* of mirror transference appears is not as important as the establishment of a relatively stable transference by the activation of the grandiose self, for this enables the patient to mobilize and maintain a working-through process "in which the analyst serves as a therapeutic buffer and enhances the gradual harnessing of ego-alien narcissistic fantasies and impulses."

250

The therapeutic mobilization of the grandiose self may arise either directly—a primary mirror transference—as a temporary retreat from an idealizing transference—reactive remobilization of the grandiose self—or in a transference repetition of a specific genetic sequence that Kohut calls "a secondary mirror transference." This very difficult concept is clearly thought out. The regressive swings in the working through are desirable and cannot be avoided, since no analyst's empathy can be perfect, any more than a mother's empathy to the needs of her child could be. The understanding that is gained from the therapeutic scrutiny of these swings is of great value to the patient.

In the treatment of these patients Kohut faces directly the technical problem of the extent to which the analyst must become "active." He feels that major forceful interference is necessary mainly in instances of borderline psychoses and the related instances of profound ego defect that result in unbridled impulsivity. The major approach to such disturbances or acting out is to alert the patient's ego that a change of behavior is indicated in the interest of self-preservation. No moral issue must be raised except that practically and realistically in view of the prevailing mores, the patient is putting himself in jeopardy by his doings.

This leads to a crucial discussion of the so-called passivity of the psychoanalyst during the psychoanalytic treatment, which Kohut correctly observes has at times been mistakenly discussed as if it were a moral issue. The essential factors of the process in the psychoanalytic cure are outlined. A contrast is drawn between inspirational therapy and psychoanalysis: "the former works through the active establishment of object relations and massive identifications, the latter through

251

the spontaneous establishment of transferences and minute processes of (transmuting) reinternalization." Kohut explains,

> If the analyst assumes actively the role of "prophet, saviour and redeemer" he actively encourages conflict solution by gross identification, but stands in the way of the patient's gradual integration of his own psychological structures and of the gradual building up of the new ones. In metapsychological terms the active assumption of a leadership role by the therapist leads either to the establishment of a relationship to an archaic (prestructural), narcissistically cathected object (the maintenance of the patient's improvement depends thereafter on the real or fantasied maintenance of this object relationship) or to massive identifications which are added to the existing psychological structures.

The analytic process attempts to keep the infantile need activated, while simultaneously cutting off all roads except the one toward maturation and reality. "Only one way remains open to the infantile drive, wish, or need: its increasing integration into the mature and reality-adapted sectors and segments of the psyche, through the accretion of specific new psychological structures which master the drive, lead to its controlled use, or transform it into a variety of mature and realistic thought and action patterns."

Kohut claims that *not* to make any active moves to foster the development of a realistic therapeutic bond may be the decisive factor on the road to therapeutic success; the endless ability to remain noninterfering while a narcissistic transference establishes itself is crucial. Furthermore, "the manifestations of the inability of such patients to form a *realistic* bond with the analyst must not be treated by the analyst through active interventions designed to establish an 'alliance.'"

These manifestations also must be examined dispassionately. Turning directly to the theories of Balint, Kohut believes that imputing to the very small child the capacity for even rudimentary forms of object-love "rests on retrospective falsifications and on adultomorphic errors in empathy." More specifically, he argues that situations in which the analyst feels that he must step beyond the basic interpreting attitude and become the patient's leader, teacher, and guide, *are most likely to occur when the psychopathology under scrutiny is not understood metapsychologically.* "Since under these circumstances the analyst has to tolerate his therapeutic impotence and lack of success, he can hardly be blamed when he abandons the ineffective analytic armamentarium and turns to suggestion (offering himself to the patient as a model or an object to identify with, for example) in order to achieve therapeutic changes."

The calm, well-trained craftsman is held up as the ideal so that, "As our knowledge about the narcissistic disorders increases, the formerly so personally demanding treatment procedures will gradually become the skilled work of the insightful and understanding analysts who do not employ any special charisma of their personalities but restrict themselves to the use of the only tools that provide rational success: interpretations and reconstructions."

Some of the implications of Kohut's theories are already being picked up by authors such as Goldberg (1972, 1973) and have led to some new ideas on the treatment of narcissistic adolescents. Much exciting work remains to be done on this subject.

In summary, there is a separate line of development along the path of narcissism—from autoerotism to primary narcissism and then to the grandiose self (which is phase-appropriate for development and which replaces the sense of perfection experienced during primary narcissism.)—that parallels the development or vicissitudes of the sexual instincts. Another normal derivative of primary narcissism is the development of the idealized parent imago. Thus, fixations due to traumatic interferences can occur along this developmental line, just as they can occur during the phases of development of the ego's capacity to deal with the sexual instincts, leading to the traditional disorders.

An unconscious attachment to and failure in integration of the archaic grandiose self or the idealized parent imago and their corresponding self–object representatives result from impaired development of narcissism. Disturbances in integration of the grandiose self means that the primitive narcissistic impulses remain walled off from the reality ego, but they continue to influence the self as manifested by wide oscillations in self-esteem. Failure in the mother's empathic relationship to the infant or child forces the child to remain continually fixated on the need for an idealized and empathic external object who will provide the missing function to help regulate tension.

In some patients, as a result of fixations to cohesive and stable narcissistic structures, transferences can take place that remobilize the grandiose self and the idealized parent imago. This kind of a transference is relatively stable and is capable of being worked through in a formal psychoanalytic fashion. In other types of patients such a stable transference cannot occur, and there is a danger of further regression, breakup of the self, and the development of fragmented autoerotic states. Such patients are borderline or psychotic patients and are not amenable to formal psychoanalysis.

254

This leads to the original thesis presented in *How Psychotherapy Heals* (Chessick, 1969). Except in obvious cases, where it is contraindicated, it is advisable to give every patient a period of trial uncovering psychotherapy for at least six months and to examine carefully the type of transference manifestations that appear, all the while maintaining an unobtrusive, patient, and sympathetic attitude unless forced to interfere by serious, poorly controlled, acting-out propensities. Many patients, if treated in this fashion, will (sometimes to our surprise) be able to tolerate the procedure and to develop more-or-less stable transference configurations that then can be worked through by the method of psychodynamic understanding and interpretation, with the resulting gradual accretion of internal control and ego dominance.

A certain substantial portion of patients, such as some delinquents and schizophrenics, will not be able to tolerate this procedure, and the psychotherapeutic intervention will have to be shifted in a supportive direction for the purpose of shoring up the relatively less-pathological defenses. Heroic techniques or massive attempts to inspire or offer oneself to the patient are to be avoided in the treatment of *any* of these patients, unless one is looking for temporary dramatic and precarious change. The psychotherapist should always keep in mind that the wish to rescue the patient, who has become so tremendously important to the therapist, is frequently equivalent to the wish to kill him (Giovacchini, 1972).

Between what Kohut calls the borderline schizophrenic and the narcissistic personality, I believe, there is a very large group of patients—the true borderline patients (Chessick 1973b). These do *not* fragment entirely when they regress in therapy, but they cannot form a stable transference neurosis that is amenable to a formal psychoanalysis, and so they must

255

be treated by intensive uncovering psychotherapy—to which they respond much better than to supportive therapy. They are more common than Kohut's, narcissistic personality disorders who, I think, represent to some extent a theoretical model rather than a common clinical entity. This remains, of course, a subject for further clinical research.

In the psychotherapy of borderline patients the art of the psychotherapist comes into play in keeping the anxiety and disruption to a workable level, but we must recognize that to the extent the therapist must step out of the analytic attitude, a basic obstacle is placed against the working through and internalization of autonomous ego functions that can eventually deal with these problems without the therapist.

I see no profound differences possible in the atmosphere of the therapist's office or in how he approaches his patients as a manifestation of some deliberate attempt to be more "holding" with one type of patient or another. It seems to me that the healthy therapist will behave himself in essentially the same way with *all* patients and provide an atmosphere that is essentially the same for all patients. It appears unscientific to depend on either a charismatic atmosphere or heroic measures for some mysterious healing element in treating patients with severe preoedipal disorders. Although some therapists *are* able to achieve this charisma and sooth their patient's anxieties and others *do* engage in heroic measures that give temporary relief to patients, a fundamental difference still exists between inspirational forms of treatmant—no matter what shape they may take—and a scientific effort to understand and treat an emotional disorder.

It is extremely vital that the psychotherapist understand this and have a firm identity of his own. Thus, when he finds

256

himself impelled to step outside the ordinary sympathetic, listening, evenly hovering, attentive attitude and do something "more active," he can be immediately aware when this is a countertransference manifestation—e.g., based on lack of metapsychological understanding or on personal factors in the therapist—and treat it accordingly. If the therapist is confused as to what psychoanalytic psychotherapy is all about and what his personal identity as a therapist is, then he will be easily fooled by his own rationalizations. The avowedly "eclectic" therapist whose inconsistent and dramatic actions are essentially a response to the many frustrations in psychotherapeutic practice is a good example of this, leading to what is foisted upon the public as "new techniques" in psychotherapy of every description.

CHAPTER 12   *Therapeutic Interaction*

*T*HE mottos for this chapter are found in Franklin's *Poor Richard's Almanac:* "By diligence and patience the mouse bit in two the cable," and "Do not do what you would not have known." If we could have ended this book with Chapter 10 the whole subject of psychotherapy would appear to be much easier and less controversial. But even our brief analysis of failures using dream series indicates the complications of the field.

However, the fact that we occasionally do not know the details of how psychotherapy heals or fails or choose to ignore how what we are doing actually works does not mean that it is impossible to understand the specific factors involved in psychic healing or in psychotherapeutic failure. Nor does it imply the impossibility of engaging in a scientific study and control of these factors. The great swing away from individual psychotherapy today arises from the invariable frustrations and failures that even the best therapist experiences. Such unavoidable frustrations take a definite psychic toll on the therapist. The result is that some therapists switch away from doing individual psychotherapy altogether; others limit their practice or try to avoid the intense concentration involved in the work by assuming an "anything goes" attitude.

Such therapists constitute a serious danger to the profession, since they communicate their disillusionment to neophytes, and many applicants training as psychiatrists or psychotherapists are already only too eager to avoid the basic difficulties involved in trying to understand and heal people with emotional problems. Tarachow (1963) points out that psychotherapists in their first few years of practice often are more enthusiastic, more eager, and more interested: "They have not become fatigued or bored . . . as the years of practice go on, the therapist finds himself contending with the ingratitude, the spitefulness, the hostilities, of patients. This could slowly take its toll and in subtle ways reduce the burning enthusiasm of the therapist. The patients know the degree of the therapist's interest and respond to this knowledge."

However, even though untrained therapists are frustrated in their efforts, or because middle-age therapists have become tired of their labors, we do not have enough reason to assume that psychotherapy cannot be effective, specific, and teachable. We must learn from our failures about our own shortcomings and about what we must warn our students.

Failure in psychotherapy can be a stepping stone to further knowledge. But the problem is immensely complicated by the number of people doing psychotherapy without the proper training or without any conception of what the physicianly or healing vocation entails. The treatment of the mentally ill can be improved only by the dedicated labors of the scientific and humane physician and healer.

Perhaps the best example of therapeutic failure comes out of the problems of the negative therapeutic reaction. I have become very interested in the negative therapeutic reaction recently, because a number of patients who were referred to me were referred because they had suddenly attempted suicide in the middle of therapy. These were patients who had never attempted suicide before. The surprising response of the therapist was to get rid of the patient. There seems to be a great fear among psychotherapists of having a record of patients who commit suicide. This fear provides the patients with a lever to act out against the therapist any time they want. When the patient attempts suicide, and the therapist responds by breaking up the therapy, we have a very serious psychodynamic situation indeed, a situation that has been described rather fancifully by Racker (1968) in terms of a neurosis of failure interacting with a countertransference situation to produce a vicious circle.

The negative therapeutic reaction was first described by Freud (1923). It is a catastrophe for both participants, especially if it is not understood. Miller (1961, 1962, 1963), in a series of papers on the subject, points out that there are acute and chronic forms of negative therapeutic reaction. The acute form resembles an agitated depression, while the chronic form manifests itself as a negative transference or massive resistance. The management of each of these forms is very difficult and requires above all a sustaining of the therapeutic relationship, not its dissolution. Thus, it is most important to distinguish between a therapeutic failure and a negative therapeutic reaction. It *is* possible to work through the latter, if the therapist is himself sufficiently possessed of understanding and has recognized that a negative therapeutic reaction has taken place.

When the negative therapeutic reaction holds sway, it is possible sometimes to recognize the profound disability that exists in a patient. Sometimes a therapist has trouble visualizing a patient as potentially healthy and as fully functioning, but the converse of this also occurs; the therapist may not realize how severely damaged the patient really is. The negative therapeutic reaction constitutes a clinical manifestation of the seriousness of a patient's condition. It often reveals itself in a contempt for the therapist, attacks on anything he says, and a silence that frustrates his need to treat and taxes his understanding to the utmost.

The defenses involved in a negative therapeutic reaction, as pointed out by Olnick (1964), are, "highly cathécted narcissistic devices, originally evoked in the face of dire necessity in infancy and childhood, and now re-evoked in the transference . . . the patients may repudiate success and fulfillment, sometimes endangering their lives with the exacerbated symptoms and actions." The biggest problem is either not recognizing the negative therapeutic reaction or becoming "infected with the patient's negativistic reaction."

Certain patients react to a valid and properly timed interpretation of a defense that contains the implicit promise of understanding and eventual autonomy—or to any situation

261

holding forth the hope of an emancipation from the old crippling form of living—not with clinical improvement but with a worsening of their condition. This exacerbation occurs in the affective climate of an often resounding, dramatized "no." Utilizing a combination of defenses that involve denial by acting out, negation, and negativism is prominent. Olnick stresses the word *dramatized* in order both to emphasize the power of the behavior and the disturbing emotions of the other person and to indicate that the negativism may be totally or partly nonverbal.

Racker (1968) discusses this at even greater length in his concept of the neurosis of failure. It is hoped that when the therapist is confronted with silence and contempt, he will normally experience these situations with only a part of his being, leaving another part free to take note of them in a way suitable for the treatment. Racker writes,

Perception of such a countertransference situation by the analyst and his understanding of it as a psychological response to a certain transference situation will enable him to better grasp the transference at the precise moment when it is active. It is precisely these situations and the analyst's behavior regarding them, and in particular his interpretations of them, that are of decisive importance for the process of therapy, for they are the moments when the vicious circle within which the neurotic habitually moves—by projecting his inner world outside and reintrojecting this same world—is or is not interrupted.

"Moreover, at these decisive points," writes Racker, (1968) "the vicious circle may be reinforced by the analyst, if he is unaware of having entered it." Racker gives an ex-

262

ample: A patient closes himself up to every interpretation or represses it at once, reproaches the therapist for the uselessness of the therapy, foresees nothing better in the future, and declares his complete indifference to everything. If one has had patients like this, one knows what the therapist goes through. It may happen that all the interpretations the therapist offers, in spite of their being directed to the central resistances and connected with the transference situation, suffer the same fate. They fall into the neurosis of failure. Nothing happens. As Racker explains:

> Now the decisive moment arrives. The analyst, subdued by the patient's resistance, may begin to feel anxious over the possibility of failure and feel angry with the patient. When this occurs in the analyst, the patient feels it coming, for his own "aggressiveness" and other reactions have provoked it; consequently he fears the analyst's anger. If the analyst, threatened by failure, or, to put it more precisely, threatened by his own superego or his own archaic objects which have found an *"agent provocateur"* in the patient, acts under the influence of these internal objects and of his paranoid and depressive anxieties, the patient again finds himself confronting a reality like that of his real or fantasied childhood experiences and like that of his inner world; and so the vicious circle continues and may even be reinforced. But if the analyst grasps the importance of this situation, if, through his own anxiety or anger, he comprehends what is happening . . . if he overcomes, thanks to the new insight, his negative feelings and interprets what has happened . . . then he may have made a breach—be it large or small—in the vicious circle.

Racker's statement correctly indicates the complexity of

263

the therapeutic process, which involves much more than the mere interpretation of resistances and content.

In my own thinking about the psychotherapy process I like to divide therapeutic interaction into working through and aftereducation. These terms are used in a variety of ways by different authors. I conceive of working through as an intellectual or "cerebral cortex" process, whereas aftereducation involves "gut factors," the heart of the therapy, an "encounter" that goes on, a deep interaction. Let us begin with the simpler, more intellectual aspects of working through and attempt to go deeper and deeper into the field of aftereducation, ending with a discussion of what seem to be the most complex therapeutic procedures and most profound emotional interactions between the patient and the therapist.

The term *working through* was first introduced by Freud (1913b). Freud pointed out that, "it is a part of the work which effects the greatest changes in the patient." Freud recognized, as we still do, the *time lag* invariably attendant on the assimilation of correct interpretations, during which certain vital but poorly understood processes take place. This time lag is most difficult to explain. It hopefully leads to the assimilation of interpretations and their consequent use in changing adaptational patterns, but how it does this remains debatable.

Fenichel's (1945) views on this subject are quite advanced. He writes that "working-through," is "demonstrating again and again the unconscious impulse, once it has been recognized, in its manifold forms and connections, and attaining thereby cessation of the pathogenic defense." The long duration of psychoanalysis is accounted for by Fenichel by the need for what he calls, "the education of the ego to tolerate

264

less and less distorted derivatives, until the pathogenic defense is undone." In other words, a certain time lag takes place from the time that the therapist begins interpreting resistances and conflicts to the time they are assimilated or made use of by the patient in changing himself or the situation. In fact, we say that a patient has only intellectual insight if he cannot make use of these insights.

The procedure differs from indoctrination in that the therapist stays conscientiously with the patient's material, and empathically resonates with the patient's unconscious. He is thus enabled to interpret the unconscious accurately and is not presenting his own preconceptions *de novo* to the patient. For a genuine assimilation of interpretations to occur, however, a *very complex process* must go on between therapist and patient. Freud (1926) insisted that not only must the ego's repressive forces be overcome, but a magnetic force he called "id resistance," which pulls unwanted ideas into the unconscious, must be overcome as well. Thus, the time lag between insight and assimilation is due to the necessity of overcoming the ego's repressive forces *and* the id resistance. Stewart (1963) reviews this and reasonably contends that it is an unclear and somewhat mystical formulation. He feels that Freud deliberately left the matter open, so that further clinical experience could enrich these concepts and permit further elaboration of them.

A general clinical psychotherapeutic description of working through has been offered by Fromm-Reichmann (1950). She points out that the human mind does not operate in terms of independent mental processes.

The individual mental or emotional experiences which the

psychiatrist and the patient must investigate and interpret, of necessity, in seeming isolation, as they are presented to the therapist's observation, are of course, part of the person's pattern of reacting and thinking, but they are interlocked with one another in multiple ways. Interpretive dissolution and understanding of some specific piece of dissociated material, therefore, can produce only a certain degree of actual change.

Fromm-Reichmann further writes: ". . . any understanding, any new piece of awareness which has been gained by interpretive clarification, has to be reconquered and tested time and again in new connections and contacts with other interlocking experiences, which may or may not have to be subsequently approached interpretively in their own right." Fromm-Reichmann insists that in the course of this working-through process, special attention must be paid to the repetitive occurrence of patterns of feelings, thoughts, actions, and behavior that are conditioned by the same underlying experience previously unconscious. This holds true especially for four areas of interpersonal experiences toward whose clarification the therapist's attention should mainly be directed: "present emotional difficulties in living, developmental history and general biographical data, previous and recent situations of personal crisis, and the vicissitudes of the doctor–patient relationship."

Shands (1960, 1970) takes an investigative approach to psychotherapy, which he correctly calls "a semiotic approach." I have discussed his theoretical conceptions in detail in *How Psychotherapy Heals* (1969) and will only summarize them here, as our primary interest is in practice and technique. He views the process of working through basically as one he calls changing descriptions. As he sees it, the psychotherapy situation is designed to, "facilitate data processing into patterns of description, both in terms of an examination of previously undescribed aspects of the series of events and in terms of the alternative description from a different point of view." The mechanisms of defense, according to Shands, are for the purpose of maintaining familiar ways of processing data, for the processing of data in a novel way tends to be experienced as unpleasant. The end process of working through has been found when the therapist and the patient agree substantially on their descriptions. Thus the patient ". . . ceases to be a patient when he consistently formulates his experience in agreement with the therapist."

In this view psychotherapy is an intensive training in the use of words to contain and convey the universe and is completed when the descriptions of the patient agree with the descriptions of the therapist. It comes to an end when the patient has accepted the descriptions of the therapist. We say he has worked through his resistances or has ceased to resist, for he formulates his experience in agreement with the therapist. The patient has been provided with a better instrument to adapt to the demands of the external world. The test of therapy thus becomes a test of whether the patient's adaptation or emotional maturity has improved. Changing the descriptions of the patient so that they come into substantial agreement with the descriptions of the therapist improves the patient's adaptational capacity, for the descriptions of the therapist are a better instrument; that is, they explain and predict the world in action more accurately and consistently.

The question then becomes one not of the truth of one of the given descriptions but of its adaptational value. The various schools of psychiatry are seen by Shands as representing a variety of description sets that have been found to have considerable adaptational value as power instruments, and so they attract followers.

A deeper approach to the same process is presented by Giovacchini (1971). He points out that primitive mechanisms such as projection and introjection, symbiotic fusion, reintegration of split-off parts of the self, and so on, are primitive preverbal processes. "At the time of their origin," he writes,

> they were constructed at psychic levels that precluded verbalization. Their archaic characteristics made them incapable of articulation. In order to make such processes communicable they have to be stated in a verbal form. The analyst contributes to the patient's treatment by putting in verbal form what the patient already knows. This adds a secondary process organization, which achieves a level of understanding that makes them capable of integration with higher integrative and reality-oriented systems.

In this approach, instead of providing the patient with a changed description set, the therapist has provided a secondary-process elaboration to the primary process or primitive mechanisms; or, as Giovacchini puts it, he has raised "primitive mechanisms to abstract levels within an internally consistent theoretical system" and shared this with the patient. This enables the patient to approach these mechanisms in a secondary-process manner and to deal with them in a more mature fashion.

The process of working through has also been approached using the concepts of learning theory, for an interpretation can be viewed as a source of information or even as an emotional experience. It is unusual to view an interpretation in this way, but Frank (1961) has pointed out that, even when it is presented in the most noncomittal terms, an interpretation reveals information about the competence of the therapist and his attitudes. A good interpretation, whether it is exact or inexact, increases the faith of the patient in the therapist and thereby reduces anxiety and heightens a sense of security. Simultaneously, it reassures the therapist as to his own competence, leading to the well-known phenomenon of the neophyte therapist bombarding the patient with interpretations of the fanciest kind, in order to reassure himself of his own competence.

This brings us into the whole area of learning theory, which views psychotherapy as a learning experience. In an excellent article reviewing this subject, Strupp (1969) points out that the traditional descriptions of the therapeutic process do not adequately reflect the immensely complex interaction between the therapist and patient. The patient's reactions cannot be described fully as transference reactions. The patient reacts to the therapist as a concrete person and not only a representative of parental figures. The therapist's reaction also far exceeds what is usually called countertransference and includes, in addition to this, interventions based on conscious deliberations and what Strupp calls "spontaneous idiosyncratic attitudes." Strupp insists that the therapist's values are conveyed to the patient, even if he consistently tries to protect "his incognito." "The patient reacts to the therapist's overt but also his nonverbal hidden intentions and the therapist reacts to the patient's reaction to him." In this situation, as Strupp sees it, the patient learns a set of lessons in psychotherapy, and his conception of psychotherapy has moved more and more radically in this direction (Strupp, 1973), which is rather unfortunately oversimplified and anti-analytic.

Strupp feels that learning in psychotherapy is mainly through imitation and identification. The therapist serves as "a model whose feelings, attitudes, values, and behavior . . . the patient learns to accept, imitate, emulate, internalize and respect. They become an integral part of his (the patient's) own view of the world and his system of values." Strupp argues that the transference situation is an extremely valuable and useful strategy in the production of such learning. He points out, however, that although there is a sizable literature on the transference situation, we possess very little systematic knowledge concerning the precise manner in which therapeutic techniques use this as a form of learning.

"Therapeutic learning," according to Strupp, "appears to be most effective when there exists a strong emotional tie between the patient and the therapist, which the therapist controls and manipulates in the interest of effecting therapeutic change. Therapeutic learning appears to be predominantly experiential, although the therapist's explanations (interpretations) of the patient's experience may aid the process." Strupp quotes Fromm-Reichmann's famous saying that the patient needs an experience not an explanation.

Here the focus begins to shift from working through as essentially an intellectual process to what is known as after-education. This concept too was originated by Freud (1938): "If the patient puts the analyst in the place of his father (or mother) he is also giving him the power which his super-ego exercises over his ego, since his parents were, as we know, the origin of his superego. The new superego now has an

270

opportunity for a sort of *aftereducation* of the neurotic; it can correct mistakes for which his parents were responsible in educating him." After-education brings us from the idea of working through and the assimilation of interpretations to the much vaguer and more difficult conception of how psychotherapy actually changes a patient.

Very few of the authorities and texts on the subject have really made a detailed analysis of how this after-education takes place. For example, Saul (1958) conceives of what goes on in this way:

> If a person sees that mature attitudes will help win the love, the security, the inner peace, and the satisfactions that he wants, then he has added impetus to mature. Sometimes the demands are so great that they can be satisfied only if they are reduced, and the patient will accept this if he sees a half a loaf of real gratification in life instead of a whole loaf in fantasy only . . . Sometimes the need can be satisfied by changing its form, for example, by sublimation . . . The problem of living is largely how to enjoy the present realities rather than pine in constant frustration for potentialities.

Saul brings up the concept of after-education again and again in his book.

Those who are interested in the subject of applying learning theory to psychotherapy are referred to Dollard and Miller (1950). Study of the literature on the learning-theory approach to psychotherapy can, however, be disappointing, because there is very little agreement as to how people learn. This makes it very difficult to try to apply learning theory to psychotherapy.

Alexander (1963) insists that in the field of psychother-

271

apy, the long overdue observation of the therapeutic process by nonparticipant observers is turning out to be the required methodological tool. This in itself, however, is not sufficient. The evaluation of the rich, new observational material calls for new theoretical perspectives. According to Alexander:

> Learning theory appears to be at present the most satisfactory framework for the evaluation of observational data and for making valid generalizations. As it continuously happens at certain phases of thought development in all fields of science, different independent approaches merge and become integrated with each other. At present, we are witnessing the beginnings of a most promising integration of psychoanalytic theory with learning theory, which may lead to unpredictable advances in the theory and practice of the psychotherapies.

This was written in 1963, and there have been none of the significant advances utilizing learning theory that Alexander hoped for. It is difficult to understand the reason for this, but perhaps it lies in the extreme complexity of psychotherapeutic interaction. Strupp has pointed out that very little is gained by attempting to switch from one set of theoretical concepts of change to another, while all the various deep aspects of therapeutic interaction are not yet understood.

In general, learning theories fall into two major families: the "stimulus–response theories," represented by those of Thorndike, Guthrie, Skinner, and Hull, and the "cognitive theories," such as those of Tolman, Lewin, and the Gestalt psychologists. The former thinkers tend to regard most learned behavior as a process of accretion, acquired through conditioning and trial-and-error sequences in which responses are reinforced by reward or success or inhibited by punishment or failure. The cognitive group, on the other hand, tend to emphasize the greater importance in learning of more rapid perceptual "insights". Marmor (1966a) feels that both types of learning take place in life. He points out, however, that a significant difference between psychotherapy and any normal learning situation is that, "in the former the task is complicated by the fact that the previously learned behavior that constitutes the neurotic pattern is often extremely resistant to change. The problem of overcoming this resistance to change is the basic challenge of the therapeutic process."

In my experience the big battles in psychotherapy come when one tries to get the patient to utilize insights—to actually *change his behavior*. Patients will undergo any kind of contortions they can to avoid actually changing. Many a psychotherapy has been derailed when the therapist feels that the patient has plenty of insight and yet nothing happens. The patient insists on maintaining his habitual, rigid patterns. Thus, the problem of overcoming the resistance to change is the basic challenge of the psychotherapeutic process. As discussed in Chapter 11, frustration with this inertia and insufficient metapsychological understanding exert great pressure on the therapist to abandon the evenly suspended attentive attitude of listening and become active and inspirational, to the detriment of further uncovering psychotherapy.

The contribution of learning theories to the major aspects of this problem come from the study of the role of cognitive insights and the patient–therapist interaction. Usually the mere acquisition of intellectual or even emotional insight does not result in any immediate alteration of the neurotic patterns. There still remains the arduous and time-consuming

273

task of overcoming the patient's tendency to cling tenaciously to his previously learned patterns of perception and behavior and of enabling the patient to generalize acquired insights to all situations in which similar principles are operative. These two tasks are essentially what has been called working through, as described by Fromm-Reichmann earlier in the chapter. It is with regard to the nature of this working-through process that the proponents of the Skinner and Hull schools of learning theory have, according to Marmor, come up with some important ideas:

> A host of experimental studies seem to indicate that the non-verbal as well as the verbal reactions of the therapist act as positive and negative reinforcing stimuli to the patient, encouraging certain kinds of responses and discouraging others. According to these investigators, what seems to be going on in the working-through process is a kind of conditioned-learning, in which the therapist's overt *or covert* approval and disapproval—expressed in his nonverbal reactions as well as in his verbal confrontations, and in what he interprets as neurotic or healthy—act as reward—punishment cues or conditioning stimuli.

Thus, the therapist's implicit or explicit approval acts as a positive reinforcement to the more mature patterns of reacting, while his implicit or explicit disapproval tends to inhibit the less-mature patterns. As with experimental studies on animals, this process requires frequent repetition before the previous overlearned conditioned responses become extinguished, and the new conditioned responses or habit patterns become firmly established. Many therapists have resisted these conceptions because they don't like to think of themselves as conditioning their patients. But whether we like it or not, there is a lot of experimental evidence in the direction of the importance of conditioning in the therapeutic process, especially with respect to what Skinner (1960) has termed *operant conditioning*.

A quick view of operant conditioning and of Skinner's views in general, can be found in a book by Evans (1968). Operant conditioning conceives of a behavior that operates on the environment and produces reinforcing effects. Operant behavior, as Skinner sees it, is a study of what used to be called the purpose of an act; but the purpose of an act, as far as Skinner is concerned, is the consequences it is going to have. So in the case of operant conditioning, we study the consequences an act has had in the past. Skinner (Evans, 1968) explains, "Changes in the probability of response are brought about when an act is followed by a particular kind of consequence." This consequence can be positive or negative reinforcement, as the case may be, but the datum you watch is the probability that a response of a given type will occur. "An operant, then, is a class of responses, and a response is a single instance of the class." These operants in Skinner's view, condition a person's behavior, and they are vital parts of the therapy process.

Adding this aspect of conditioning to the main factors in therapeutic interaction discussed so far, we now have the following set:

1. Release of tension through catharsis and by virtue of the patient's hope, faith, and expectancy;
2. Cognitive learning of the trial-and-error variety;
3. Reconditioning by virtue of operant conditioning, by

275

virtue of subtle reward or punishment cues from the therapist, and by what is well known as "corrective emotional experiences (Alexander, 1956);

4. Identification with the therapist;

5. Repeated reality testing, which is the equivalent of practice in the learning process.

According to Marmor (1966b), these five elements are the most significant factors on the basis of which changes take place in a psychotherapeutic relationship.

There seems to be more to the process of therapeutic interpretation, however, than is covered by these five factors. We might begin with some little-known ideas from the French psychoanalyst Nacht (1962, 1963), who studies that mysterious area of nonverbal conditioning in psychotherapy. According to this analyst, "the deep inner attitude" of the therapist produces a major reconditioning effect on the patient. "It functions to reduce the patient's fear of closeness, bit by bit." It is very difficult to describe this operation to those who have not experienced it, but in principle it represents still another form of subtle conditioning, although less amenable to scientific investigation and certainly poorly investigated. This deep inner attitude or participation is much more than just the therapist's physicianly sense of vocation. It provides an atmosphere of peace and participation that of itself leads to growth, via either introjection of a much better parent or direct gratification out of the therapeutic amosphere itself, as also described at length by Balint (1968) and reviewed in Chapter 11.

Thus Nacht (1963) speaks of the "gratifying presence" of the therapist, in which a silent and peaceful union can be established, satisfying an essential need in the patient. This is qualified by the warning not to allow the patient to attach "too firmly" to this kind of relationship, as eventually he must be brought to separation. Techniques implementing Nacht's conception seem to require an intuitive capacity in the therapist. They are interesting but vague and undefined. Certainly we do know that the atmosphere of the therapist's office, combined with his personality and inner attitude toward the patient, does provide a reconditioning or at least a neutralizing effect on previous destructive experiences in the patient's early childhood. This is especially true regarding deep anxiety produced by a highly ambivalent and intense relationship to one or both parents. This neutralizing effect—that is to say, the neutralizing effect provided by the atmosphere, the therapist's office, personality, and inner attitude—can by itself be gratifying and liberate energy for growth. Thereby it can set the stage for introjection of the therapist.

Surprisingly little work has been done toward conceptualizing this mainly unconscious and important interaction between the patient and the therapist. I would like to attempt this here, with full knowledge of the subject's controversiality. Tower (1956) attributes vital significance to an unconscious interaction between the transference of the patient and the countertransference structure of the therapist. She writes, "The treatment situation between patient and analyst at its deepest and nonverbal level, probably follows the prototype of the mother–child symbiosis . . . and involves active libidinal exchanges between the two through unconscious nonverbal channels of communication." To put it another way, Tower conceives of certain basic emotional attitudes toward the patient being generated into a consistent pattern or structure over the months and even years of working with the

277

patient. This is called the countertransference structure. It interacts with the transference or the transference neurosis of the patient at various unconscious levels and is vital to the outcome of the treatment.

Other authors such as Menninger (1958) have implied a similar point of view, but rather than deeply exploring the subject, they back away from it. Whitaker and Malone (1953) point out that all psychotherapy involves a therapist and a patient, who have both therapist and patient vectors in them that work on the level of the apparent as well as unconscious relationship between patient and therapist. Therapist vectors are responses to the needs of the immature child part of the other person. Most often the responses of the therapist are therapist vector responses to the patient. At times, however, the patient responds with therapist vector responses to the (we hope) relatively small residual child part of the therapist. Patient vectors are demands for a feeling response from the other person, much as a hungry child demands response from his parents.

It follows that patients will get well only if the patient vectors of the therapist do not make excessive demands on the patient's therapist vectors. Assuming that the therapist had an adequate therapy of his own, thus reducing his patient vectors to a minimum, Whitaker and Malone then make a rather startling point. They insist that it is vital for successful therapy that the therapist bring in his patient vectors along with his therapist vectors. This they call a total participation with the patient. The therapist thus expands the frontiers of his own emotional growth during the therapy. If he refuses to participate totally in this fashion, it is felt by the patient as a severe rejection, and the therapy is not successful.

The contrast has to be made clear between what Whitaker and Malone call the gross pathological patient vectors of the immature therapist and the minimal or sliver type of residual patient vectors in the mature therapist. There are unfortunately some texts on psychotherapy that advise the therapist to dump all his problems on the patient. This approach is, of course, absurd.

There is a parallel between the intellectual process of working through and the emotional process of after-education. In the successful psychotherapy, according to Whitaker and Malone, a core symbolic process is passed through resembling the mother–child symbiosis. (This emphasis on the mother–child symbiosis occurs also in the quotation above from Tower, where the transference neurosis interacts with the counter-transference structure.) In this core process the therapist gains further emotional integration and the patient introjects a much more satisfactory parent, thus breaking up the neurotic structure.

Racker's (1968) concept of breaking up the vicious circle of the neurosis of failure should be thought of in the present context. We have previously discussed the interaction between the therapist and the patient in which a breaking up of the vicious circle must be attained through an understanding by the therapist of what is going on. According to Whitaker and Malone this dissolution of the vicious circle cannot happen unless the therapist is emotionally participating in the symbiosis with both his therapist vectors and his patient vectors.

The subject of this symbiotic fusion in psychotherapy has been sadly neglected. It has been suggested that the reason for this involves defenses in the psychotherapist against his

279

own incorporative fantasies, as well as against recognizing those of his patients. At the deepest intrapsychic levels in fantasy, this kind of fusion certainly contains elements of mutual introjection—a buried and primitive process. It must be admitted that in order to discuss this matter rationally, a therapist must be prepared to admit at least the possibility (a) that he gains in ego integration or emotional growth from his relationship with the patient and (b) that he has patient vectors—that is, he unconsciously reaches out for a symbiotic fusion with the patient. Not all therapists are willing to make such an admission.

What goes on at very deep levels between the patient and therapist? Communicating (through derivatives in the ego) with the unconscious is always proportional to success. The greater the extent to which the patient communicates to us his hidden repressed and unconscious ideation, the greater are our chances of successful therapy. Understanding the unconscious of the patient is proportional to success as far as the therapist is concerned.

The therapy process produces a conflict in both the patient and the therapist. In the patient there is a conflict between his conscious wish to exercise the ego functions of perception, communication, and judgment, on the one hand, and his unconscious ideation with the associated affect charges plus the transference out of the repetition compulsion, on the other. In other words, the patient's mature ego functioning—which would enable the patient to communicate his unconscious and to make judgments to change his behavior—is interfered with by his neurotic structure and infantile core.

The therapist also develops a conflict, arising out of the situation in therapy, where he is trying to exercise ego func-

280

tions. These are ego functions with which he perceives what the patient is communicating and with which he judges what is going on in the patient. They involve his capacity to communicate back to the patient through interpretations what he understands. The therapist's ego functions are interfered with by the countertransference structure. These countertransference structure problems arise out of the repetition compulsion of the therapist, associated with the therapist's unconscious ideation that has been stirred up by his encounter with the patient. The interference that takes place is an interference that reduces the energy available for conflict-free functioning of the ego.

The working-through process, then, could be understood as a reduction of this interference in both parties. That is, in a successful working through, the patient becomes increasingly capable of communicating unconscious material via secondary processes to the therapist, and the therapist becomes increasingly capable of understanding the unconscious material from the patient and interpreting it back to the patient. It has been pointed out that countertransference interferes both with understanding the patient's material and with the capacity to interpret it back to the patient. The therapist listens with evenly hovering attention to the patient's material. He tries to understand the patient's unconscious material and interpret it back, but this is interfered with by the countertransference structure. Thus, the therapist must undergo a continuous self-analysis of his countertransference structure.

The motivating force for this self-analysis lies in the gratification the therapist obtains from the symbiotic fusion with the patient, as well as from the crucial secondary-process

281

gratifications of experiencing the maturation of his patient "and the intellectual pleasure of comprehending how it is being achieved" (Kohut, 1971). These gratifications drive the therapist forward to increased ego integration, to better self-analysis, and to a finer empathic capacity. By resolving his conflict to some extent, he receives and understands new information from the patient's unconscious. He communicates this to the patient via his better capacity to interpret newly won understanding.

The interpretations, communications to the patient, work in both an intellectual way and a gratifying way to loosen and reduce the interference from the patient's conflict. As the patient's ego becomes stronger and more capable of integrative functioning via what he gets from the therapist, this, in turn, allows the patient to reveal more unconscious material. The reward of a correct interpretation is often the production of dreams, new memories, and the release of affect that was not present before. It enables the patient to get deeper and deeper into a symbiotic fusion with the therapist, which, in turn, affords more gratification and more intellectual material for the therapist to work with, and motivates the therapist to further self-analysis and, thus, to greater resolution of the interference of his countertransference structure. This then leads to better ego functioning in the therapist and more communication and interpretation to the patient.

So we go around and around in an ascending spiral—the opposite of Racker's "neurosis of failure." The resolution of the therapist's conflict between his countertransference structure and his mature ego functioning becomes the cornerstone to producing the resolution of the patient's conflict between his

282

wish to hide and repress unconscious material and his wish to communicate it to the therapist and to change.

In a successful psychotherapy, therefore, both parties gain increased ego integration, although, of course, the patient gains a great deal more than the therapist, since the patient has a great deal farther to go. The motor that drives this whole system forward is the mutual gratification derived from the deep symbiosis, as well as secondary-process gratifications of understanding, respect, and alliance between the patient and the therapist.

How deceptive the facade of the facility of therapeutic interaction is can be comparably gauged by the story of Dr. Euwe. Dr. Euwe, a world champion chess player and mathematician, reports a conversation that he overheard on a streetcar. The conductor of the streetcar asks a passenger, "How did Euwe make out yesterday, did he lose?" The passenger says, "No, the game was adjourned, but I think Euwe had a bad game." The conductor replies, "I'm afraid he is beginning to decline. Every one passes his peak sooner or later." The passenger remarks, "It does seem to be rather tiring for him." The conductor ends up with a tirade: "Tiring, what do you mean tiring? Do you know what's tiring? —When you have to stand up all day on the streetcar selling tickets and giving the correct change—that's physical and mental labor. But a chess player—he just sits in his chair until the game is over" (Reinfeld, 1951).

The immense complexity of therapeutic interaction has opened up a whole new field for scientific investigation. I have suggested the name of metapsychiatry for this field (Chessick, 1969), since it deals with the theoretical foundations of psychiatry and psychotherapy. In order to characterize therapeu-

283

tic interaction in an increasingly precise manner, we must examine these theoretical foundations carefully, conscientiously keeping in mind Artistotle's maxim, "It is the mark of an educated mind to expect that amount of exactness in each kind which the nature of the particular subject admits" (*Nicomachean Ethics*).

CHAPTER 13 *Metapsychiatry*

*T*HEORETICAL understanding of psychotherapy is a neglected subject that promises to help disengage us from some of the unnecessary and acrimonious controversy in our field. The founder of the subject was Freud (19), who defined metapsychology as the study of the assumptions on which the system of psychoanalytic theory is based. Statements on this subject are scattered throughout Freud's writings, with the main sources constituted by Chapter VII of *The Interpretation of Dreams* (1900), the "Addenda" to *Inhibitions, Symptoms and Anxiety* (1926) and the various papers on metapsychology (as they have come to be called). Rapaport (1967) points out the unfinished nature of all this and reviews the basic tenets of metapsychology in a brilliant fashion, so there is no reason to repeat the subject here.

A more general epistemological question regarding the relationship of metapsychological propositions to "reality" and to scientific method has been repeatedly raised, sometimes seriously and sometimes in a pejorative fashion. Avoiding the issue by regarding psychodynamic propositions as heuristic or "as-if" hypotheses has been suggested (Chessick, 1961). More recently the term *metapsychiatry* was introduced (Chessick, 1969) to ask certain questions:

1. What is the position of psychotherapy in Western philosophical tradition?

2. To what extent can psychotherapy be said to be a science and yield scientific knowledge?

3. To what extent is it philosophy or art?

Thus, we might ask whether generalizations based on the clinical data of psychotherapy represent scientific knowledge. Where do such propositions stand with respect to knowledge by intuition, knowledge by philosophy, or knowledge obtained through the method of science? I have maintained (Chessick, 1969) that three kinds of propositions are often mixed together under "knowledge" that should be separated according to the method used to obtain them. *All* propositions are matters of opinion regarding "truth" or "reality," and there are no absolutely apodeictic propositions that are not at the same time tautological.

Through rigorous use of scientific method, for example, Koch's postulates, we approach certainty with the greatest probability. However, many areas of study simply do not lend themselves to scientific experimentation in the rigid sense but must depend on the common accumulated historical experience of mankind: For example, slavery is always undesirable, or, participatory democracy is the most advanced form of government. I call such propositions "philosophical," and they are arrived at by the method of philosophy (Adler, 1965; Chessick, 1971a) and suffer from a lesser certainty. Propositions with the least certainty, such as the insights of Nietzsche or religious claims, are arrived at by the method of intuition; these are sometimes brilliant but never testable.

Generalizations from the clinical data of psychotherapy are on the borderline between philosophical knowledge and scientific knowledge because, although some experimental manipulation is possible in restricted situations, no crucial experiments can be devised that could lead to the definitive acceptance or rejection of a system of generalizations, such as the Freudian or Sullivanian, from the clinical data of psychotherapy. The ultimate acceptance or rejection of major propositions from such "schools" of thought will have to depend partly on restricted types of experiments and clinical observation and partly on the accumulated historical experience of psychotherapists, naturalists, child psychologists, and so on.

An outstanding example of metapsychiatry is provided by Kohut (1971) in a footnote. How does one decide whether a specific form of psychotherapy is primarily scientific or primarily inspirational? He suggests asking three important questions:

1. Do we have a systematical theoretical grasp of the processes involved in therapy?

2. Can the treatment method be communicated to others, learned, and practiced without the presence of its originator?

3. Does the treatment method remain successful after the death of its creator?

This latter question frequently separates out therapies that primarily depend on the charisma of their originators.

One of the most important areas of metapsychiatry to

287

have generated much controversy and needless acrimony lies in the understanding of "what goes on" in psychotherapy between patient and therapist, often labeled therapeutic interaction. I have attempted to reduce this controversy by putting various partial claims in perspective in the "special theory of psychotherapeutic interaction" (Chessick, 1971a). It is designated as a special theory because for practical clinical application it can be reduced to standard psychoanalytic metapsychology, just as Einstein's equations could be reduced to Newtonian physics for practical terrestial purposes. Let us briefly review this theory.

The psychotherapist is caught between what has been called by C. P. Snow "the two cultures." Even if he is a sensitive and conscientious therapist, he will be criticized by the scientists for engaging in an unscientific discipline. Alternately he will not be accepted by artists, because there are many aspects of his work that are scientific and that restrict him in his creativity. Yet he must be immersed in the arts and he must have a wide knowledge of the humanities. Stumpf (1966) reminds us of one of the most interesting and neglected philosophers, Charles S. Pierce, who lived from 1839 to 1914. Pierce pointed out, writes Stumpf, that,

> Beliefs guide our desires and shape our actions. But beliefs are "unfixed" by doubts. It is when the "irritation of doubt" causes a struggle to attain belief that the enterprise of thought begins. Through thought we try to fix our beliefs so that we shall have a guide for action. There are several ways in which we can fix our beliefs, according to Pierce. There is the method of *tenacity*, whereby people cling to beliefs, refusing to entertain doubts about them, or to consider arguments or evidence for another view. Another method is to invoke *authority*, as

288

when persons in authority require the acceptance of certain ideas as true on pain of punishment. Still another method is that of the metaphysician or philosopher . . . who, according to Pierce, would settle questions of belief by asking whether an idea was "agreeable to *reason.*"

Pierce disagrees with all these approaches because they cannot really fix or settle belief. They all lack a connection with experience and behavior, and he advised the method of science, whose chief virtue, he thought, is a realistic basis in experience. The method of science requires that the person state not only what he believes but also how he arrives at it. The procedures he follows should be available to anyone who cares to retrace the same steps to test whether the same result will occur. "Pierce again and again emphasizes this public or community character in the method of science . . . the method of science is highly self-critical. It subjects its conclusions to severe tests, and wherever indicated conclusions of a theory are adjusted to fit the new evidence and new insights." This, says Pierce, "ought also to be the mental attitude of any one in relation to his beliefs."

Pierce felt that science required a high degree of cooperation between all members of the scientific community. "This element of the method, this cooperation, is yet another force that prevents any individual or group from shaping truth to fit its own interests. Conclusions of science must be conclusions that all scientists can draw. Similarly, in questions of beliefs and truth, it should be possible for anyone to reach the same conclusions." In the last analysis, there have to be some practical consequences to any idea or belief.

The essence of science is that it is a method of doing something. Before men are able to do, they must have a belief and a belief, in turn, requires thought. Only thought that is tested by the criteria of experience and experiment can provide us with the surest basis of belief, thought Pierce. This, in turn, will establish our habits of action. Now the usual explanation of the difficulties of psychotherapy is to assume that they are a consequence of our ignorance in the scientific field. This implies that as more knowledge or more scientific understanding in psychotherapy accumulates, the practice of psychotherapy will become more and more scientific and approach the classical doctor–patient model in medicine.

I have argued (Chessick, 1971a) that this generally held assumption is wrong and accounts for much of the confusion and acrimony within our field as well as for many unfair and invidious comparisons that are made with the so-called more scientific branches of medicine. It is based on a misconception about the nature of knowledge—a misconception that has existed for centuries as a squabble between the proponents of science and the proponents of the humanities, the traditional rivals of Snow's two cultures.

The standard views on the subject by Snow (1963) and Bronowski (1959) have perpetuated this misconception. Snow tries to distinguish scientists and humanists in terms of personality differences between the two, with some bias for the scientists as against the so-called literary intellectuals. This again implies that with time, understanding, and patience the two cultures can get together and merge into one. Bronowski is even more specific. He finds "a profound likeness" between the creative acts of the mind in art and science and tries to urge a synthesis of art and science into one kind of investigation.

Actually, science reveres matters of fact and basically

290

relies on some sort of formulation of principles and causation. The humanities are dramatic, emotional, and oriented to human purposes in a sense in which the impersonality and supposed objectivity of science can never allow. The avowed and willing anthropocentralism of the humanities is far removed from the neutral causations of science. Scientists and humanists think differently and use completely separate languages.

Levi (1969, 1970) has pointed out there are not one but two maps of reality: one sober, factual, and claiming to be the custodian of the literal truth; the other mythical, playful, but claiming to be pointing the way to a deeper wisdom. These two maps of reality compete for allegiance in the divided mind of every individual man. Levi tries to base this on the philosophy of Kant, who distinguishes between two vital faculties of the mind. This is stretching the point and there is much disagreement about Kant's conception of human cognition. At any rate, the first of these vital faculties discussed in Kant's *Critique of Pure Reason* was labeled the cognitive understanding, and dealt with what Kant called the analytic presuppositions of mathematics and physics, the principles behind scientific assertions, the rational presuppositions of the natural sciences, the pure concepts of the understanding. The second faculty is labeled reproductive in *The Critique of Pure Reason* by Kant (1963) and changed to creative in *The Critique of Judgment* (1968). This deals with the dialectic of illusion, the heuristic fictions of the mind, the creative imagination, or—in terminology used by Levy—the humanistic imagination, since there is creativity in science as well.

Thus scientific understanding and humanistic imagination are fundamentally different and are grounded in different nuclear operations of the mind. The need to construct chains of causal explanation and the need to construct heuristic, often dramatic and anthropomorphic, explanatory fictions are both fundamental cognitive needs of the human person.

Any map of the psychic interaction or the therapeutic interaction between therapist and patient will have to be bilingual. Each of the two languages selects out two centers for the psychic fields, therapist and patient. In *the language of scientific understanding* the therapist is described in terms of his set of ego operations, countertransference structure, combination of therapist vectors and patient vectors, and his conduct and therapeutic technique. The patient is described in terms of a set of ego operations, a genetic–dynamic formulation, Freud's (Arlow and Brenner, 1964) structural theory, transference, and a combination of patient vectors and therapist vectors. A scientific understanding of the process of psychotherapy would have to present a steady mutual influencing, continuous throughout the psychotherapy process, both on a conscious and unconscious level, of the psychic fields of the therapist and the patient on each other, using the usual Freudian terminology.

In *the language of the humanistic imagination* the same psychic fields are described in terms of power strivings, security operations, caring, being there, I and Thou, encounter, basic anxiety, and so on, depending on which inspirational school of psychotherapy or which philosopher one wishes to follow. The point is there are, and always will be, two fundamentally different and competing ways of describing the interaction between the psychic fields of the therapist and the patient in the process of psychotherapy. The theory of psychotherapeutic interaction maintains that these two fundamentally different ways of describing the continuing mutual influence of the psychic fields on each other are *both* necessary and useful maps. They are not in competition with respect to truth or falsehood but, rather, arise from the perpetual and fundamental human need to describe reality in two fundamentally different ways—the language of scientific understanding and the language of the humanistic imagination.

Freud, because of his unusual and wide erudition, had a tendency to switch back and forth between these two languages—assuming that his readers could follow what he was doing—in order to present as immediate and complete a description of the clinical phenomena as he possibly could. In addition, his readers had, because of their European backgrounds, a much more humanistic education than the average physician has today. What happened, of course, is that the two languages became confused in the minds of his lesser followers, and even more in the minds of general readers. Thus, a number of problems that I have elsewhere (Chessick, 1961) described as pseudoproblems arose and gave rise to all kinds of animosities and foolishness, a situation that unfortunately continues to this day.

As an example of how the special theory of psychotherapeutic interaction can be applied, let us turn again to the controversial issue of the treatment of patients with ego defects and begin in *the language of scientific understanding.* When Freud (1923) originally presented the concept of the ego, he simultaneously introduced two extremely important notions into our basic understanding of ego formation. The first of these was the notion of *introjection,* in which he suggested, "there quite often ensues an alteration of his ego which can only be described as a setting up of the object inside the ego, as it occurs in melancholia; the exact nature of this substitu-

293

tion is as yet unknown to us." This process, especially in the early phases of development, was regarded as being extremely important by Freud, and it leads to his famous statement, "The character of the ego is a precipitate of abandoned object–cathexes and that it contains the history of those object–choices."

The second important concept introduced by Freud was the notion that if the ego's

> object-identifications obtain the upper hand and become too numerous, unduly powerful and incompatible with one another, a pathological outcome will not be far off. It may come to a disruption of the ego in consequence of the different identifications becoming cut off from one another by resistances; . . . Even when things do not go so far as this, there remains the question of conflicts between the various identifications into which the ego comes apart, . . . whatever the character's later capacity for resisting the influences of abandoned object–cathexes may turn out to be, the effects of the first identifications made in earliest childhood will be general and lasting.

These two conceptions, representing a remarkable theoretical innovation by Freud, still remain the cornerstone of our understanding of ego psychology today. Regrettably, little agreement on further understanding has developed within the whole subject of the ego and the introjects, especially the early introjects that form its foundation (see Guntrip, 1971).

The most thorough study of the subject of introjection available is by Schafer (1968). He writes,

> An introject is an inner presence with which one feels in a continuous or intermittent dynamic relationship. The subject

294

conceives of this presence as a person, a physical or psychological part of a person (e. g. a breast, a voice, a look, an affect,) or a person-like thing or creature . . . Relations with introjects are as variable in their nature as those existing between any two persons. For example, the introject may act on the subject in a manner that is nourishing, loving, sensual, helpful, joyous, placating, hurtful, depriving, restraining, mournful, oppressive, and so forth. . . . The qualities of this inner presence are usually modeled after one or more dynamically significant characteristics of an external object. . . . Both the coming into being of an introject and its continued existence represent attempts to modify distressing relations with the external object.

Giovacchini (1967b) pointed out,

The role of introjects, since Freud first focused upon it, has become increasingly important, not only as a significant aspect of ego development but because of its relevance to therapeutic considerations. Ego psychology has caused us to focus upon psychic functions and to view the development of the personality, not only in terms of its genetic antecedents but also as a balance between a variety of systems that can be considered from the viewpoint of a hierarchical continuum. The introject is included as an intrinsic aspect of ego structure.

Giovacchini insists that "somehow" introjects are "instrumental" in ego formation, both in terms of establishing a coherent identity and in initiating a process "that enables the psyche to deal with both instinctual pressures and the outer world," that is, the acquisition of adaptional techniques. The concepts of the good introject and the disruptive introject (sometimes called the hostile or malevolent or malignant introject) are simply a rephrasing of Freud's language. Giovacchini writes,

> Disruptive introjects do not lead to ego differentiation. They interfere with the development of specific areas of adaptation. Such lack of development or maldevelopment may prevent the patient from obtaining gratification from persons who may be willing to help him. The patient is not able to utilize or assimilate experiences which another person that does not have the same type of constricting introjects finds indispensable for his emotional development.

There is little understanding and agreement on the exact method in which the introject is formed and precisely how it functions in specific stages of ego development to either enhance or impair the adaptative functioning of the ego and the synthetic functioning of the ego, with a subsequent impaired development of a healthy sense of self.

It is generally agreed, however, that at least in the borderline patient there is a profound lack of a sense of self-love or "beloved self" (Modell, 1968) or as Saul (1970) puts it, there is a lack of "inner sustainment," without which even the best technical interpretations will fail. This generally known situation in the borderline patient, along with the sense of alienation and identity diffusion (Erikson, 1959) and the well-known difficulties in responding to positive experiences of these patients, can all be understood clearly on the basis of what might be called hostile, malevolent, or constricting introjects formed early in life and developing what Saul and Pulver (1969) have called a "warping" of the childhood nucleus.

The task of psychotherapy with the borderline and the

psychotic patient becomes infinitely complicated by the fact that the patient neither has a firm grasp of his own sense of identity nor is he able, because of the introjects, to respond to supportive, kindly, or benevolent measures as we logically would expect a starved and lonely person to do. It is now theoretically clear why attempts at directly gratifying the borderline patient have been repeatedly shown to fail. Directly trying to mother the borderline patient causes serious chaos and often produces a paradoxical response, leading to frustration on the part of those who originally approached the patient with benevolence and good will (Chessick, 1968).

The concept of "unfreezing" these malevolent introjects was, to my knowledge, first introduced by Winnicott (1958, 1966). I believe that the key to any successful uncovering psychotherapy with the borderline or the psychotic patient is in the capacity of the therapist, and the therapeutic atmosphere he creates for all his patients, to permit and enable the patient to unfreeze disruptive and restrictive introjects warping the basis of his early ego formation. On the other hand, Guntrip (1968) points out that, "The major source of resistance to psychotherapy is the extreme tenacity of our libidinal attachments to parents whatever they are like. This state of affairs is perpetuated by repression in the unconscious inner world, where they remain as subtly all-pervasive bad figures generating a restrictive, oppressive, persecutory, inhibiting family environment in which the child cannot find his real self, yet from which he has no means of escape."

The only reasonable approach to these patients in uncovering psychotherapy would have to be an unfreezing of early ego formation; clearly this can only occur if a controlled regression is permitted to take place. It must be pointed out that

297

regression cannot be forced by the therapist. It must occur as the natural consequence of the sense of security within the therapeutic alliance that is allowed to form between a relatively healthy therapist and whatever mature aspects are available in the observing ego of the patient. Winnicott (1958) enumerates some of the obvious factors that allow this regression to take place, which resembles our discussion in Chapter 3. It might be first mentioned that "the whole thing adds up to the fact that the analyst *behaves* himself or herself, and behaves without too much cost simply because of being a relatively mature person."

The factors encouraging a regression useful in psychotherapy are:

1. A consistent and frequent being at the service of the patient, at a time arranged to suit mutual convenience;

2. Being reliably there, on time, "alive, breathing";

3. For the limited period of time, keeping awake and becoming preoccupied with the patient;

4. The expression of love by the positive interest taken and "hate in the strict start and finish and in the matter of fees";

5. The attempt to get into touch with the process of the patient, to understand the material presented and to communicate this understanding by interpretation;

6. Use of a method stressing a nonanxious approach of objective observation;

7. Work done in a room that is quiet and not liable to sudden unpredictable sounds and yet not dead quiet. Proper lighting of a room, not by a light staring in the face and not by a variable light. In some instances the patient lies on a couch that is comfortable, in other instances, depending on

the situation (Chessick, 1971b), a face-to-face situation with the patient is necessary.

8. Keeping moral judgment out of the relationship as well as any uncontrollable need on the part of the therapist to introduce details of his personal life and ideas;

9. The therapist's staying, on the whole, punctual, free from temper tantrums, free from compulsive falling in love, and so on, and in general neither hostile and retaliatory nor exploitative towards the patient;

10. Maintaining a consistent, clear distinction between fact and fantasy, so that the therapist is not hurt or offended by an aggressive dream or fantasy: in general eliminating any "talion reaction" and insuring that both the therapist and the patient consistently survive their interaction. Winnicott feels that this setting reproduces the earliest mothering techniques and invites regression. If it is consistently offered, an unfreezing takes place as a natural consequence of the regression that occurs.

A verbatim and dramatic example follows from my clinical material of a young woman in the third year of intensive psychotherapy, illustrating the to-and-fro battle between the gradually maturing ego and the adhesive force of the constricting maternal introject:

> Last week the dream about my mother and me began in a store where my mother had gotten beat up. I went into the store to help her. I went into a rage wanting to kill the person responsible for hurting my mother. The next thing I knew I was seeing a girl sprawled out on the floor naked. She had no breasts at all and no hair on her vagina. No one would have anything to do with her, she seemed repulsive. Next, I was

299

behind a curtain with my chest exposed. My breasts were very large. My left breast (which happens to be the larger one) was all bruised and discolored. I wanted to show it to my mother but I was afraid she would get mad because, first of all, my chest was exposed, and, secondly, because she would want to know how I got bruised (which I did not know myself).

I feel as though the beginning of the dream was my own slave-guilt defending my mother. I believe it was really my healthy side that was hurting her. I also think the girl lying on the floor naked was myself as a child. At that time I did feel my body was repulsive. I was not sure about the part with my left breast being bruised, large, and discolored. I believe you might be right about it representing my mother. I have always felt aroused through my breasts and dissatisfied that they were not as large as my mother's. The bruises and discoloration could represent my own distorted, discolored views of sex being ugly, repulsive, and cruel. Not to mention a downgrading of one's character.

Ever since I have started to get well I have had the feeling at times of losing control of my healthy mind. As I told you in the fantasy I had in our last session concerning my behavior with Eddie the previous night, while lying on the bed after an unsuccessful try at "baby making" (which is what it really boiled down to), Eddie came into the bedroom and told me he was sorry—it was at that moment I could feel "her" come. In the fantasy I pictured her standing over the bed and then entering me and taking over. (When he told me he was sorry I felt as though I had him in a very vulnerable position—I could therefore "punish" him for not doing what I wanted him to do by saying whatever I could to hurt.) This I think is a basis for my fear of my mother, that is, punishment for not doing or acting or being what she wanted you to be was to be hurt in whatever way she deemed fit, and God only knows she could come up with some pretty good ways. One of her favorites was *guilt* and a feeling that I had drastically and almost unforgivably let her down. I say "almost" unforgivably because she always forgave me, after all I was her great "masterpiece" of seduction and slavery, she would not let me get away without a fight. It is really funny to think I was always trying to be above everyone else and I was really one of the lowliest and most pitiful human beings on earth—a slave.

To get back to the fantasy. After I felt she had entered me I could not control anything I said for a period. I spouted off with whatever hurting I could think of—no limit to the intensity. I could feel myself trying to stop it (just like a person who feels themselves ready to vomit and is trying desperately to stop it—even to the point of clamping their hands over their mouth—to no avail). I was able to stop her at a point but not until she had left a bucket full of puke all over the one I love and that includes you and Eddie. I think I was trying to hurt you primarily and knock him around a bit too, but unfortunately for Eddie he got both shares that night. When I did finally stop I could still feel the remnants of her in me (like when you have a climax in sex you still feel the spasms after the big jolt is over). I could feel it when I had to struggle to say I was sorry. I then won out and told Eddie to please try to understand me and ignore everything I say when I get like that. At that point it was as if she were hovering over me and looking mad and mean, because I had given in, which she would not approve of. I think I felt this feeling of my mother coming into me before. At many times in the past I have felt uncontrollable urges to inflict pain on men, usually those closest to me and most vulnerable.

Because of this "pact" with my mother, my mind was completely wrapped around her. After I had been in therapy a while, it seemed almost as if there was another mind devel-

301

oping right next to the first. For the longest time the sick mind didn't bother the healthy one, because the healthy one was too weak. But, as it got stronger, as therapy went on, it started to worry the sick mind, and that's when the trouble started. I feel now that my healthy mind is strong enough to survive, but not strong enough to keep my mother from "entering" me and blocking out all sense of control from my healthy mind so that I can't prevent what I can see coming.

When Eddie told me he was sorry, I felt as though something was going to happen to me that I couldn't prevent and when it did I would explode at him. It was then that I believe my mother took over. It didn't even sound like me to myself. It was almost as if I was somewhere else hearing these things come out of my mouth and not being able to stop them. When it was over I started to cry and felt sick and tired like something had been taken out of me, like my healthy mind had been literally sat on and smothered. I think the constant struggling with this force is what made me feel exhausted and so relieved when I calmed down and was myself again.

I think as a child I was afraid of my mother. I didn't have the strength to resist and at the time had no reason to, it seemed a suitable arrangement. I didn't know any other way of life, I was boxed in a cage. Now I know it's that same mind and will that scares me now—the power of it, that is. I can really see why it's so hard to break it, each time she's "in" me less, but even for those moments I turn into something really ugly and vicious.

This crucial unfreezing of malevolent introjects through a controlled regression contains within it two major constructive and therapeutic events. The first of these is the loss of destructive introjects; the second is the substitute introjection of the psychic field offered by the therapist. However, the regression contains also a major *destructive* event, for such a regression stirs up omnipotent expectations on the part of the patient: a yearning for what the therapist can do to restore, magically and in a primary-process manner, to the patient all the missing experiences from his infancy, and make good for the patient all the negative experiences of his infancy. I shall proceed to discuss first this destructive event and then the constructive events in detail.

Either the inevitable frustration of the omnipotent expectations of the patient stirred up by regression, *or also* narcissistic blows that occur to the patient in his real life during the long process of psychotherapy can lead to a series of events that result in a failure of the treatment. The psychotherapist must be aware that the danger of regression induced by the therapeutic setting can lead to failure, and he must have an understanding of the typcal kinds of consequences that are produced as a result of the frustration of the omnipotent expectations and from serious narcissistic blows.

Such consequences are typically:

1. Acting out, in which the patient quits the treatment or in which he finds quickly a third person to meet his unbearable infantile cravings for holding and body contact as described by Hollender (1969, 1970);

2. The need for revenge, in which the patient through passive aggression stalemates the treatment, stalemates his life, or allows his life situation to fail, making psychotherapy impossible;

3. Projection of destructive introjects onto the therapist with fear and hatred of him all coming as a consequence of the frustration of the patient's omnipotent expectations, which may lead to a break up of the therapy;

4. An autistic retreat on the part of the patient into sadistic sexual fantasies; or;

5. At worst, even hallucinations and delusions, as a consequence of ego fragmentation, described in Chapter 11, which may even require hospitalization.

Let us turn now to the therapeutic and constructive consequences of regression in the treatment setting. The loss of malevolent introjects as a consequence of regression can be noted if the therapist carefully studies both changes in ego function and superego function in the patient. Destructive introjects in the ego manifest themselves by poor adaptive techniques. Introjects of the parents include many elements of the relationship with them that involve methods of mastery. As there is a loss of destructive and restrictive introjects, there is a corresponding improvement in the patient's capacity to adapt to the external world, to function more efficiently, and to observe himself more realistically. Similarly, as introjects are discharged from the superego by projection and then interpreted, there is a lessening of the hostile punitive aspects of the superego, and the patient becomes more reasonable with himself and others and begins to develop a sense of beloved self.

One of the most tricky and debatable aspects of psychotherapy is the subject of the introjection of the therapist's field. There is general agreement that a correct interpretation with a subsequent increase in knowledge is not only an intellectual acquisition by the patient but a therapeutic experience (Fromm-Reichmann, 1950). It is also clear that the therapist must take a humane, reasonable, and nonanxious secondary-process approach with all patients, in contrast to *any* kind of role playing or *any* unusual, abnormal inconsistent, phony, or socially bizarre behavior that we might call a primary-process approach. A primary-process approach, as explained in Chapter 9, tends to fix the patient on primary-process thinking and adaptative techniques, which represent a great danger as the patient attempts to deal with the external world. Most seriously, the immediate gratification through primary-process behavior in the therapy tends to stop the development of ego function and fixates the patient on this level (Giovacchini, 1965).

More is introjected from the therapist in a properly conducted treatment than the healthy experience of a correct interpretation (Greenson, 1972). First of all, the therapist's nonanxious observing attitude, his compassionate, studious, and sincere approach to the patient, becomes a part of a healthy introject in the patient's ego. Most tricky of all, it seems imperative that we recognize the countertransference structure (Tower, 1956) as an important aspect of the therapist's attitude forming his psychic field, which is *also* introjected by the patient. If this countertransference structure, as defined in Chapter 7, is, for the most part, not malevolent and murderous, it at least does not represent a serious impediment to ego growth through introjection of the therapist's psychic field. We hope then, that through the introjection of the psychic field of the therapist—based on correct interpretations, a compassionate secondary-process approach, a non-anxious observing attitude, and a relatively benign counter-transference structure—there is ego growth, manifested by better functioning of the various subsystems of the ego.

It is ego growth through this process that allows the destructive dangers of the regression induced by the therapeutic setting to be overcome by the patient's gradually increasing ego strength. They *will* be overcome providing certain ominous situations do not occur, such as;

1. If the omnipotent demands are not too overwhelming and immediate.

2. If the patient does not immediately quit or unconsciously set out to destroy therapy before any work can be done.

3. If the destructive introjects that have made up the early ego formation of the patient are not so constricting and malevolent that a total rigidity and incapacity to get free of them is present.

4. If the psychic field of the therapist is mature enough.

It is clear that a certain realistic limitation is placed on our therapeutic efforts by the first three of these factors, and some cases will inevitably fail because of them. It is in the area of the psychic field of the therapist that *the most hope exists* for an improvement of our results.

In *Why Psychotherapists Fail* (Chessick, 1971a) I have already discussed in detail the production of the optimal psychic field of the therapist. In addition to this generally optimal psychic field, there is certain specific work that the therapist must do with every patient and in every psychotherapy. It is easy to see that a countertransference structure is stirred up in the therapist (a) by each regressive step in the patient, confronting the therapist with a new set of feelings, demands, and reactions; (b) by intercurrent realistic or narcissistic blows in the life of the psychotherapist—after all, this is over a long-term psychotherapy, in which both therapist and patient are experiencing numerous events in their actual living; and (c) by the very length of time of therapy, representing a "time frustration" to the secret omnipotent hopes of the psychotherapist.

All of these factors operate to provoke the tendency in the therapist to exploit or retaliate or both, even in such minor ways as the tone of one's voice or letting the patient out a minute early. Thus a *constant self-analysis of the counter-transference structure* must be going on within the therapist in order to keep the psychic field up to a maximum of maturity. This should take place at the same time as efforts are made to understand the patient and to interpret this understanding back to him. So, *in the language of scientific understanding*, "learning from one's patients" means expanding one's own ego capacities through the continual self-analysis of countertransference structures precipitated by either the various phases of the patient's regression or by intercurrent events in the real world of the patient and/or the therapist.

It has occurred to me that this psychic interplay may be given mathematical form as follows:

Let i_{th} = various partial benevolent and adaptive introjects from the psychic field of the therapist

Let i_p = malevolent and constricting parental introjects

Let A_ϕ = ego subsystems not developmentally constricted by i_p or "autonomous ego functions"

$$(1) \quad \text{Then} \sum_{th=1}^{th=n} i_{th} - \sum_{p=1}^{p=n} i_p + \sum_{\phi=1}^{\phi=n} A_\phi = \vec{F_t}$$

where $\vec{F_t}$ is the drive vector existing in the patient toward maturity and ego integration at time t.

Let r_{th} = experiences of frustration of magical expectations from the therapist

307

THE TECHNIQUE AND PRACTICE OF INTENSIVE PSYCHOTHERAPY

Let r_e = experiences of frustration out of various narcissistic blows from external reality in patient's life, during the years of psychotherapy

Let G_ϕ = the net of unknown adhesive forces, perhaps genetic, perhaps "id-resistance" producing "inertia" to psychic change (Chapter 9)

$$(2) \quad \text{Then} \sum_{th=1}^{th=n} r_{th} + \sum_{e=1}^{e=n} r_e + \sum_{\phi-1}^{\phi=n} G_\phi = \overleftarrow{F}_t$$

where $\overleftarrow{F}_t$ is the drive vector existing in the patient toward clinging to the illness and ego fragmentation at time t.

$$(3) \quad \text{Then} \quad \overrightarrow{F}_t - \overleftarrow{F}_t = P_t$$

where P_t is the "progress" (or deterioration) of the psychotherapy process at any time t.

This formulation allows for a methodical evaluation of any psychotherapy at time t, and the minute study of the interacting fields of the patient and therapist rests on a breakdown of each sigma $\left(\sum \right)$ into its constituent elements, 1, 2 . . . . . . n, providing a guideline for investigation or research into each element. Since n is *not* infinite, this becomes a possible, although difficult, task.

This is not enough. In *the language of the humanistic imagination,* the patient must continuously experience the "presence" of the therapist. Each therapy session must "count," as Saul (1958) puts it. Each session must represent an encounter between the psychic field of the therapist—which in its maturity, extends trust, confidence, and hope—and the need–fear dilemma of the patient, who has fallen

308

away from living and being with another person. This deep inner attitude on the part of the therapist can be maintained only as a function of continual reduction of constricting countertransference structures, just as a healthy nervous system permits the maintenance of an alert and attentive mind. The purpose of this for the patient is described by Saul (1970):

> For the unsustained, the analyst must provide the experience which the patient lacked in childhood: that of having an interested, sympathetic, understanding person always available in his life. Without such an attitude, technically correct interpretations may be interpreted by the patient as disapproval. Accurate interpretations also require an attitude of human understanding, of being on the patient's side, of having confidence in him . . . The analyst's confidence is partly internalized and can move even the "hollow" ones in the direction of a sense of sustainment, of identity, a good self-image and self-acceptance.

It follows from these theoretical considerations that the phenomena described in the language of the humanistic imagination, such as "presence," or "being there" or "I-thou," and so on, represent *epiphenomena* of the successful working through in the psychotherapist of the various phases of countertransference structure called forth by the phases of the patient's psychotherapy.

Thus the "encounter" value of the therapy at any given time E_t may be written:

$$(4) \quad E_t = f(P_t).$$

A graph of this function, in usual clinical experience, would be a logarithmic curve, which explains why, during a certain

309

interval, a dramatic interchange and rapid unfolding may appear after a long plateau period. Obviously if P_t is not a positive (forward) value, the patient cannot *experience* the encounter (E_t) since the destructive aspects as described above would prevail. Also, the capacity to experience the encounter (E_t) is clearly proportional to the value of P_t. This is an extremely important fact.

The reverse is *not* true, and here is where an increasingly common amateur error takes place. One cannot force "presence" or an encounter down a patient's throat. Hugging and touching and going through all kinds of "immediacy" gestures with a patient will not fool the patient; they mask serious countertransference problems in the therapist. Only the natural and inevitable unfolding of a human encounter in the forward progress of psychotherapy, as both the patient and the therapist work through their respective tasks, can produce a genuine growth experience for both. *There are no short cuts.*

CHAPTER 14 *Goals and Termination*

Growth, maturation, and the expansion of personality in the direction of capability of self-realization, the giving and accepting of love, and forming durable relationships of intimacy are all continuous experiences in living. Their perpetuation and renewal should be an ever-present goal throughout the lives of all former patients. After the termination of treatment they should be able to reach out through their own endeavors for the accomplishment of these goals. This was what Freud referred to when he said that psychoanalysis and the therapeutic method aiming at the facilitation of growth and maturation in the human are "interminable" in essence as long as the patient lives and as long as changing mental processes and fluctuating emotional experiences are at work within him and his environment.

311

From this statement by Fromm-Reichmann (1950), the entire discussion of termination and goals of therapy could be deduced. The end phase of psychotherapy and the beginning phase of psychotherapy were compared by Freud in a famous analogy to the game of chess. Freud (1913a) pointed out that anyone who hopes to learn the noble game of chess from books will soon discover that only the openings and endings admit of an exhaustive systematic presentation and that the infinite variety of moves that develops after the opening defy any such description. This gap in instruction can only be filled by a diligent study of games fought out by masters. The same situation applies to psychotherapy. As we approach the end phase or the termination of psychotherapy it becomes somewhat easier to present clear-cut strategies and tactics. This termination phase, like a chess game, obviously depends on the goals of therapy in general.

It is common knowledge that patients come to psychotherapists for a variety of reasons, most often hoping to be the beneficiary of the therapist's supposed omniscience and omnipotence. Wheelis (1958) and many other authors have emphasized the recent marked shift in what patients are seeking from psychotherapy, from the removal of symptoms to the removal of "vague conditions of maladjustment and discontent." He writes, "The change is from symptom neurosis to character disorders. . . . To get well these days is to get well from loneliness, insecurity, doubt, boredom, restlessness, and marital discord." The entire concept of character disorder remains fuzzy and difficult, and there is little agreement on the correct method of treatment of these cases. No other type of patient so consistently, dramatically, and urgently raises the so-called existential questions in psychotherapy. In fact,

312

two of the most famous existentialist books, Sartre's *Nausea* (1964) and Camus' *The Stranger* (1957), depict people who are alienated and alone.

The confusion, which seems to be rampant these days, about what psychotherapy can and cannot do, is illustrated by the frequent synonymous use of three phrases by philosophers, psychiatrists, and many lay persons. These terms—mental health, happiness, and the good life—are assumed to be either identical or overlapping in meaning. The conditions they describe, it is assumed, can be attained by essentially the same methods. For example, it is said that the good life leads to happiness, that mental health leads to the good life, and so on. Character disorders and borderline patients bring these terms up again and again, for they are vaguely unhappy and discontent, certainly looking for what they would call a good life and hoping that getting well and finding mental health will mean finding happiness and a good life.

In our present age, society seems to be reinforcing this confusion. The current fashion of bringing the psychiatrist —who is, I am sorry to say, all too often willing—into every conceivable kind of community situation as an "authority" reinforces the assumption that the psychiatrist has the key to the variegated difficulties of living that Freud called "everyday misery."

Within therapy, patients with character disorders and especially borderline patients watch the psychotherapist intensely—in every sense of the conscious and unconscious meaning of that phrase—to see what kind of a person he is, what kind of a life he leads, and whether he has appeared to have found happiness. This can lead to considerable confusion, since an unhealthy therapist sends a double message to the patient, if he pretends that he is omnipotent or has the answers to the perpetual human quest for the good life and happiness.

Fromm (1955) has proposed that the only meaning life can have is what an individual gives it by unfolding and realizing his personal, potential, and characteristically human powers of reason, love, and productive work. Camus (1955) has portrayed this human predicament as a lucid invitation to live and to create in the very midst of the desert.

The vague phenomena characterized as so-called existential anxiety, as discussed in Chapter 8, are much more complex than originally believed by the existential philosophers because they often represent a displacement from anxiety over unconscious conflicts. Thus, as conversion symptoms were the fashion in the Victorian era, existential nausea is the current vogue. It follows that unconscious mental conflicts must be resolved before a person can be considered to be genuinely concerned with problems of the good life and happiness. In all fairness, I have to point out that some authors take the opposite viewpoint. For example, Tillich (1952) argues that all neurotic problems are really based on what he calls existential anxiety. From the clinical point of view, this appears to be a philosophical absurdity that reduces the term "existential anxiety" to meaninglessness.

Mental health is a condition that must be achieved prior to the pursuit of either the good life or happiness, just as physical health, a certain minimum material prosperity, and political freedom are necessary. Otherwise the energies of the individual are bound up in the problems of survival alone. A person can have mental health without having the good life and happiness, but he cannot have the good life or happiness without a reasonable degree of mental health. The pathologi-

314

cal, destructive, interfering, and alienating mechanisms of defense must be given up by the ego before the individual has the good life and happiness. Otherwise his life remains in bondage to the repetition compulsion.

Freud (1937) in one of his most famous late papers has made this quite clear in the context of discussing the task of psychotherapy.

> The mechanisms of defense served the purpose of keeping off dangers. It cannot be disputed that they are successful in this; and it is doubtful whether the ego could do without them altogether during its development. But it is also certain that they may become dangers themselves. It sometimes turns out that the ego has paid too high a price for the services they render it. The dynamic expenditure necessary for maintaining them, and the restrictions of the ego they almost invariably entail, prove a heavy burden on the psychical economy. Moreover, these mechanisms are not relinquished after they have assisted the ego during the difficult years of its development. No one individual, of course, makes use of all the possible mechanisms of defense. Each person uses no more than a selection of them. But these become fixated in his ego. They become regular modes of reaction of his character, which are repeated throughout his life whenever a situation occurs that is similar to the original one. This turns them into infantilisms, and they share the fate of so many institutions which attempt to keep themselves in existence after the time of their usefulness has passed. . . . The adult's ego with its increased strength continues to defend itself against dangers which no longer exist in reality; indeed, it finds itself compelled to seek out those situations in reality which can serve as an approximate substitute for the original danger, so as to be able to justify, in relation to them, its maintaining its habitual modes of reaction. Thus we can easily understand how the defense

mechanisms, by bringing about an ever more extensive alienation from the external world and a permanent weakening of the ego, pave the way for, and encourage the outbreak of neurosis.

Guntrip (1968) conceives of the ego primarily in terms of schizoid mechanisms and very deep introjects and projective identifications. Thus, when he thinks about the goals of psychotherapy, it is in terms of changes in such internal representations. As Guntrip sees it, the patient has such a fear of losing these malevolent introjects that he regards the therapist as someone who is going to rob him of his parents, even though it is also true that he looks to the therapist to rescue him from them. Thus, the patient has to go through an awful period in which, if he loses his internal bad objects while not yet feeling sure enough that his therapist will adequately replace them, he will feel that he is falling between two stools, or, as one patient vividly expressed it "plunging into a mental abyss of blank emptiness."

It takes the patient a very long time to feel that the therapist can really be and is a better parent with respect to giving him a relationship in which he can become his own true self. There is a tremendous responsibility placed on the therapist, as Guntrip sees it. It is a view similar to the one I have discussed in previous chapters on therapeutic interaction (see Chapters 12 and 13). Guntrip points out that long after the patient is consciously and intellectually persuaded that the therapist could be a better parental image, the child deep within cannot feel it. "In this uncertainty, even accepting the therapist's help may still feel like a fundamental disloyalty to parents and arouse guilt. . . ."

Clinically, this is very important for us to keep in mind. The patient cannot be weaned from, and become independent of, internalized bad parental objects—and so cannot become healthy and mature—unless he can consolidate and introject a goood relationship with the therapist as a real object. Therefore, what really concerns the patient, and the only thing that is really of absolutely crucial importance however much other things may crop up, is the question of "whether the therapist as a real human being has a genuine capacity to value, care about, understand, see, and treat the patient as a person in his own right" (Guntrip, 1968).

Essentially in psychotherapy we attempt either to ameliorate the childhood warp through various supportive techniques or actually to reduce the extent of the warp through intensive uncovering techniques. The more serious the warp, the more vital will be the human interaction between patient and therapist as a factor in the cure. There are limitations to our techniques that must be recognized (Wilson, 1971), based on early severe ego and somatic disturbances.

The goals of psychotherapy are clearly connected with the emerging and always latent capacity for mature love. Fromm-Reichmann (1959) describes our goals of treatment as,

". . . aiming psychotherapeutically at the development of growth maturation, and inner independence of the patient; at his potential freedom from fear, anxiety, and the entanglements of greed, envy, and jealousy in his interpersonal relationships; and at his capacity for self-realization and for forming durable relationships of intimacy with others and of giving and accepting mature love."

317

She defines "mature love" along with Sullivan, as discussed in Chapter 2, as "the state of interpersonal relatedness in which one is as concerned with the growth, maturation, welfare, and happiness of the beloved person as one is with one's own. This capacity for mature love presupposes the development of a healthy and stable self-respect."

It should now be clear that psychotherapy has actually nothing to say about the good life or about happiness, except for the fundamental comment that mental health is a necessary precondition to attaining these phenomena. The psychotherapist or psychiatrist is no more trained or equipped to lead people to the good life or happiness than anybody else. His solutions are no better, and he is no more a winner in the battle of life than many other people. We expect only that the childhood nucleus will be "a little less fractious, unruly, and disruptive in those whose profession it is to help others in life's journey" (Saul, 1958).

The most reliable test of mental health is the capacity to exchange mature love with other persons. If the individual is unable to exchange mature selfless love with others, there is no point whatever in talking about the good life and happiness. For individuals who are unable to love, life becomes an empty charade occupied by shadow people, without meaning and purpose. They complain of perpetual boredom and go madly in all directions to find an escape from the horror of their condition. This condition has been described innumerable times in literature, in philosophy, and in psychiatry.

The question of what love is can be answered in many ways from many psychological systems. Anyone capable of love and who has experienced the give and take of mature love

318

knows intuitively what I am talking about—the sense of fusion, of belonging, of the exchange of feelings with another person or persons on the deepest possible level of intimacy. Problems involving the capacity to love others must be resolved before any discussion of happiness or the good life can be meaningful.

The patient, however, will not keep still about matters of the good life and happiness; in fact, as he improves and energies become released, he begins the process of searching and scanning—so typical in adolescents—for his own identity, his own good life, and his own happiness. In the later stages of therapy, an intellectual phase of this nature is often necessary. The patient is then, eager to engage in search and discussion, intellectualization, and identification with the therapist on these matters. This phase, from the psychodynamic point of view, is a more mature version of the mother–child symbiosis. It permits solidification of identity and sets the stage for eventual separation from the psychotherapist.

In order to know when the therapy is reaching a termination phase, the therapist must have an idea of what sets the stage for termination, what he is looking for, and what clues he can find to let him know termination is becoming a possibility. Fromm-Reichmann (1950) writes that termination is approaching when the patient and therapist are becoming "satisfied with the results of their psychotherapeutic collaboration" and "when the patient has gained a sufficient degree of lasting insight into his interpersonal operations and their dynamics to enable him, in principle, to handle them adequately." The evaluation of the patient's personality by both patient and therapist should coincide to a very large degree at the end of the treatment.

319

The best measuring rod of the patient's having attained sufficient insight into interpersonal processes will be a successful dissolution of the transference and the distortions regarding people and interpersonal situations. This should include the patient's increased ability to get along with the significant people of his childhood. The patient must gain a marked degree of awareness of the causes of previous overattachment or hatred toward the mother and father and other significant people. He need not love them, but his awareness should be sufficient to enable him to clarify and channel psychopathological hatred and love within himself. Fromm-Reichmann emphasizes this, and she is quite right about it, because there does seem to be a misconception in the mind of the public that learning to hate one's parents is considered a therapeutic accomplishment. This is absolutely not true. The true therapeutic goal is gaining independence from one's previous hateful or loving attachments to one's parents and gaining nondefiant self-valuation and independence free from parental judgment.

One of the aims of psychotherapy should be to enable the patient to sit down and have a cup of coffee with his parents in a friendly and nonexplosive or supercharged fashion. Of course, this depends on the personality of the parents, because some parents will simply not accept the changes that have taken place in psychotherapy. Their ego integrity sometimes depends on the sickness of their children, and, therefore, they insist on a total rupture with the patient—and sometimes the death of the patient or suicide—as a price of the patient's changing. Clinically speaking, this is the exception rather than the rule, and most parents in time accept the situation and learn (with much protest) to adjust and adapt to the changes in their children.

In order to understand the strategy and tactics of termination we must distinguish and clarify between consultation for the patient, consultation for the therapist, change of therapists, interruption of treatment, and termination. Sometimes these things get confused, and it is very important that the patient has a clear understanding what is being done and why. The indications for consultation for the therapist are usually involved with countertransference and the emerging evidences of countertransference. Sometimes the patient wants a consultation. This comes up most frequently at the beginning of therapy, and a consultation can be very useful in the sense that it increases and strengthens the patient's determination to work with the original therapist if the consultant is in agreement. Under no circumstances should a therapist ever bitterly oppose a patient's wish for a consultation. This is unethical. On the other hand, every effort should be made to understand the reason why the patient is requesting the consultation.

There are also times when a change of therapists is a good idea, but these times are far less frequent than is usually thought. I do not go along with the idea that change from a male therapist to a female therapist, or vice versa, is often useful. To me the most important indication for change of therapists is when the therapist has developed a rigid countertransference structure that does not yield to consultation. It is in the patient's best interest at that point to change therapists, and he may realize it before the therapist.

Interruption of treatment often has a useful function, if there seems to be a stalemate over a prolonged period of time and consultations don't help. It can serve to mobilize the patient's difficulties and lead to an increase in the patient's motivation to work them through. Therefore, interruption of treat-

321

ment can be a useful strategy in psychotherapy and can also be useful in situations where there has been an acute upset that is now in remission. The therapist wishes to wait a while and let things solidify before he goes into the depths of the unconscious with the patient.

It should be obvious that our conception of what sets the stage for termination in psychotherapy involves certain moral and value judgments. We cannot get away from this no matter how we try. When we observe that the patient is showing the capacity to exchange mature love, to function effectively, and to develop a certain sense of social consciousness and libidinal investment in those around him involving his family, his community, and so forth, we invariably—if we are not engaged in a countertransference bind for which we have to hang onto the patient—begin to think of termination.

Often the patient suggests termination first, and not all such suggestions should be taken as transference! They often can be genuine, especially if they appear along with our clinical observations of the patient's much increased capacity to engage in healthy object relations. Because there are resistances to the loss entailed by termination, it often occurs that a dream suggests the idea of termination to the patient or the therapist first. Sometimes the therapist has to be the one to suggest termination.

The strategy of suggestion is usually to bring the problem up to the patient and get the patient's observations about it. If the termination idea is a good one, the patient will be able to work on it and often will accept it. It is necessary either to set a date substantially in advance of the termination time or, as I prefer to do, taper the therapy off in frequency.

It is important not to terminate a therapy too quickly or

to permit a patient to do so. The reason for this is that certain vital phenomena which must be worked through, always manifest themselves in a natural and normal termination process. Often a flareup of the symptomatology or new symptoms may appear, sometimes in a dramatic fashion. This can be generally regarded as an effort to avoid the termination and is based on the mourning process that *must* take place.

A patient who approaches termination of a successful psychotherapy is being asked to give up an extremely meaningful object relationship. DeWald (1964) points out,

> This experience of loss of the object may be accompanied by sadness, grief, and anger at the object over the felt rejection. In a nontherapeutic situation of loss of an important object, the individual must go through the process of grief and mourning to a varying degree, depending on the significance of the object. But the anticipation is that when there has been an elaboration and resolution of the grief-work, there will again be a readiness and capacity to invest in new objects. In the usual situation of loss, the absence of grief and mourning is an indication of their repression and they may then persist indefinitely or serve as the source of subsequent neurotic disturbance.

Thus, in the termination phase we must provide the patient with an opportunity to elaborate and work through the grief and mourning reaction in whatever intensity the patient will experience it. If there is no such reaction, something has gone wrong, something is being repressed, or most likely we are terminating the patient prematurely. A major source of resistance is the wish to avoid the sadness and grief and to avoid the work of mourning the therapeutic relationship. Patients may wish to terminate immediately, rationalizing this in various ways. Such a plan usually represents the wish to avoid the experience of grief and the mobilization of conflict that is an invariable aspect to termination. The patient may attempt denial of the importance and meaning that idea that the termination represents any type of significant loss. "Another frequent manifestation of resistance is the attempt to find a substitute object who will replace the therapist and thereby permit the patient to ward off he impact of the loss as well as to perpetuate the transference wishes. This may involve such things as seeking out another therapist or physician, or falling love, or making use of a spouse or a friend to serve as the therapist," writes DeWald (1964).

In some cases of supportive therapy, or where I am dealing with a patient who has a very fragile ego structure but cannot continue therapy, I set a definitive date for a return appointment, perhaps six months later. I personally use appointment cards with my patients, and I have found this to be one of the best places where they come in handy. The patient gets a little white card with the date and time of his six-month return appointment on it. Some of the severe borderline patients I have worked with in a supportive effort to enable them to function and get along without any profound hopes of change, have taken that little white card, put it in their wallet or purse, and used it as a symbolic introject or "transitional object" that has kept them going over the six months they don't see me. The only alternative to this kind of strategy with severely damaged ego structures is an interminable psychotherapy that drains the finances of the patient indefinitely.

This, however, is the exception rather than the rule.

Usually either a gradual tapering off or a setting of a definite termination date at some time in the future is handled quite well by the patient, and the grief and mourning aspects are worked through in the usual fashion. In addition to this, I like to leave the door open. A patient should never be terminated with the idea that he cannot come back, unless there is a very specific reason for doing so. Even when patients prematurely terminate their therapy insisting that you are the world's worst psychiatrist and so forth, always leave them with an invitation to return if they feel they have changed their minds. Often they do return. A therapist must leave time in his schedule to take on a patient who has left therapy, thought it over, and decided to return. Such patients should never have the experience of being told that the door is open and then rejected when they try to come back through it.

It is also my conviction that psychotherapy is really a never-ending process. The question of termination is not, "When is your psychotherapy over?" but "When is it no longer necessary for us to have formal meetings in order that your psychotherapy process may go on in a continuous fashion?" The answer to this is in terms of the patient's capacity to invest in other people around him. The catalysis for the continued psychotherapy that goes on in the head of the patient, hopefully all his life, is the introjection of the therapist's attitude, and the reality gratification that the patient has gained through improved interpersonal relations that motivate him constantly to expand his capacities for ego operations.

Very frequently the question comes up, "Can we be friends?" or "Could you love me now as a wife or a husband?" Patients often pose this during the phase of termination. There are a number of instances where apparently genuine

325

friendships have developed between the therapist and the patient at the end of therapy, and even some situations where the therapist and the patient have married. The latter in my opinion invariably represents countertransference neurotic problems on the part of the therapist and can never be genuinely beneficial for either party.

The question of personal friendship is a little more difficult, and it is conceivable that in some situations it could be possible for such friendships to take place. In the anonymity of the big city it is in the patient's best interest that such personal friendships not be encouraged by the therapist. The patient should have plenty of opportunities to make friendships in social situations and should not have to depend on the therapist for gratification of the need for friendship. More significantly, it is in the patient's best interest if the therapist always remains potentially the professional so that if things go wrong or a stress takes place later in the patient's life, he can return to psychotherapy in the same setting, atmosphere, and situation as he had before, without any kind of contamination by a social relationship with the therapist. I explain this frankly to patients. There are numerous patients I have been able to tell at the end of psychotherapy that there is nothing about them that would cause me to reject them as friends, but I feel it is in their best interest that I remain available in the professional capacity that originally brought them to me, in case they need me in the future.

Sometimes we make mistakes and think the patient is ready to terminate when he is not. The best ways to determine whether an error has been made in discussing termination are to watch the patient's dreams and to watch for the appearance of acting-out phenomena. If termination has been discussed prematurely, the patient may have a variety of dreams that point to it.

More seriously, one often sees dreadful types of acting out when premature termination is pushed. The most typical reason for premature termination is that the therapist is trying to get rid of the patient for one reason or another. This often leads the patient to suddenly fall in love with someone else, seek a substitute, and get involved in situations from which it is very difficult to emerge. One must distinguish between the mistake of premature termination and the usual flareup that can take place when termination is discussed. The way to distinguish this is simply to watch it in terms of time and severity. An ordinary flareup, as a function of termination, is usually worked through in the therapy, interpreted, and dies away. However, in a situation of premature termination the severity of the symptoms and the acting out get *worse*. They are not amenable to working through, and interpretations do not seem to affect them at all. In these situations therapy is being terminated prematurely, and the patient is experiencing an object loss he cannot handle at the time.

WHAT MANNER OF PERSON IS THE PSYCHOTHERAPIST?

There is, of course, a moralistic aspect to the termination of therapy, setting of goals, and in our whole approach to the patient in intensive psychotherapy. Certain value judgments cannot be avoided. London (1964) goes to the absurd extreme of arguing that psychotherapists have both a scientific and moralistic function. The scientific function according to him, is that of manipulator of behavior. The moralistic function is that of a "secular priesthood." He admits that many psychotherapists will object to such descriptions of their functions.

If indeed we are not a "secular priesthood," what are we? Psychotherapists can be divided roughly into two groups. Let us call them the optimists and the pessimists. The extreme of the pessimists is typified by Freud's (1937) paper on *Analysis Terminable and Interminable,* whereas Wolberg's (1969) well-known textbook, *The Technique of Psychotherapy,* is a good example of the optimistic viewpoint. The pessimists believe that most emotional problems yield only bit by bit to a long psychotherapy; that a hard nuclear infantile core must be reached for a therapy to succeed; that certain basic conservative principles of treatment are necessary to reach this infantile core, involving an intense one-to-one relationship between therapist and patient; and that the art of therapy consists largely of correctly recognizing and interpreting crucial manifestations of transference at the appropriate times.

The optimists see other factors operating throughout life to form and re-form the personality. They emphasize cultural and later influences and give a general impression that things are not so bad and not so hard. Even popularized guidebooks read by the individual will help change him. Many factors are given equal weight, all sorts of schools are described together, and, since there is so much disagreement, it is implied that almost anything goes.

Eclecticism, unless it is carefully defined, can lead to both confusion and to an insidious sense of nihilism on the part of the novice. In other instances it can lead to a false sense of the ease of psychotherapy, encouraging untrained and poorly trained semiprofessionals to try all kinds of innovations and acting out under the guise of "therapy." In such a situation anyone can be a therapist. There is no authority to say, what can or cannot be carried out in the office, what is or what is not scientific or correct technique, and so on. The effect of this kind of eclecticism is that psychotherapy becomes a mystical and indescribable process. The differentiation between the goals of psychotherapy and the goals of life become completely blurred, and the patient does not know what to expect, apart from some kind of mystical experience.

In order to avoid the pitfalls of falling prey to the latest therapeutic fashion, the psychotherapist should have considerable knowledge of philosophy, history and literature. Philosophers have for centuries been struggling with the same problems psychotherapists now contend with. An outstanding example of this is the much-maligned Nietzsche, who tried to present a new and different image of humanity. Nietzsche (1968) dealt in his works with the importance of man overcoming himself and developing a creative and dynamic personality, becoming a person who could look at the absurdities of human life and feel laughter and exaltation in spite of it. Nietzsche also recognized the chaos of the passions and asked us to harness this chaos but not to lose it and regard it as an enemy to be sternly repressed.

Knowledge of such philosophical considerations, as well as of the arts and myth-making are important to the psychotherapist and has been heavily stressed by many authors. The therapist must be weaned from the idea that he is the cold-blooded scientist skillfully dissecting the patient's mind on the basis of scientific knowledge. He must become aware that a variety of solutions to problems are available, some of them dating long before psychotherapy. We are after all, part of the Western philosophical and cultural tradition, and part of our influence in the didactic therapeutic experience is through imparting the attitude of "civilisation" (Clark, 1969). Ehrenwald (1966) proclaims: ". . . every individual therapist, will have to do more than acquire the professional skills and experiences required by his academic curriculum. He will have to devote equal attention to acquiring the spiritual discipline, to develop the cultural awareness and the sense of values which forms the matrix of his evolving personal myth and therapeutic presence. The gift of (therapeutic) intuition may be one of the by-products of this development."

There are problems of psychopathology and problems of human living or, as Freud put it, neurotic suffering and everyday misery, and the psychotherapist must be able to distinguish between them. We all share the universal problems of human living—the ultimate mystery of our being in the world and the tragedy of our impending death. When faced with these kinds of problems the psychotherapist has little to offer the patient, except his own personality, his life experience, and his knowledge of the various kinds of solutions he knows to be available. This is the rationale for having historical perspective, a knowledge of Western culture and perhaps some idea of the Eastern approaches to life as well. Such information is actually more helpful than science in grappling with man's inevitable personal fate.

It is inconceivable that a psychotherapist with no knowledge of philosophy or Western culture and with no interest in the humanities could do a successful job of intensive psychotherapy. The patient would be working with a shadow person. The most obvious model for the psychotherapist to follow would be Freud himself.

Innumerable courses and seminars are no substitution for intensive psychotherapy of the therapist. No amount of knowledge can substitute for the massive countertransference reactions that invariably take place when the therapist is not in possession of deep self-knowledge. Because of the lack of theoretical constructs in our field at this time, we can only borrow from many sources such as philosophy, clinical experience, and common sense as to what will produce an optimal type of psychotherapist. It is easy to see this will involve, in addition to selection of talented individuals, good supervision, and adequate training in psychodynamics and therapeutic technique, the development of a humane, optimistic, and mature individual who has the leisure to create and to promote in himself an attitude of empathy and interest in his patients. It is obvious that the production of the optimal psychotherapist will require a revolution in current training in psychotherapy and require a much more thorough commitment of time and effort, even during psychiatric residency training.

However, some reviewers of my *Why Psychotherapists Fail* (1971a) entirely missed the main point. The goal of a humanistic curriculum is not to produce a Renaissance man out of service to some philosophical or esthetic ideal. A humanistic education for the psychotherapist is not a luxury, but a logical extension of the fundamental theoretical notions behind the special theory of psychotherapeutic interaction. As described in Chapter 13, this theory argues that a complete understanding of the patient and of psychotherapeutic interaction cannot *ever* be achieved by a purely technical scientific education in dynamic psychiatry, no matter how thorough.

If it is correct, a corresponding education in the language of the humanistic imagination will *have to* be provided for the psychotherapist, since two complementary languages, grounded on different nuclear operations of the mind, are used for the description of psychotherapeutic interaction: the scientific and the humanistic. Therapists must be educated in both, or their understanding and interpretation capacities will be imparied.

We also hope for a humanizing effect from the study of literature, philosophy, and the arts, but we must fully realize that the primary source of this would be from the personal psychotherapy of the therapist. Whenever psychiatrists have become pervaded with the humane spirit, there has been advancement in the field. There is a direct relationship between cultural focus on the individual human as worthy of attention and the improvement of our lot on earth.

Perhaps some of the credit for renewed interest in all this is due to the existentialist movement, which has provided traditional psychotherapy with a considerable challenge. By offering the "phenomenological method" it has even challenged the basic scientific methodology on which psychotherapy is based.

Just as I have delineated between optimists and pessimists among psychotherapists, there is a moralistic and value judgment to be made about the question of the entire view of man held by psychotherapists. Two philosophical paradigms of this view come to us from Jaspers and Schopenhauer. Jasper's view of man is contained for example, in a quotation from his excellent little book, *The Way to Wisdom* (1954):

> The truth is that man is accessible to himself in two ways: as object of inquiry ,and as existence endowed with a freedom that is inaccessible to inquiry. In the one case, man is

conceived as object, in the other as the nonobject, which man is and of which he becomes aware when he achieves authentic awareness of himself. We cannot exhaust man's being in knowledge of him, we can experience it only in the primal source of our thought and action. Man is fundamentally more than he can know about himself.

This is a rather mystical and optimistic view of the concept of man. In many ways it stands in direct opposition to the Freudian view or the Schopenhauerian (Gardiner, 1967) viewpoint, which might be defined something like this: The entire perspective in terms of which we are disposed to view our personalities and behavior is distorted. We customarily think of ourselves as being essentially free and rational agents, whereas, in fact, the principle sources and springs of our conduct consist of deep underlying tendencies and drives about whose character we are often wholly unaware. Consciousness, Schopenhauer (Gardiner, 1967) wrote, "is the mere surface of our mind, of which as of the earth we do not know the inside, only the crust." In consequence, we often put an entirely false construction on the behavior in which these basic impulses are expressed. Schopenhauer also suggested that the ignorance we display, the rationalizations that in all innocence we provide, may themselves have a motive, although not one we are aware of. Thus he frequently wrote of the "Will" as preventing the rise to consciousness of thoughts and desires that, if known, would arouse feelings of humiliation, embarrassment, or shame.

Taylor (1964) reminds us that "Schopenhauer compared the life of man to the journey of someone riding a raft upon swift, turbulent rapids, struggling to avoid every shoal and rock throughout the whole course of the journey, only to reach the escarpment at the end, from which he is hurled down into an eternal nothingness." The life of man or every other creature he found mainly to be a struggle against death, and yet time itself rushes every living thing along to its death as its only possible ultimate goal. According to Schopenhauer we are so accustomed to viewing animal life in the light of innumerable creatures casually perishing in the woodlands by a chance fire that it is hard to realize it is no different with human life.

> If we declare human nature to have some special transcendent worth—to be, in Kant's terms, "an end in itself"—it is from our own wishful thinking. It is not from the lessons of nature and history, for these contradict us daily. A man is often felled at the height of his powers by a bacterium; a civilization is robbed of one of its geniuses by the most trivial trick of fate; cities are abolished by earthquakes; millions are slaughtered at the caprice of a tyrant and their bodies piled into pits and burned like grasshoppers.

It is obvious that the differences in the view of man between Jaspers and Schopenhauer will be reflected in a psychotherapist's thinking and is going to make a profound difference in his approach to emotional problems and setting of goals for psychotherapy. The psychotherapist must be aware of these approaches and think through his own views after a careful study of the leading thinkers.

The urgency of training future psychotherapists in the humanities and abstract studies, and immersing them in the arts as well as the so-called scientific subjects, now has a theoretical foundation (Chessick, 1971a). The psychotherapist, to do an optimal job, must be familiar with both the language of scientific and of the humanistic understanding. He must be able to shift back and forth with facility between these maps of psychic interaction, so that what he misses on one map, he finds on the other. This increased grasp of the situation will surely improve the psychic field he has to offer the patient and sharpen his capacity for perception.

To be in tune with one's own unconscious and the unconscious of others depends on one's state of ego functioning and partly on a certain innate ego capacity. Professional persons with the capacity to empathize with others and to enter into a feeling relationship with others on a deep level need to be encouraged to achieve good training as psychotherapists. Organizations such as the American Board of Psychiatry should be able to separate those truly qualified to do psychotherapy by virtue of ability, training, and experience from those who are not. We must try to develop ideal programs and certification for truly qualified individuals who intend to do psychotherapy, free of the patient care needs of participating hospitals. We also have the responsibility to sponsor social legislation to relieve the financial burdens of those who need psychotherapy and to prevent the unqualified from the practice of psychotherapy.

The didactic therapeutic relationship remains the primary model for all clinical psychiatrists. Knowledge of the intricacies and the complexities of this relationship with all its theoretical and therapeutic implication of the unknown is the unique tool of the psychiatrist. This knowledge fundamentally includes understanding the major forces that have contributed to the development of the psychiatrist, as well as the patient. The shift of residents toward eclecticism during their training is a function of pedagogic failure, a failure of an educational program that does not give proper focus and proper perspective.

335

It is helpful and desirable if the psychotherapist has first had a physician's education, but the distance between being educated as a physician and finally becoming a psychotherapist is every bit as great as the distance between entering college and being a graduate physician. Our education in psychotherapy now has to be based on what we conceive to be the optimal model of a psychotherapist. When we look at therapeutic interaction in a variety of ways we see that the fundamental demand from the psychotherapist, besides a very thorough personal psychotherapy, is the capacity to be humane and to possess as wide an understanding as possible of human problems. The therapist must be able to put himself in the shoes of a variety of people. For example, Russell (1965) writes:

> I will try to say . . . what I feel that I personally have derived from the reading of history. I should put first and foremost something like a new dimension in the individual life, a sense of being a drop in a great river rather than a tightly bounded separate entity. The man whose interests are bounded by the short span between his birth and death has a myopic vision and a limitation of outlook which can hardly fail to narrow the scope of his hopes and desires. . . . Cocksure certainty is the source of much that is worst in our present world, and it is something of which the contemplation of history ought to cure us, not only or chiefly because there were wise men in the past, but because so much that was thought wisdom turned out to be folly—which suggests that much of our own supposed wisdom is no better.

CHAPTER 15   *Epilogue:*
Psychotherapy
and Beyond

*I*MPORTANT contemporary authors such as Camus and many other existentialists have argued that the fundamental question of human life and philosophy boils down to the question of whether or not to commit suicide. For example, in *The Floating Opera*, Barth (1956) portrays a man—a convinced nihilist, lawyer, rake, saint, and cynic—who struggles perpetually with himself over this question.

At the same time a remarkable countertheme runs throughout Barth's novel, which the protagonist calls his *Inquiry*, a title taken from Hume's famous philosophical treatises. This *Inquiry* is never finished:

To be sure one doesn't want to live as if each day may be his last, where there is at least some chance that it may be only

337

his next. One needs, even in my position, something to counterbalance the immediacy of a one-day-at-a-time existence, a life on the installment plan. Hence my *Inquiry*, properly to prepare even for the beginning of which, as I see it would require more lifetimes than it takes a lazy Buddhist to attain Nirvana. My *Inquiry* is timeless in effect; that is, I proceed at it as though I had eternity to inquire in. And, because processes persisted in long enough tend to become ends in themselves, it is enough for me to do an hour's work, or two hours' work, on my *Inquiry* every night after supper, to make me feel just a little bit outside of time and heartbeats.

So, I begin each day with a gesture of cynicism, and close it with a gesture of faith; or, if you prefer, begin it by reminding myself that, for me at least, goals and objectives are without value, and close it by demonstrating that the fact is irrelevant. A gesture of temporality, a gesture of eternity. It is in the tension between these two gestures that I have lived my adult life.

The purpose of this epilogue is to discuss and further explore the tension between temporality and eternity as a universal phenomenon and to study the role of psychotherapy in helping patients resolve inevitable existential problems of this nature. A clearer conception of the limitations of psychotherapy, as well as of the role of psychotherapy in the perspective of the stages of a person's lifetime development, can arise from such a discussion.

There are many ways to approach the developmental stages of a lifetime. One of the most famous of these is encapsulated by Kierkegaard, who saw life as a series of agonizing "criterionless" decisions.

338

The agony of existence is suffered by the individual and propels him to decisions that then influence the next stages of development of his life. To exist for Kierkegaard is to struggle, to strain, to encounter opposition, to experience passion. It is to make decisions, not to drift with the tide. Existence and selfhood are identical—to exist is to become and to make choices. This, of course, is one of the basic tenets of existential philosophy.

The passionate commitment to specific options of choice is seen by Kierkegaard as the point at which the agony of decision disappears. Kierkegaard attempts to propel this concept further, because, although he recognizes that passionate commitment may be satisfactory psychologically, it is not satisfactory ethically from his preconceived point of view. He insists that not only must the commitment be deliberately chosen, but it must be a religious Christian commitment, his solution to man's existential problems.

Kierkegaard (Jones, 1969) emphasizes "a fundamental difference—which everyone can experience within himself—between choosing and merely wishing or wanting. . . . Choosing is inner; it is not at all dependent on successfully making a change in the state of affairs. It is distinguished from mere wishing and wanting in that it is an act of will; that is, it involves a commitment, a movement, of the personality."

Kierkegaard (1946) distinguished three kinds of choices in life, the three ways of choosing or attitudes toward choice. He called these the esthetic, the ethical, and the religious. In the esthetic life (an extremely unfortunate phrase) choice is not taken seriously. The esthetic man takes the view "it doesn't matter"—whatever he chooses, it will all be the same

339

or all be equally bad. The esthetic life is characterized by Kierkegaard as either a hedonistic happy-go-lucky existence, a cynical life, or a poetic and romanticized existence.

In contrast, the ethical life is a serious one. At this level man lives not by whim or impulse but by an ethical code. Choice becomes problematic and serious, since ethical men must decide how their code applies to the various complex situations in which they find themselves. From Kierkegaard's point of view the particular code to live by is less important than the fact that the person has chosen to live by that code —if, indeed, he has chosen his code rather than merely drifted into it as part of the inheritance from his culture.

Kierkegaard (1947) believed a third stage was also possible and necessary. He called this the "leap of faith" into a passionate commitment to the Christian religion. A beginning example of this, given by Kierkegaard, is the decision of the incisive logician Socrates to believe in immortality although there was and could be no proof. Kierkegaard argued that as long as a person lives by autonomy and a sense of being alone in the world, he is in despair, even if he is passionately serious about doing good and meticulously lives the ethical life. In fact, the more serious a person is, the more he is in despair because he realizes that as long as he relies on his own judgment he can never be sure that he is right. The solution to this despair or doubt, according to Kierkegaard, is the assurance of faith.

I am going to utilize these concepts here in a way that will undoubtedly *not* be satisfactory to all, since we are, after all, in the open-ended region of opinion and philosophy. From the point of view of the psychotherapist, the issue of faith is very important. For example, Erikson (1959) describes the stages in development and characterizes the earliest stage as fundamentally the development of basic trust. He emphasizes the potentially great importance of the faith of the mother if the serenity that it entails is transmitted to the child. He says:

> It is not the psychologist's job to decide whether religion should or should not be confessed and practiced in words or rituals. Rather the psychological observer must ask whether or not in any area under observation religion and tradition are living psychological forces creating the kind of faith and conviction which permeates the parent's personality and thus reinforces the child's basic trust in the world's trustworthiness. The psychopathologist cannot avoid observing that there are millions of people who really cannot afford to be without religion, and whose pride in not having it is that much whistling in the dark. On the other hand, there are millions who seem to derive faith from other than religious dogmas, that is fellowship, productive work, social action, scientific pursuit, and artistic creation. And again there are millions who profess faith, yet in practice mistrust both life and man. With all of these in mind, it seems worth while to speculate on the fact that religion through the centuries has served to restore a sense of trust at regular intervals in the form of faith, while giving tangible form to a sense of evil which it promises to ban. . . . Whosoever says he has religion must derive a faith from it which is transmitted to infants in the form of basic trust; whosoever claims he does not have religion must derive such basic faith from elsewhere.

This is a very powerful statement and deserves careful study by the clinician. I would like to substitute at this point for the terms *basic faith* or *religion* the terms *philosophical faith,* or *search for transcendence,* taken from Jaspers (1971).

341

It is philosophical faith or the search for transcendence that is buried in the quotation from Barth at the beginning of this chapter. A man who is in despair and considering suicide finds himself starting each day drinking alcohol and closing each day in a gesture toward immortality, working on a timeless study of a philosophical or psychological nature—persisting in it as if he were immortal. This represents an attempt to feel outside, or to transcend, time and physical mortality. It eventually affords the character the psychological strength to resist his existential despair.

The importance of basic trust cannot be sufficiently overemphasized in the clinical practice of psychotherapy. In fact, Strupp (1972) sees it as the essence of psychotherapy. As he views the therapeutic process, the patient develops trust in the therapist's integrity and begins to see him as a person who is genuinely interested in the patient's self-development and maturity. The whole procedure of psychotherapy is contingent on the development of this trust. Psychotherapy, according to Strupp, can actually be viewed as a "technology" eliminating the barriers against openness, honesty, and trust. This is why psychotherapeutic changes must *always* occur in the context of an interpersonal relationship, in which the major task of the therapist is to bring about an experience of trust that alone permits him to apply the requisite leverage for therapeutically influencing the patient.

In many ways psychotherapy may be understood as a lesson in the development of basic trust that unfortunately has not developed in the patient because of a faulty mother–child symbiosis.

What happens next? What are the limitations? How far can we go? Certainly what happens next is an "integration," producing what Erikson (1959) calls a sense of ego identity: "The sense of ego identity, then, is the accrued confidence that one's ability to maintain inner sameness, and continuity . . . is matched by the sameness and continuity of one's meaning for others. Thus, self-esteem confirmed at the end of each major crisis, grows to be a conviction that one is learning effective steps toward a tangible future, that one is developing a defined personality within a social reality which one understands."

Notice the emphasis on the future and on the process of life as a dynamically progressive panorama in Eriskon's brilliant thinking. The emerging ego-identity bridges the early childhood stages founded on basic trust, and, if this does not develop, the result is the well-known phenomenon of identity diffusion he describes.

According to Erikson the maturity of the adult stages consists of three important phases: intimacy and distantiation versus self-absorption, generativity versus stagnation, and integrity versus despair and disgust. A patient's improvement through psychotherapy is charted by his progress in the ability to love and to work. Love here is not merely genital love but a general expansiveness and generosity. Similarly, work implies not routine or all-encompassing labor, but a productiveness that permits the individual to exist simultaneously as a loving and sexual being. The therapist further sees generativity or the interest in establishing and guiding the next generation, as an important sign of the patient's having reached maturity in psychotherapy. Various forms of altruistic concern and a creativity, which is not necessarily absorbed by parental responsibility, are other signs of the patient's growing health and maturity.

343

At the end point of the psychotherapy, the therapist looks for what Erikson calls integrity, as compared with the despair and disgust that the patient so often begins with. This state of mind is defined as

> the acceptance of one's own and only life cycle and of the people who have become significant to it as something that had to be and that by necessity permitted of no substitutions. It thus means a new and different love of one's parents, free of the wish that they should have been different, and an acceptance of the fact that one's life is one's own responsibility. It is a sense of comradeship with men and women of distant times and different pursuits, who have created orders and objects and sayings conveying human dignity and love.

This is in contrast to despair, in which the individual is constantly feeling that the time is short, too short to start another life and try out alternative roles to integrity. This despair is often presented as disgust, misanthropy, and chronic contemptuous displeasure against particular institutions and particular people, common attitudes constituting presenting symptoms in the clinical practice of psychotherapy.

It is clear from all this that intensive psychotherapy far surpasses any simplistic conceptions of behavior modification. In this context, Strupp (1972) points out, the whole question of therapeutic outcome assumes a ring of superficiality. The quest for self-knowledge and individuation is a quest for meaning, not simply for adaptation or adjustment to conditions as they are. If he is successful, the therapist launches the patient on a different course of life, inevitably inculcates

344

some of his own values; fosters self-examination, self-knowledge, and honesty; and participates in the individual's personal development.

The end point of the psychotherapy is reached as these problems are dealt with and resolved and the individual becomes freer to examine his place in the world, to struggle with existential issues, and to evolve his own philosophy of life. In this endeavor he greatly profits from whatever wisdom and perspective and insight the therapist has acquired through his own and hopefully richer life experience.

To what extent does the patient identify with the wisdom and insight of the therapist and to what extent is there a limitation on what the therapy can do in helping the patient resolve existential questions? More generally, what evidence is there that human life has a *forward force*, as it is variously described by authors like Goethe, Kierkegaard, and Erikson. Is man actually propelled to examine his place in the world, trouble himself with existential issues, and evolve his own philosophy of life? It is the thesis of this epilogue that evidence has begun to accumulate that life *does* have such a forward force and that this forward force is actually built into the human organism. Limitations of therapy arise from the fact that all we can do as therapists is repair and enhance ego function in the patient by freeing the ego from internal conflicts, providing an atmosphere in which this forward force can take over.

This is a significant matter in viewing our work as psychotherapists. It takes psychotherapy almost totally out of the realm of suggestion and manipulation and places it back primarily into the realm of evoking the patient's constructive potential. Psychotherapy then emerges as a practice based

345

on the assumption that many patients have the inner moti-vating force, not only to get well and to heal, if given the opportunity to do so, but to go forward and reach philosophi-cal faith or transcendence as they become more mature and move along the stages of life.

It is *extremely important* to define philosophical faith and the search for transcendence in a way other than invoking religion, for it is perfectly possible for patients to seek phil-osophical faith and transcendence in ways that do *not* involve organized religion, any religion, or even a deity at all. The belief in a religious system *definitely is not* to be used as a mark of maturity (or immaturity) or of a successful (or un-successful) psychotherapy.

What evidence is there for a constructive potential innate in man? For built-in developmental patterns, knowledge, and understanding in the human mind? And what exactly do I mean by the innate human reaching out for philosophical faith and transcendence? To answer this, we must turn mo-mentarily to recent developments in contemporary thought.

Chomsky's (1972) work has brought about a linguistic revolution that has altered our mode of thinking and that has important ramifications for the clinical psychotherapist. Without going into the technical details of Chomsky's work in linguistics, his most spectacular conclusion about the na-ture of the human mind indicates support for the claims of the seventeenth-century rationalist philosophers such as Des-cartes, Leibnitz, and others (providing one doesn't take these claims too precisely) that there are innate ideas in the mind.

The classical philosophical argument has always been one between the rationalist's claim that human beings have knowledge that does not derive from experience but is prior

346

to all experience and determines the form of the knowledge to be gained from experience, as against the empiricist's contentions—from Locke down to contemporary behavioral learning theorists—that the mind must be treated as a *tabula rasa* containing no knowledge prior to experience. The empiricists place no constraints on the form of possible knowledge, except that it must be derived from experience by such mechanisms as association of ideas or the habitual connection of stimulus and response. For the empiricists and behaviorists all knowledge comes from experience. For the rationalists some knowledge is implanted innately prior to experience.

It is quite possible to argue that Chomsky has produced some convincing refutation of empiricists and behaviorists, and, although he has not vindicated the classical rationalists once and for all, at least he has produced convincing evidence for Kantian synthetic *a prior* schemata (Hook, 1969).

His argument centers around the way in which children learn language. If all the various rules of grammar built into languages are necessary for linguistic confidence, how does a child ever acquire language? In learning to talk, how does the child acquire that part of knowing how to talk that is described by the grammar and that constitutes linguistic competence? Chomsky asks us to notice certain features of the learning situation. The information the child is presented with when other people address him or when he hears them talk to each other is limited in amount, fragmentary, and imperfect. There seems to be no way the child could learn the language just by generalizing from his inadequate experiences from the utterance he hears. Furthermore, the child acquires the language at a very early age, before his general intellectual faculties are developed. Indeed the ability to

347

learn a language is only marginally dependent on intelligence and motivation. Stupid children and intelligent children, motivated and unmotivated children, all learn to speak their native tongue. Formal teaching of the first language is unnecessary. The child may have to go to school to learn to read and write, but he does not have to go to school to learn how to talk.

In spite of all this, the child who learns his first language claims Chomsky, performs a remarkable intellectual feat. In internalizing the grammar he does something akin to constructing the theory of the language. The only explanation for all this says Chomsky, is that the mind is not a *tabula rasa* but rather *the child has the form of the language built into his mind before he ever learns to talk.* The child has a universal grammar programmed into his mind and brain as part of his genetic inheritence. He may be spoken of as having a perfect knowledge of universal grammar, together with a fixed schematism he uses in acquiring language. A child can learn any human language on the basis of varied and imperfect information. That being the case, he must have the form common to all human languages as part of his innate mental equipment.

As further evidence and support of a specifically human language faculty, Chosmky points out that animal communications are radically unlike the human languages. Animal systems have only a finite number of communicative devices, and they are usually controlled by certain stimuli. Human languages by contrast all have an *infinite generative capacity,* and the utterances of sentences are not predictable on the basis of external stimuli. This *creative aspect* of language use is peculiarly human.

348

The heart of the argument is that the universal grammar is so complicated and so specific in its form, and so unlike any other kind of knowledge, that no child could learn it unless he already had the form of the grammar programmed into his brain; that is, unless he had a perfect knowledge of universal grammar. This is entirely different from the behaviorist's postulations of readiness to learn, or disposition, or motivation, important to learning theory.

There seems to be an innate faculty of language that is simply waiting to unfold in the child and enables him to put together speaking capacities on the basis of very imperfect information. The general principles that determine the form of grammatical rules and rules for languages such as English, Turkish, or Chinese are to some considerable degree common to all human languages. Chomsky claims that the principle structures underlying languages are so specific and so highly articulated that they must be regarded as being biologically determined, constituting part of what we call human nature, and being genetically transmitted from parents to children.

If this is so, it will grossly affect our attitudes toward psychotherapy in terms of what our patients do with the experience they get from us. Chomsky presents the most powerful scientific argument so far against the behaviorist approach or the learning theory approach to psychotherapy. Chomsky (Lyons, 1970) claims that the behaviorist's impressive panoply of scientific terminology and statistics is no more than camouflage covering up their inability to encounter the fact that language simply is *not* a set of habits and *is* radically different from animal communication.

"It is Chomsky's conviction that human beings are different from animals or machines and that this difference should

349

be respected both in science and in government; and it is this conviction that underlies and unifies his politics and linguistics, his philosophy, and his psychology," writes Lyons. This message will find an immediate response from all those who subscribe to a belief in the brotherhood of man and the special dignity of human life.

There is, however, something more in the Chomskian revolution in linguistics that commands the attention of psychotherapists. One of the most striking facts about language is its creativity. By the age of five or six children are able to produce and understand an indefinitely large number of utterances they have not previously encountered. The behaviorists and learning theorists, however successful they might be in accounting for the way in which certain networks of habits and associations are built up in the behavior patterns of animals and human beings, are totally incapable of interpreting creativity, an aspect of human behavior manifest first and most clearly in language. Chomsky further claims that the whole terminology of behaviorism, response, conditioning, and reinforcement, though it can be made precise, is really so loose when actually applied to language that it could cover anything and is devoid of empirical content.

Thus, we are led by Chomsky's considerations to the whole subject of mechanistic determinism. Although Chomsky describes himself as a mentalist, this mechanistic determinism—especially in terms of behaviorism or physicialism—is challenged by Chomsky's findings. Like Descartes, he believes that human behavior is, in part at least, undetermined by external stimuli and internal physiological states. Chomsky would, however, disagree with Descartes and other philosophers, who are usually called mentalists, because he does not subscribe to irreducibility between body and mind.

Taking this discussion one step further, it is not difficult to accumulate evidence, for example, from modern physics (Chessick, 1971a) that there is an *indeterminacy* built into all our world that forms the object of scientific investigations, at least at an atomic level. The indeterminacy principle of Heisenberg in quantum physics is taken as a principle that represents an absolute and final limitation on our ability to define the state of things by means of measurements of any kind that are possible or even ever will be possible. If this is true, the future behavior of a system, as far as we are concerned, can be predictable only to a certain degree of accuracy corresponding to the limits set by the indeterminacy principle and to no higher degree, regardless of what kind of measurement we could carry out. This implies that as we keep on refining our measuring devices more and more, we discover that the indeterminacy principle provides an absolute and final law that applies to all processes that can possibly take place in the scientifically knowable world. Furthermore, as these measurements are refined, a breakdown of causality in connection with phenomena becomes apparent. This breakdown actually applies to any real and observable physical phenomena, because the observing apparatus' sensitivity will eventually be able to show only a statistical behavior for groups but will be totally unable to predict how individual measurement will fluctuate from one case to the next.

Thus, one is led to the conclusion that the precise manner of occurrence and irregular fluctuations at an individual particle level cannot be traced by means of experiments to *any kinds of causes at all*. In fact, the question of causation loses

351

meaning at this point. It is assumed that in any particular experiment, the precise result that will be obtained is completely arbitrary in that it has no relationship whatever to anything else that exists in the world or that ever has existed. In the area of physics it is possible to show that the question of attempting to define specific individual variations and movements, at least at the subparticle level, loses its meaning and cannot be answered in terms of cause and effect or stimulus and response. This is a conclusion Einstein could never accept—"I cannot believe that God plays dice with the universe." The entire matter is discussed at length by Bohm (1957), and the reader is referred to this discussion for more details about causality and chance in modern physics.

To bring this unpredictability into the area of psychotherapy, I offer the following argument: It is not very difficult to observe in the stages of life, phases that begin with a hedonistic or pleasure principle orientation and move to an ethical and reality principle orientation. This is normally followed by development of a sense of identity or a sense of self, and—if basic trust has been present—a feeling of ego-identity or self-authentication, a sense of self-esteem, and inner sustainment, to use phrases from various authors that suggest essentially the same thing. As we move in psychotherapy through the developmental phases from the pleasure principle to the reality principle and toward self-authentication, the creative or generative capacities of the ego take over the treatment. The therapist drops into the background, and the patient takes over. As this happens, the therapist can no longer determine the course to be taken. It is *not possible* to predict or to mold a genuine movement to specific individual self-authentication—or beyond.

352

There is a built-in, unfolding forward pattern in people, which is really the most important of their forces and at the same time an unpredictable one. If the therapist can clear away the obstacles that are present in the patient at the level of developing basic trust and in moving from the pleasure principle to the reality principle, he should then be able to observe the taking over of the creative or generative forces that are built into the patient. These then carry the patient forward into the search for self-authentication—and beyond. The therapist will not be able to predict in any mechanistic or deterministic or stimulus–response manner *what form* that self-authentication—and more—will take. The application of cause and effect at that point breaks down, and the therapist can only withdraw in wonder, watching the unfolding of the patient's personality.

I believe that a *further* step occurs at least in some cases, that is, a fourth step—from self-authentication to the search for transcendence. Jaspers, both a psychiatrist and philosopher, stressed the term *philosophic faith*. This consists of the conviction that man is open to transcendence, that personal freedom is to be maintained and respected, that man as he finds himself is still inadequate but can rely on help from that transcendence in which the world is grounded and supported. His main argument for this concept of philosophical faith is a negative one. To reject philosophical faith means to hold that the immediate world is all there is, that man's destiny is fully determined, that man is perfectible and alone, that the world is self-supporting.

The same debate is going on in the mind of the protagonist of Barth's book. Even if we grant that the Chomskyian revolution has taken place, and that the stages in life's way are

353

propelled by inward forces and indeterminate in their outcome, a crucial question nags perpetually at us. Is the search for transcendence simply a regressive rearch for some kind of blissful union with the good mother, a "cosmic consciousness" that the infant in us wishes once more to restore; some kind of opiate for facing the uncertainty of life and certainty of death? Or is there actually an unfolding, as the ego becomes freed from its conflicts, of a forward drive toward seeking transcendence? *Of course, the answer to this crucial metaphysical question is that one can never know the answer.*

The search for transcendence as we observe it in others seems to be an act of philosophical faith. Even asking the above question is an act of cynicism or temporality. *We all must live with this uncertainty and never know if it is all a delusion,* just as solipsism in philosophy can never be proven wrong.

The argument can be made more precise, however, and it is worthwhile to do so, by utilising Jaspers' (1971) concept of the *cipher,* borrowed from Kant and Pascal. This concept is based on the premise that reason cannot know the nature of the world directly, but that, instead, ultimate reality or transcendence must be read in the secret language of appearances. Kant spoke of the ciphers by means of which nature speaks to us, and the German romantics expressed themselves similarly. For Jaspers, ciphers are not identical with appearances but are a language spoken to us through them by transcendence, not following a deliberate method but almost presented as a gift that we must be able to read and grasp.

The direct language of transcendence is not a language that is universally intelligible, but the incompleteness of the empirical world points above and beyond every rational certitude. This pointing itself is a cipher. It has the immediacy of an experience. A similar example of a cipher is found in the study of various philosophical systems. Each of these systems has a core of truth over and above itself, and in all great philosophies one can experience these ciphers if one *immerses one's self thoroughly* in the specific philosophies. Thus, in a sense Jaspers' thought may be regarded as a philosophy of philosophy.

The concept of transcendence is seen as the object of man's perpetual groping for portents and meanings beyond the merely human. What the individual reaches for is something greater than himself as an object, something dimly sought for and yet never met face to face. Man can think and has indeed always been thinking about things he cannot know, define, or even clearly conceive. It is very frustrating, indeed.

According to Jaspers, transcendence speaks to man in man's only immediate world, the world of appearances and so-called material objects. The transcendent voice speaks to us through the cipher: "Yet everything objective is a possible cipher if it is adopted in transcending, brought to mind in a way that will make transcendence appear of it." Examples of ciphers beside scientific, religious, and philosophical systems, are the subjective feelings of man's unity and fusion with nature, a oneness with the external world, the cipher of our sense of psychic freedom; even art and esthetic experiences are examples of cipher opportunities.

I would like to suggest that the experience of intensive long-term psychotherapy could also be a cipher. It cherishes the individual human being and is unlike any other human enterprise in contemporary society. It persists in a critical and personal examination of an individual and his place in the world. And, finally, it releases the inward force toward reaching transcendence, while serving at the same time, as a cipher of transcendence in itself. Like all other ciphers it presents for both the patient and the therapist a mundane experience, in which there is made possible a jump from fear to serenity.

References

Adler, M. (1965), *The Conditions of Philosophy.* New York: Atheneum.

Alexander, F. (1948), *Fundamentals of Psychoanalysis.* New York: Norton.

—— (1956), *Psychoanalysis and Psychotherapy.* New York: Norton.

—— (1963), The dynamics of psychotherapy in the light of learning theory. *Am. J. Psychother.,* 120:440–448.

Allen, A. (1971), The fee as therapeutic tool. *Psychoanal. Q.,* 40:132–140.

Altman, L. (1957), On the oral nature of acting out. *J. Am. Psychoanal. Assoc.,* 5:648–662.

—— (1969), *The Dream in Psychoanalysis.* New York: International Universities Press.

Arlow, J., and Brenner, C. (1964), *Psychoanalytic Concepts and the Structural Theory*. New York: International Universities Press.

Balint, M. (1953), *Primary Love and Psychoanalytic Technique*. New York: Liveright.

———— (1968), *The Basic Fault*. London: Tavistock Publications.

Barth, J. (1956), *The Floating Opera*. New York: Avon Books.

Baum, O. (1969–1970), Countertransference. *Psychoanal. Rev.*, 56:621–637.

Beers, C. (1970), *The Mind That Found Itself*. Garden City, N.Y.: Doubleday.

Bird, B. (1957), A specific peculiarity of acting out. *J. Am. Psychoanal. Assoc.*, 5:630–647.

Bleuler, E. (1911), *Dementia Preacox or the Group of Schizophrenias*. New York: International Universities Press, 1952.

Bohm, D. (1957), *Causality and Chance in Modern Physics*. Philadelphia: University of Pennsylvania Press.

Bonine, W. (1962), *The Clinical Use of Dreams*. New York: Basic Books.

Born, M. (1968), *My Life and My Views*. New York: Scribners.

Brenner, C. (1955), *An Elementary Textbook of Psychoanalysis*. New York: International Universities Press.

Brodey, W. (1965), On the dynamics of narcissism. I. Externalization and early ego development. In *Psychoanalytic Study of Child*, 20:165–193.

Bronowski, J. (1959), *Science and Human Value*. New York: Harper and Row.

Bychowski, G., and Despert, J. (Eds.) (1961), *Specialized Techniques in Psychotherapy*. New York: Basic Books.

Calef, V. (1971), Concluding remarks. *J. Am. Psychoanal. Assoc.*, 19:89–97.

Camus, A. (1955), *The Myth of Sysiphus*. New York: Knopf.

———— (1957), *The Stranger*, transl. S. Gilbert. New York: Knopf.

Chessick, R. (1961), Some problems and pseudo-problems in psychiatry. *Psychiatr. Q.*, 35:711–719.

—— (1965), Empathy and love in psychotherapy. *Am. J. Psychother.*, 19:205–219.

—— (1968), The crucial dilemma of the therapist in psychotherapy of borderline patients. *Am. J. Psychother.*, 22:655–666.

—— (1969), *How Psychotherapy Heals.* New York: Science House.

—— (1971a), *Why Psychotherapists Fail.* New York: Science House.

—— (1971b), The use of the couch in psychotherapy of borderline patients. *Arch. Psychiatr.*, 25:306–313.

—— (1972a), Angiospastic retinopathy. *Arch. Psychiatr.*, 27:241–244.

—— (1972b), Externalization and existential anguish. *Arch. Psychiatr.*, 27:764–770.

—— (1973a), Defective ego-feeling and the quest for Being in borderline patients. *Int. J. Psychoanal. Psychother.*, in press.

—— (1973b), The borderline patient. In *American Handbook of Psychiatry*, ed. S. Arieti, New York: Basic Books.

Clark, K. (1969), *Civilisation.* New York: Harper and Row.

Copleston, F. (1965), *The History of Philosophy*, Volume VII, Part 2. New York: Image Books.

Chomsky, N. (1972), *Language and Mind.* New York: Harcourt, Brace, Jovanovich.

DeWald, P. (1964), *Psychotherapy.* New York: Basic Books.

Dollard, J., and Miller, N. (1950), *Personality and Psychotherapy.* New York: McGraw-Hill.

Ehrenwald, J. (1966), *Psychotherapy, Myth and Method.* New York: Grune & Stratton.

Ellenberger, H. (1970), *The Discovery of the Unconscious.* New York: Basic Books.

359

Erikson, E. (1959), *Identity and the Life Cycle.* New York: International Universities Press.

Evans, R. (1968), *B. F. Skinner. The Man and His Ideas.* New York: Dutton.

Fenichel, O. (1945), *Psychoanalytic Theory of the Neuroses.* New York: Norton.

Frank, J. (1961), *Persuasion and Healing.* Baltimore: John Hopkins Press.

French, T., and Fromm, E. (1964), *Dream Interpretation.* New York: Basic Books.

Freud, A. (1965), *Normality and Pathology in Childhood.* New York: International Universities Press.

Freud, S. (1893), *Studies On Hysteria.* In *Standard Edition*, Volume II. London: Hogarth Press, 1962.

——— (1900), *The Interpretation of Dreams.* In *Standard Edition*, Volumes IV and V. London: Hogarth Press, 1962.

——— (1901), *The Psychopathology of Everyday Life.* In *Standard Edition*, Volume VI. London: Hogarth Press, 1960.

——— (1905), *Fragment of an Analysis of a Case of Hysteria.* In *Standard Edition*, Volume VII:3–124. London: Hogarth Press, 1962.

——— (1911), Formulations on two principles of mental functioning. In *Standard Edition*, Volume XII:213–226. London: Hogarth Press, 1962.

——— (1912), Recommendations to physicians practicing psychoanalysis. In *Standard Edition*, Volume XII:109–120. London: Hogarth Press, 1962.

——— (1913a), On the beginning of treatment. In *Standard Edition*, Volume XII:121–144. London: Hogarth Press, 1962.

——— (1913b), Remembering, repeating and working through. In *Standard Edition*, Volume XII:145–156. London: Hogarth Press, 1962.

——— (1914a), On the history of the psychoanalytic movement.

In *Standard Edition,* Volume XIV:3–66. London: Hogarth Press, 1957.

———— (1914b), On narcissism. In *Standard Edition,* Volume XIV: 67–104. London: Hogarth Press, 1957.

———— (1915a, 1916), *Introductory Lectures on Psychoanalysis.* In *Standard Edition,* Volumes XV and XVI. London: Hogarth Press, 1963.

———— (1915b), Observations on transference love. In *Standard Edition,* Volume XII:157–171. London: Hogarth Press, 1962.

———— (1917), A metapsychological supplement to the theory of dreams. In *Standard Edition,* Volume XIV:217–236. London: Hogarth Press, 1957.

———— (1923), *The Ego and the Id.* In *Standard Edition,* Volume XIX:3–68. London: Hogarth Press, 1961.

———— (1926), *Inhibitions, Symptoms and Anxiety.* In *Standard Edition,* Volume XX:77–178. London: Hogarth Press, 1962.

———— (1930), *Civilization and Its Discontents.* In *Standard Edition,* Volume XXI:59–148. London: Hogarth Press, 1961.

———— (1933), *New Introductory Lectures on Psychoanalysis.* In *Standard Edition,* Volume XXII:3–184. London: Hogarth Press, 1964.

———— (1937), Analysis terminable and interminable. In *Standard Edition,* Volume XXIII:209–254. London: Hogarth Press, 1962.

———— (1938), *An Outline of Psychoanalysis.* In *Standard Edition,* Volume XXIII:141–208.- London: Hogarth Press: 1964.

Fromm, E. (1955), *The Sane Society.* New York: Rinehart.

Fromm-Reichmann, F. (1950), *Principles of Intensive Psychotherapy.* Chicago: University of Chicago Press.

———— (1959), *Psychoanalysis and Psychotherapy.* Chicago: University of Chicago Press.

Gardiner, P. (1967), Arthur Schopenhauer. In *Encyclopaedia of* of *Philosophy*, ed. P. Taylor, 7:325–332. New York: Macmillan.

Gill, M. (1951), Ego psychology and psychotherapy. *Psychoanal. Q.*, 20:62–71.

Giovacchini, P. (1965), Transference, incorporation and synthesis. *Int. J. Psychoanal.*, 46:287–296.

—— (1967a), Frustration and externalization. *Psychoanal. Q.*, 36:571–583.

—— (1967b), The frozen introject. *Int. J. Psychoanal.*, 48:61–67.

—— (1971), The delicate touch of analytic dedication. *Psychiatr. Soc. Sci. Rev.*, 5:22–28.

—— (1972), Technical difficulties in treating some characterological disorders. *Int. J. Psychoanal. Psychother.*, 1:112–128.

Gitelson, M. (1949), Panel discussion on countertransference. *Bull. Am. Psychoanal. Assoc.*, 5:46–49.

Glover, E. (1955), *The Technique of Psycho-Analysis*. New York: International Universities Press.

Goldberg, A. (1972), On the incapacity to love. *Arch. Gen. Psychiatr.*, 26:3–7.

—— (1973), Psychotherapy of narcissistic injuries. *Arch. Gen. Psychiatr.*, 28:722–728.

Graves, R. (1955), *The Greek Myths*, Volume I. Baltimore: Penguin Books.

Greenson, R. (1965), The working alliance and the transference neurosis. *Psychoanal. Q.*, 34:155–181.

—— (1968), *The Technique and Practice of Psychoanalysis*. New York: International Universities Press.

—— (1972), Beyond transference and interpretation. *Int. J. Psychoanal.*, 53:213–217.

Greenspan, S., and Cullander, C. (1973), *A Systematic Metapsychological Assessment of the Personality*. Int. J. Psychoanal. 21:303–327.

Guntrip, H. (1968), *Schizoid Phenomena, Object Relations and the Self*. New York: International Universities Press.
——(1971), *Psychoanalytic Theory, Therapy and the Self*. New York: Basic Books.
Hartmann, H. (1958), *Ego Psychology and the Problem of Adaptation*. New York: International Universities Press.
Havens, L. (1965), On the anatomy of a suicide. *N. Engl. J. Med.*, 272:401.
Healy, W., et al. (1930), *The Structure and Meaning of Psychoanalysis*. New York: Knopf.
Heidegger, M. (1962), *Being and Time*, transl. J. Macquarrie and E. Robinson. New York: Harper and Row.
Hendon, H. (1963), On the psychodynamics of suicide. *J. Nerv. Ment. Dis.*, 136:236.
Hendrick, I. (1948), *Facts and Theories of Psychoanalysis*. New York: Knopf.
Hollender, M., et al. (1969), Body contact and sexual enticement. *Arch. Gen. Psychiatr.*, 20:188–191.
—— (1970), The need or wish to be held. *Arch. Gen. Psychiatr.*, 22:445–453.
Hollingshead, A., and Redlich, F. (1958), *Social Class and Mental Illness*. New York: Wiley.
Hook, S. (1969), *Language and Philosophy*. New York: New York University Press.
Ibsen, H. (1881), *Ibsen's Plays*. New York: Modern Library.
Jacobsen, E. (1964), *The Self and the Object World*. New York: International Universities Press.
Jaspers, K. (1954), *The Way to Wisdom*. New Haven: Yale University Press.
—— (1964), *The Nature of Psychotherapy*. Chicago: University of Chicago Press.
—— (1969), *Philosophy*, Volume I, transl. E. B. Ashton. Chicago: University of Chicago Press.

———— (1970), *Philosophy*, Volume II. Chicago: University of Chicago Press.

———— (1971), *Philosophy*, Volume III. Chicago: University of Chicago Press.

Jones, E. (1953), *The Life and Work of Sigmund Freud*, Volume I. New York: Basic Books.

Jones, W. (1969), *A History of Western Philosophy*. New York: Harcourt, Brace, and World.

Kahn, M. (1969), On the clinical provision of frustrations, recognitions, and failures in the analytic situation. *Int. J. Psychoanal.*, 50:237–248.

Kant, I. (1963), *Critique of Pure Reason*, transl. F. M. Mueller. New York: Doubleday (Anchor Books).

———— (1968), *Critique of Judgment*, transl. J. H. Bernard. New York: Hafner.

Kierkegaard, S. (1946), *The Concept of Dread*, transl. W. Lowrie. Princeton: Princeton University Press.

———— (1947), *A Kierkegaard Anthology*, ed. R. Bretall. Princeton: Princeton University Press.

Kohut, H. (1971), *The Analysis of the Self*. New York: International Universities Press.

Kubie, L. (1971), The retreat from patients. *Arch. Gen. Psychiatr.*, 24:98–106.

Kuhn, T. (1962), *The Structure of Scientific Revolutions*. Chicago: University of Chicago Press.

Levi, A. (1969), *Literature, Philosophy and the Imagination*. Bloomington: Indiana University Press.

———— (1970), *The Humanities Today*. Bloomington: Indiana University Press.

Lewin, B. (1950), *The Psychoanalysis of Elation*. New York: Norton.

Lipschutz, D. (1955), Transference in borderline cases. *Psychoanal. Rev.*, 42:195–200.

London, P. (1964), *The Modes and Morals of Psychotherapy*. New York: Holt, Rinehart and Winston.

Lyons, J. (1970), *Noam Chomsky*. New York: Viking Press.

Marmor, J. (1966a), Theories of learning and the psychotherapeutic process. *Br. J. Psychiatr.*, 112:363–366.

—— (1966b), The nature of the psychotherapeutic process. In *Psychoneurosis and Schizophrenia*, ed. G. Usdin, 66–75. Philadelphia: Lippincott.

—— (1971), Dynamic psychotherapy and behavior therapy. *Arch. Psychiatr.*, 24:22–28.

May, R. (1950), *The Meaning of Anxiety*. New York: Ronald Press.

Mendel, W. (1970), An editorial: The seduction of the therapist, *Existent. Psychiatr.*, 7:3–7.

Menninger, K. (1958), *Theory of Psychoanalytic Technique*. New York: Basic Books.

Meyer, A. (1951), *Collected Papers*, Volume II (*Psychiatry*). Baltimore: John Hopkins Press.

Miller, C. (1961), Differential diagnosis of the negative therapeutic reaction and therapeutic failure. *Am. J. Psychother.*, 16:452–459.

—— (1962), The negative therapeutic reaction. From *Current Psychiatric Therapies*, Volume II. New York: Grune & Stratton.

—— (1963), Clinical management of the negative therapeutic reaction. *Am. J. Psychother.*, 17:641–650.

Modell, A. (1968), *Object Love and Reality*. New York: International Universities Press.

Mullahy, R. (1948), *Oedipus, Myth and Complex*. New York: Hermitage Press.

—— (1970), *Psychoanalysis and Interpersonal Psychiatry*. New York: Science House.

Munroe, R. (1955), *Schools of Psychoanalytic Thought*. New York: Dryden Press.

Nacht, N. (1962), Curative factors in psychoanalysis. *Int. J. Psycho-Anal.*, 43:206–211.

—— (1963), The non-verbal relationship in psychoanalytic treatment. *Int. J. Psycho-Anal.*, 44:328–333.

Nagera, H. (1969), *Basic Psychoanalytic Concepts of the Libido Theory*. New York: Basic Books.

Noyes, A., and Kolb, L. (1963), *Modern Clinical Psychiatry*. Philadelphia: Saunders.

Nietzsche, F. (1968), *Thus Spoke Zarathustra*. In *The Portable Nietzsche*, ed. W. Kaufmann, 103–439. New York: Viking Press.

Olnick, S. (1964), The negative therapeutic reaction. *Int. J. Psycho-Anal.*, 45:540–548.

Orr, D. (1954), Transference and countertransference: A historical survey. *J. Am. Psycho-Anal. Assoc.*, 2:621–670.

Odier, C. (1956), *Anxiety and Magic Thinking*. New York: International Universities Press.

Pachter, H. (1961), *Paracelsus: Magic into Science*. New York: Collier Books.

Racker, H. (1968), *Transference and Countertransference*. New York: International Universities Press.

Rapaport, E. (1956), The management of an erotized transference. *Psychoanal. Q.*, 25:515–529.

Rapaport, D. (1967), *Collected Papers*. New York: Basic Books.

Reich, A. (1973), *Psychoanalytic Contributions*. New York: International Universities Press.

Reinfeld, F. (1951), *A Treasury of Chess Lore*. New York: Dover.

Rogow, A. (1970), *The Psychiatrist*. New York: Putnam.

Reusch, J. (1961), *Therapeutic Communication*. New York: Norton.

Russell, B. (1965), *Portraits from Memory*. New York: Simon and Schuster.

Sartre, J.-P. (1964), *Nausea*, trans. L. Alexander. New York: New Directions.

Saul, L. (1958), *The Technic and Practice of Psychoanalysis*. Philadelphia: Lippincott.

—— (1970), Inner sustainment. *Psychoanal. Q.*, 39:215–222.

—— (1971), *Emotional Maturity*. 2nd ed. Philadelphia: Lippincott.

——,and Pulver, S. (1966), The concept of emotional maturity. *Int. J. Psychiatry*, 2:446–469.

Schafer, R. (1968), *Aspects of Internalization*. New York: International Universities Press.

Schilder, P. (1951), *Psychotherapy*. New York: Norton.

Searles, H. (1965), *Collected Papers*. New York: International Universities Press.

Shands, H. (1960), *Thinking and Psychotherapy*. Cambridge: Harvard University Press.

—— (1970), *A Semiotic Approach to Psychiatry*. Cambridge: Harvard University Press.

Sharpe, E. (1951), *Dream Analysis*. London: Hogarth Press.

Singer, E. (1970), *Key Concepts in Psychotherapy*. New York: Basic Books.

Skinner, B. (1960), *Science and Human Behavior*. New York: Macmillan.

Sklansky, M., et al. (1969), *The High School Adolescent*. New York: Association Press.

Snow C. (1963), *The Two Cultures*. New York: New American Library (Mentor Books).

Stewart, W. (1963), An inquiry into the concept of working through. *J. Am. Psychoanal. Assn.*, 11:474–499.

Stone, L. (1961), *The Psychoanalytic Situation*. New York: International Universities Press.

Strupp, H. (1960), *Psychotherapists in Action.* New York: Grune & Stratton.

—— (1969), Towards a specification of teaching and learning in psychotherapy. *Arch. Psychiatry,* 21-203-212.

—— (1972), On the technique of psychotherapy. *Arch. Gen. Psychiatry,* 26:270-278.

—— (1973), *Psychotherapy: Clinical, Research, and Theoretical Issues.* New York: Aronson.

Stumpf, S. (1966), *Socrates to Sartre.* New York: McGraw-Hill.

Sullivan, H. (1947), *Conceptions of Modern Psychiatry.* Washington, D.C.: White Foundation.

—— (1953), *The Interpersonal Theory of Psychiatry.* New York: Norton.

—— (1954), *The Psychiatric Interview.* New York: Norton.

Tarachow, S. (1963), *An Introduction to Psychotherapy.* New York: International Universities Press.

Taylor, R. (1964), Schopenhauer. In *A Critical History of Western Philosophy,* ed. D. J. O'Conner, 365–385. New York: Macmillan.

Tillich, P. (1952), *The Courage To Be.* New Haven: Yale University Press.

Tower, L. (1956), Countertransference. *Am. J. Psychoanal. Assoc.,* 4:224–255.

Voth, H. (1972), Responsibility in the practice of psychoanalysis and psychotherapy. *Am. J. Psychother.,* 26:69–83.

Wheelis, A. (1958), *The Quest for Identity.* New York: Norton.

Whitaker, C. and Malone, T. (1953), *The Roots of Psychotherapy.* Philadelphia: Blakiston.

Whitehorn, J. (1955), Understanding psychotherapy. *Am. J. Psychiatry,* 112:328.

Wile, D. (1972), Negative countertransference and therapist discouragement. *Int. J. Psychoanal. Psychother.,* 1:36–67.

Wilson, P. (1971), On the limits of the effectiveness of psycho-analysis. *J. Am. Psychoanal. Assoc.*, 19:552–564.

Winnicott, D. (1958), *Collected Papers*. New York: Basic Books.

——— (1965), *The Family and Individual Development*. London: Tavistock.

——— (1966), *The Maturational Processes and the Facilitating Environment*. New York: International Universities Press.

Wolberg, L. (1969), *The Technique of Psychotherapy*. New York: Grune & Stratton.

Zeligs, M. (1957), Acting in. *J. Am. Psycho-anal. Assoc.*, 5:685–706.

Zetzel, E. (1956), Current concepts of transference. *Int. J. Psycho-Anal.*, 37:369–376.

Zilboorg, G. (1941), *A History of Medical Psychology*. New York: Norton.

Index

Index

371

373